Turning the Wheel

In Search of Seasonal Britain
on Two Wheels

To, Chris,
enjoy the journey!

Best
Wishes, Kevan
Jan '12

Turning the Wheel

In Search of Seasonal Britain
on Two Wheels

Kevan Manwaring

BOOKS

Winchester, UK
Washington, USA

First published by O-Books, 2011
O-Books is an imprint of John Hunt Publishing Ltd., Laurel House, Station Approach,
Alresford, Hants, SO24 9JH, UK
office1@o-books.net
www.o-books.com

For distributor details and how to order please visit the 'Ordering' section on our website.

ISBN: 978 1 84694 766 7

Design: Stuart Davies

Printed in the UK by CPI Antony Rowe
Printed in the USA by Offset Paperback Mfrs, Inc

We operate a distinctive and ethical publishing philosophy in all
areas of our business, from our global network of authors to
production and worldwide distribution.

CONTENTS

'Our time on this earth is sacred, and we should celebrate every moment.'
Paulo Coelho

'Everything begins over again at its commencement every instant. The past is but a prefiguration of the future. No event is irreversible and no transformation final. . . . In a certain sense, it is even possible to say that nothing new happens in the world, for everything is but the repetition of the same primordial archetypes; this repetition, by actualizing the mythical moment when the archetypal gesture was revealed, constantly maintains the world in the same auroral instant in the beginnings.'
Mircea Eliade, *The Myth of Eternal Return*

'For those to whom a stone reveals itself as sacred, its immediate reality is transmuted into supernatural reality. In other words, for those who have a religious experience all nature is capable of revealing itself as cosmic sacrality.' Mircea Eliade, *The Sacred and the Profane*

'Declare today "sacred time" —off-limits to everyone, unless invited by you. Take care of your personal wants and needs. Say no, graciously but firmly, to others' demands.' Oprah Winfrey

'No day can be so sacred but that the laugh of a little child will make it holier still.' Robert Green Ingersoll

'Everything that lives is holy.' William Blake

'The ritual calendar, in an age in which most kinds of community have been atomised by central government and the mass media, is becoming a celebration of private relationships and the individual lifecycle. Humanity has come to replace the natural world at the centre of the wheel of the year.' Ronald Hutton, *The Stations of the Sun*

'...if enough of the world's exploding population will seek to live in symbiosis with the planet there is hope for us yet.' Janet and Colin Bord, *Earth Rites*

'Fortune, good night; smile once more. Turn thy wheel.'
William Shakespeare

'I'm hip about time. But I just got to go.' *Easy Rider*

Dedicated to Jennifer
my companion in sacred time

By Stoney Littleton Long Barrow
3400 – 2400 BCE/Easter Monday 2007 CE

*The deep silence after a long ride is intoxicating. As opposed to alien-
ating you, riding a motorbike actually sensitizes you to nature. To take
off your helmet, feel the wind on your face, the sun on your back after
being cooped up and cooking in leathers, to take off your boots and
stretch your legs. It's a wonderful feeling. One experiences the wild
euphoria of the pilgrim. It's a great way to travel and an even better way
to arrive. After a tiring return from my trip (wrong turnings, draining
energy) I parked up and, crossing the little foot-bridge over the brook,
climbed the hill to the long barrow. Breathless, I lay back in the grass by
the dark passage tomb entrance swirling with ammonites, savouring the
ecstatic song of the skylark, the deep peace, the ancient landscape. This
neolithic machine of solstice rebirth, with me, like an astronaut
marooned in the Stone Age, sprawled next to it.*

My time as a bard on a bike had begun.

Introduction

Why is it we feel the need to celebrate? I ask myself this in the immediate aftermath of my fortieth, still suffering the mother of all hangovers. I can hazard my own answer – albeit a hazy one – although I suspect something universal drives us to mark the turning of the seasons, of the years, and I intend to explore Britain in search of reasons why. Doing this in my fortieth year seems especially resonant; forty seems to mark something significant in one's life journey – a watershed. It is a true coming of maturity. If one hasn't put away childish things by now, it's your last chance if you want to grow old gracefully – then again, why do we need to conform to social norms? Isn't life meant to *begin* at forty – not become deadly serious? And yet these benchmark birthdays synchronise briefly with everyone else, even if we have our own trajectories and velocities in between. Some seem to become middle-aged in their twenties. Some remain teenagers until their twilight years. Some grow old too fast. Some never grow up. For me, forty represents a time to take stock – to assess what I have achieved in my life and what I still want to achieve. Almost like any other birthday or New Year, in fact, but it seems laden with extra significance. Perhaps as one reaches a possible halfway point (though there's no guarantee it will be of course – one might get knocked over by a bus the next day), it is somewhat sobering and galvanising. Right, a voice in one's head rings out, time to *really* get your act together – you may have only a couple of decades left with the necessary energy to achieve what you need to. Of course, if you haven't 'got your act together' by forty, you're possibly on a losing streak – but, hey, there are always late developers, the tortoises in life who win the race in the end, surprising us all! A good friend of mine didn't get her first book published until the age of 54 (after writing five) and then went on to have thirty books published. With an ageing majority, such 'autumn achievers' will become increasingly common. Older people shouldn't be looked on as liabilities, but as assets. I am only too aware that this is a consoling fiction for me as I become, in my own words, an 'old git'. Another friend, Verona, put it more poetically in a birthday card to me:

Autumn is a wonderful time and this symbolic age heralds an entry into a colourful period of maturity – and abundant harvests of all that's been nurtured up to this point.

The autumn of my life... Gulp. Sounds a bit depressing – like 'it's downhill from now on' – but actually, if one thinks about autumn, it actually starts with the *beginning* of the harvest in late summer. Yes, this feels like a time to start 'reaping what I have sown', to begin gathering in my personal harvest.

And my fortieth birthday party was a ritual enactment of that.

I decided to hold a 'Bardic showcase' to celebrate my first four decades, inviting friends to perform. This seemed like my ideal way to spend the evening (with some serious dancing and merry-making thrown in). And I thought that if I could get forty fine friends there to show for forty years life on this planet then I would feel like I have truly achieved something, for friendship is perhaps the greatest harvest.

And you know what? It happened.

I guess years of just 'doing my thing' had paid off, and now I was seeing the organic reciprocation of that – beautiful friends being warm and generous, showering me with blessings.

I had one of the best nights of my life (and one of the worst hangovers), but for days afterwards I was grinning and bursting out laughing as I recalled incidents from the evening – golden memories that give me a warm glow and will keep me going for years.

I felt I had well and truly marked my big four zero – by celebrating all the friends I had made along the way. It was as much a celebration of them, their friendship, as anything. Having them all gathered together was incredible. This is what 'tribe' is about – community, marking the rite-of-passage of one of its members with gift-giving, feasting, song (*Happy Birthday to you...*), poetry and mirth, dance and 'catharsis'. By the end, I did indeed feel different! I felt truly blessed and honoured by those I hold dear. I was overwhelmed by their generosity and goodwill towards me. I was reminded not of how special I am, but *how special they are* – and how special are the meaningful connections we make in our lives.

Having celebrated this significant 'round number' I felt ready, after a couple of quiet days, to return to the wheel, feeling like what I did, day to day, mattered – how I treated people and governed myself in the world: what I gave of myself. Filled to the brim, I felt able to give – like the Cauldron of Vocation ('sings and is filled with song') – even simply through a smile; giving a stranger the time of day; responding in a positive, rather than instinctively negative manner, to an unexpected demand; feeling able to carry on. It had been a tough few years for me and this celebration really felt like a symbolic end of that period – the escape hatch from the Underworld. Difficulties will always arise, but things have shifted. I had made it back into the light and affirmed life with the joyous act of living.

A meal with friends, a nice long soak, a nap, reading a book, watching a favourite film with a loved one, curled up together, a hug, a kiss – all these are moments of sacred time. Every moment has this potential. It is an act of awareness. Being fully present in the moment, appreciating being here, being alive.

Making and marking sacred time is something humankind has been doing for a long time; perhaps it's one of the things which *make* us human: the ability to reflect and to look forward; to think beyond ourselves; to see the patterns and pre-empt them; to use art and other tools to record and create calendrical cycles. Although their precise purpose remains enticingly myste-rious, ancient ritual sites across Britain, from Seahenge to Silbury Hill, have clearly been forged to mark something in time. Stonehenge is aligned with the summer and winter solstices, as well as lunar cycles; both Newgrange and Stoney Littleton Long Barrows are aligned with the winter solstice; Silbury Hill is connected with Lammas; the Stones of Callanish with the lunar cycle and the Great Year... The list goes on.

And there are many modern sites that perform a similar function, from grand, national horological monuments (Big Ben, the Millennium Dome and Eye, the Greenwich Meridian, the scheduled public art for the London Olympics in 2012) and events (the Opening of Parliament, the Changing of the Guard, the Grand National, the Lord Mayor's Parade, the laying of poppy wreaths at the Cenotaph, carols from King's College, the Henley Regatta, the Oxford/Cambridge Boat Race), to smaller, localised events (cutting of yews, the beating of bounds, the placing of foliage, the dressing of wells, wassailing, processions and carnivals, races and contests). There is a plethora of such sites and customs, suggesting the turning of the wheel is a national pastime. It is something we have been doing for a long time.

The ancient peoples of the British Isles built great monuments in circular patterns, such as Stonehenge and Avebury, to create sacred space and mark the passing of time. They noticed over many years of careful observation the cycles of the moon, sun and stars, and marked these on what are, in effect, giant stone chronometers. They sought to synchronise with the greater turning. On this journey, on two wheels (my 2001 Triumph Legend 900TT) across Britain and Ireland, I shall endeavour to do the same, as I search out the places and people who mark the seasons and cycles in their own special way, in rituals, ceremonies and festivals, both private and public, large and intimate, ancient and modern. Along the way I will experience and relate moments of sacred time found in the unlikeliest of places and circumstances, showing how 'sacred time' is a state of mind that can be experienced not only at sacred sites, but in the everyday, in the familiar. A collection of reflections about being fully alive in the twenty-first century and all that means, as much a modern travelogue, *Turning the Wheel* offers:

- A useful overview of seasonal Britain for the visitor and the resident, making an ideal 'starting point' for days out/holidays/touring.
- A celebration of Britain's cultural and creative biodiversity.
- A 'taster' of alternative modalities, showing different lifestyles, ways of being and seeing, dreaming and doing.
- An informal manual for making and marking sacred time, for creating one's own 'holy days'.

Everyone loves a party; celebrations are our tribal way of making and marking 'special time', outside time, when, briefly, we step off the wheel at the same time as acknowledging its turning. Great Britain and Ireland seem to have more than their fair share of such seasonal celebrations. Some are well known, some are obscure, all are eccentric expressions of both being alive and being British in a modern country in an ancient land, encapsulating something simultaneously unique and universal: creative expressions of cultural and community identity — the UK's DNA.

Part of the purpose of this book is to make conscious these opportunities for sacred time; to not be simply swept along by them; to witness them and participate; to create a map not of place, but of time – an organic, highly personal attempt at Four Dimensional cartography. Yet, inevitably, any such endeavour is going to be finite, unfinished, and flawed. The map of Britain's sacred time is always going to be a work-in-progress. Revisions and additions are being added every day. Every private celebration, which creates in its small way, 'special time', adds to it: a birthday party, a wedding anniversary, a Christening, a day when a lost loved one is remembered, when a 'family tradition' is repeated – a favourite walk, followed by lunch in a favourite pub; a special meal; the bringing out of family relics; the interruption of temporal normality by the rituals that break down the walls of time; even a retro fancy dress party does this in its own mundane way. Every old classic pop song is a kind of time machine, taking us back to the time when we first heard it, danced to it, had a peak experience to it. These moments can occur when we least expect them – in the middle of the day, listening to the radio while doing the washing up. A song will come on with strong associations for us and 'time will stop'; we'll be swept back into the past, lost in a Proustian reverie, triggered by a musical Madeleine. Einstein said time is relative, and such moments show how malleable time is: how 'time flies when we're having fun'; how it can expand and condense, freeze and dance.

Riding my Triumph Legend, time certainly flies by. My 'time travelling on two wheels' may seem whimsical, but at the heart of this book is a wish to not only appreciate the many inspiring sites in Britain, but also modern culture. I hope to celebrate grassroots creativity and the locally distinctive, as manifest in the many fabulous seasonal events that bind communities together.

Turning the Wheel is not an attempt at a comprehensive gazetteer of calendrical Britain – that has been done elsewhere (e.g. *The Stations of the Sun* by Ronald Hutton) and I don't wish to reinvent or replicate. Instead, I have opted for a subjective 'eye witness' approach, hoping that what is lost in overview is made up for in an evocation of what it actually feels like to be at one of these colourful celebrations. If it gives the reader a taste and whets their appetite then it would have done its job.

But where to start?

There are so many seasonal customs and festivals in Britain, it would be nigh on impossible for one person to experience them all in a lifetime, let alone one year – for many, inevitably, occur on the same day. One couldn't physically get to Up-Helly-Aa, up in Shetland, and the Carhampton Wassail, close by each other in the dead of winter at different ends of the country (not without a teleport device or time machine). Choices have to be made. And so I set myself realistic parameters of what I could experience in my fortieth year. I have made a couple of exceptions where an event I could have gone to was cancelled (e.g. Cheese Rolling, Gloucestershire; Mari Llwyd, Chepstow), in which case I have drawn upon previous experience. Nevertheless, sticking to my general remit – what I can experience on two wheels in a year – I feel I have managed to cover a reasonable amount of ground. It has certainly made for a colourful and entertaining year! I have included verbatim extracts from the journal I have kept during this period, written often *in situ* or immediately afterwards. As such, these field notes are perhaps muddy and crumpled at times, but capture my experience as authentically as possible.

I hope you find this book useful and inspiring.

See you on the road.

Kevan Manwaring, Bath/Stroud

AUGUST

Birthday Bardic Showcase
22nd August
Oh, my head...!

I turned forty last Wednesday (had a lovely dinner party in my garden with close friends) and decided to push the boat out with a big bash at Chapel Arts Centre, in central Bath, on Saturday. Having had a few quiet birthdays, I mulled over how I would like to spend my fortieth and decided that I could think of no more agreeable a way of celebrating than having a Bardic showcase featuring my friends, and so, with this in mind I set to work.

I planned it months in advance, but as ever, everything seemed to need doing at the last minute. After a fraught week it all fell into place.

My good friend from Iceland, Svanur Gisli Thorkelsson secured the venue, prepared the buffet and MCed the evening – what a giant! He had returned from his homeland the day before (I half expected a beard rimed with hoar-frost, fresh back from the 'land of ice and snow', but he was, as ever, freshly shaven). We caught up over a quick drink at the Green Park Brasserie and then we set to work.

We 'hunted and gathered' for the buffet in the sterile wilderness that is Sainsbury's, while Jonathan, the venue manager for the night, set up the sound and lights.

Everything was prepared, ready and looking great (cabaret-style seating, atmospheric lighting, a show-reel of embarrassing photos, good tunes...) by the time the first guests arrived.

And the party began!

Svanur introduced the evening and got everybody to sing *Happy Birthday* to me in Icelandic!

Then I came on and did a couple of 'old classics' of mine: my poems *Maid Flower Bride* (for all the women who've blessed my

9

life – and had to put up with me!) and *One with the Land* (my green man 'rap' – for all the guys). I got everyone to join in on the second one, and it seemed to work. Relieved of my Bardic duties, I then got down to the serious business of making merry.

I sat back and was entertained by my dear, talented friends...

Jay Ramsay, poet and psychotherapist from Stroud, did some wise and heartfelt poems, delivered with complete authenticity and passion.

Brendan the pop poet, and sixth Bard of Bath, did a couple of his classics on request.

Saravian, alluring jazz siren, performed some lovely cool numbers.

Anthony Nanson, fellow storyteller of Fire Springs, performed an amazing feat of memory with his wonder voyage of Bran mac Ferbal: a lost island myth close to my heart!

Then... no Bard of Glastonbury (lost in the mists of Avalon...?) and so we went straight to the break, as we were running a 'bit behind'.

This was fine as it allowed people to chat, for me to mingle with my guests and be inundated with more presents, rapidly filling up the front of the stage. Oh, and drink more champagne (mixed with mead in a dangerous concoction called 'Druid's delight' – although after the hangover it gave me I think it should be renamed 'Bardic blight')!

Things were going swimmingly – the second CD, 'Dancin' Pants', had kicked in and the atmosphere was buzzing. The hall looking pretty full and there had only been a couple of technical hitches. We couldn't get the Chapel's system to play my first prepared CD; ironically it was called 'Let the Ceremony Begin'! And the projector proved temperamental; at one point the photo show-reel disappeared completely and Jonathan struggled to get it back. He finally gave up, but suddenly, during the second half we had my desktop projected onto the stage. I struggled to re-launch the show-reel, my cursor wavering behind the heads of the performers. Hilariously, I wasn't able to see the image clearly as I didn't have my glasses – a telling sign of my age! – so I just had to hit and hope, and fortunately it kick-started the photos again.

There was a fantastic crowd, but also tellingly absent friends. I missed my dear old Dad (rest his soul), as well as my brother and sister not being there – but many of them were represented in the photos, which was an inadvertent portrait of my relationships/friendships over the years as much as anything.

After the break, we had Marko Gallaidhe, a man you don't meet every day, dressed in his trademark black with plenty of silver bling, long white hair flowing from beneath his dark trilby. He was somewhat caught on the hop, so while he made his way to the stage everyone sang me *Happy Birthday* (in English this time), which was very touching. I felt truly blessed.

After Marko did a couple of fine tunes (*Danny Boy* and *Between the Tweed*) Richard Selby came up and did a great story.

Another Fire Springer followed, Kirsty Hartsiotis, with a tale and a beautiful poem by her mum, inspired by me, called *Bard Song*, which blew me away.

Then, it was the turn of Wayland, who I was delighted to see had made it down from his Smithy in Oxfordshire to perform a fine story. A former Bardic student of mine, he has come into his own as a good performer.

The first of a pair of friends from Northampton came next, Jimtom Say...? – a true shaman Bard who shared some of his incredible poetry and a song.

Peter Please was next on, but was nowhere to be seen. Then he turned up – right on cue, just arriving from his singing group, and, a true pro, was able to go right on stage and deliver his great stories.

Finally, it was the turn of my oldest friend, Justin, who delivered a blazing set of poetry and music, culminating in a poem especially written for me, for my big day, based (bizarrely, but brilliantly) upon the Billy Joel tune *He Didn't Start the Fire – 2009: A Kevan Odyssey*! Hilarious and impressive:

> *He didn't start the fire, but he his Bardic learning helped me keep it burning.*
> *He didn't start the fire, but he helped me light it … though I tried to fight it!*

I thanked everyone and then… it was time to dance! I was looking forward to this and it was great to 'cut some rug', even if we risked looking like the adults that were embarrassing to watch dancing when you were a kid! But that was all part of an old git rites-of-passage I guess! It was great to get down with my friends.

Alas, all good things… After a few stomping tunes, we'd passed the curfew and the music was turned down, but I had allowed for this, arranging to go around the corner to the Lounge. About twenty of us left for this 'promised land' – Sara insisted I led my merry band, mead horn in hand. We piled downstairs, where we took over the room. Unfortunately the music was rather jarring – hard techno – so I went back to get my CDs, only to discover their machine 'couldn't play them'. Instead, Marko did a rousing ballad after I had revived him with a glass of wine. And then Justin led the Southern Baptist song, *Down to the River*, which we all joined in with a drunken religious fervour! It felt like the foundation of some kind of guerrilla folk republic, but it was short-lived, as the music came back on. Fortunately, this time it was decent Latin Jazz, and suddenly we were up dancing. I got to dance with a lovely lady who swirled about in my arms. It was a great way to end the evening. After that, things went downhill – Justin got a round of tequilas in (at least a dozen shots) then managed to knock them all flying as the waitress carried them over on a tray. Maybe should have seen that as a sign… It was definitely the straw that broke the camel's back. I staggered to the gents and had to be 'talked out' by my friend,

Svanur. He got me out of the building, only for me to collapse in a heap on the pavement. A taxi was called, but refused to take me – not surprisingly in my bilious state. Another taxi turned up, pulling up behind the first one. Justin told the first taxi driver to 'F@#* off!'; in a tizz, he reversed into the back of the taxi behind, leading to an altercation. It was rapidly turning into some kind of slapstick comedy. Fortunately, a third taxi agreed to accept me as a passenger. My mates hauled me in and I was whisked away, the streets of Bath a blur of neon. We pulled up in front of my flat – someone paid – and I was frogmarched down the steps to the front door. They flopped me on my bed, pulled off my boots and threw the duvet over me – bless 'em! The room slowly stopped spinning and blissful oblivion followed.

The next day, oh boy, how I suffered! In the immortal words of Withnail, 'I feel like a pig shat in my head'. A weak, pathetic bed-ridden thing unable to hold anything down or even hold a conversation for long, I wallowed in my self-inflicted misery. Fortunately, the guys got it together (three of them had crashed in my living room). My old friends Justin and Jimtom went back to clear the place and collect my stuff – stars! Amazingly I hadn't lost anything valuable in my drunken stumblings. They dropped Wayland off at the station and hit the roads themselves... onto another party! I went to bed.

Despite my sufferings – it had all been worth it. Without a doubt, one of the best night's of my life. I glow with happiness at the memory of it all. Never had I felt so truly blessed. It felt like the first forty years of my life had ... meant something.

That evening, slowly recovering, I savoured opening the many presents I had been showered with – a pile of beautiful things, for which I am deeply touched, but, of course, true friendships forged (old and new) are the greatest gift of all.

To all those who made the effort to come, and made it such a success – thank you!

And apologies to the taxi driver!

My birthdays are not always so raucous (although, I suspect my experience is far from unique). I doubt I'll have another such shindig until my fiftieth. The last time I made such an effort was for my thirtieth (as a culture we seem to like round numbers), when I held a gathering at a local woodland, Rocks East Woodland, at which I invited all my friends from Bath (my home town then for the last four years) and from my old home town of Northampton. Having established myself in my adopted city – winning the Bardic Chair of Bath in 1998 – I felt ready to do this, to reclaim my past. I had not intended to cut myself off completely, but had needed to initially 'snap the elastic' (which notoriously pulls people back to the town – so far, fourteen years on, I have eluded that urge). Yet I had left some dear friends behind and I was missing them, and so I invited them down to my party in the woods. We camped in a circle and gathered around the main fire in the evening to share stories, songs and poems (as I am wont to do). It was very moving for me (and a little surreal) to see friends old and new gathered and mingling – an early dress rehearsal for *This is your Life*. The mead horn was no doubt passed around and there was certainly much merriment. The event became established as a kind of annual reunion for five or so years (my friends nicknamed it 'Kevfest'), until I decided that I didn't want myself or my birthday to be the focus of it. I encouraged others members of our circle to take it on, but it petered out. I can still vividly remember the last time we all stood in a circle at the end of the camp, holding hands, looking at each other, tears welling up – I didn't want to leave and lingered, perhaps sensing the finality of it – the 'breaking of the fellowship'. A couple of years later one of our number committed suicide and this has stopped it dead. We all met up at the funeral (a woodland burial, with Pagan, Christian and Buddhist service to honour our friend's varied beliefs), but it has been almost too painful to meet up since. Perhaps that will change.

Another birthday, I found myself leading a hand-fasting. A former storytelling student of mine, John, and his partner, Colette, wished to get hand-fasted at Swallowhead Spring, by Silbury Hill. John, having been on one of my 'Way of Awen' weekends in Wales, asked me if I would lead the ceremony. I had never done this before (although I had attended several) and never intended to be celebrant, but when friends ask, and the date they have chosen happens to fall on your birthday, I decided it was too special to decline. I like to set myself challenges. And so I met up with them a couple of times and discussed what they would like. Taking on board their wishes, I designed a ceremony for them, one that would work with the sacred landscape immediately abutting Swallowhead Spring. The womenfolk would gather there, preparing the bride and her sacred grove; she would wait behind a screen of willows to be invited into the circle at the right time, the 'goddess manifesting'. The men-folk would gather up the hill inside West Kennet long barrow, where we would prepare the bridegroom with drumming and chanting. We would then process down the hill in ritual fashion, led by drums. We would approach the stream running alongside the edge of the grove, where we would be challenged by a representative of the women. We would only be allowed to enter if she was convinced of the bridegroom's honourable intentions. A friend would speak on his behalf, vouching for his good heart and true love. If the women deigned to let us enter their sacred grove, we would process over the stepping stones. We would form a circle, blending the two parties. Everyone would hold hands and 'arrive'. The quarters would be called, with volunteers invoking the elements. I would lead an Awen, inviting in the fifth element of spirit. And then the bride would be invited to step forward from under the arch of willows – the 'goddess' revealed in all her glory. I would then invite the couple into the centre and ask them to exchange vows. I would 'bind' their hands with a cord. They would step over a besom as a symbolic threshold and would be scattered with oats and rice for fertility. Cakes and ale would be passed around and there would be the sharing of songs and poems, prayers, good wishes and other offerings, before we closed the circle and shared a picnic.

All this went according to plan. We were blessed with glorious sunshine. The ceremony flowed with the land and its energies. Holding a hand-fasting at Swallowhead Spring, at the source of the Kennet, felt very symbolic. I used the metaphor of the river as the journey of love, on which they were embarking together. We chanted 'the river is flowing', and for once this over-familiar campfire classic seemed resonant and full of beauty. Everybody felt included and had an opportunity to contribute. The success of such an event is in ensuring everyone has input, and thus 'ownership'. Therefore, delegation of duties is essential. Allow people to share their talents, their creative gifts – in costume, food, music, logistics (e.g. the site was marked out with red and purple ribbons – the respective liveries of bride and groom). Careful planning enables the Awen to flow on the day. Create a beautiful, loving, solid framework – with 'those who know' holding the space – and good things will manifest. The couple were very happy with how things went. The groom, John, later wrote: *'Thank you so much for the beautiful, sensitive, powerful way that you guided our hand-fasting ceremony. It was the most powerful part of our day and everyone we have spoken to has said how deeply moved they were by the ceremony.'* The photographs show lots of beaming faces and an event that looks very beautiful and magical. I was honoured to be given the privilege of performing such a sacred duty for this couple. It was a very memorable way to spend a birthday.

But the wheel turns and the new season brings other celebrations to attend, as well as the demands of making a living – challenging us to find the sacred in the everyday.

SEPTEMBER

Awen Autumn – Gathering in the Harvest
30th August – 1st September

It's been a busy time preparing for the new season/term. It has felt as though I've been gathering in the harvest in terms of projects and plans coming to fruition. But, at the same time, I've been wringing the last few drops of summer as the holidays come to an end. The sizeable lady hasn't sung yet!

Saturday, I held an Awen Summer Gathering around my place. Awen authors (from the small press I run, founded in 2003) and kindred spirits converged in my garden to discuss ideas and plans for the small press. Jay Ramsay talked about his inspiring initiative, *Angels of Fire*, and Peter Please (Away Publications), Skip Palmer (Tuff Talk Press) and David Lassman (Bath Writers' Workshop; Jane Austen Centre) shared their experience and expertise. Loads of great ideas were shared – and with such talented people to collaborate with, anything is possible!

Sunday, I performed in a 'Cascade of Words and Music' at Prior Park – a local National Trust property – an event organized by local Poetry Society Stanza Rep, Nikki Bennett , to celebrate its centenary. Featured poets included the ever fabulous Rose Flint and Crysse Morrison, plus storytellers Anthony Nanson and Peter Please. It was a little drizzly and overcast, but that didn't dampen the spirits of the connoisseurs of verse gathered – the venue couldn't be more conducive to romantic musings (the Palladian Bridge was used in the recent film of *Pride and Prejudice*; and novelist Henry Fielding lived on the edge of the estate, inspired in part by Ralph Allen in his writing of *Tom Jones*). I tried out some new poems and the response was very positive. It was nice to have a drink afterwards with Anthony,

Svanur and Ola – the latter a wordsmith from Bonn, Germany, but able to converse with my Icelandic friend in his native tongue. Talented polyglots!

Monday, I took a day off from it all and went on a blat to Stoney Littleton Long Barrow and the white horse of Westbury – after it stopped raining – enjoying a ride out on my wheels, a year on from when I first purchased her in Plymouth, thanks to my dear friends Nigel and Jenny.

Tuesday, I set up an exhibition of Awen titles in Bath Central Library (with help from the industrious Mr Lassman) to kick-start Awen Autumn – a whole season of events connected to my small press: book launches, talks, workshops, performances... More than you can shake a spear at!

That evening, Fire Springs gathered around the Cauldron to record a sampler CD to send to potential venues. No rest for the Bardic!

Wednesday, Bath Writers' Workshop restarted with my session at the New Inn, workshopping poetry, prose fiction and creative non-fiction. We had eight – regulars and new faces. David and I have coordinated a whole program of creative writing events for the coming months: surgeries, seminars, courses and guest writers. David has prepared a snazzy newsletter, called 'Follow Your Bliss' after Joseph Campbell's famous dictum, and I have built our website: www.bathwriters-sworkshop.co.uk

Tomorrow, off to Great Yarmouth to give a talk at a conference on The Sea in Legend and Tradition about my book *Lost Islands*. Before then I've prepared another title for publication – *The Angel in the Forest*, Niamh Clune. There's also Mary Palmer's posthumous poetry collection launch on Tuesday (8th September) at Waterstone's, Bath, with readings from family and friends (proceeds to Dorothy House Hospice) and mine, for the third Windsmith novel, *The Well Under the Sea*, on a boat, Pulteney Princess, on September 22nd.

Now, I better get some sleep before the long ride ahead!

Tall Ships and Tall Tales
Time & Tide, Great Yarmouth, 4th – 6th September

Over the weekend, I went on a long ride-out (500 mile round trip) across England to Great Yarmouth, to give a talk at the Folklore Society's annual conference – this year held at the Time and Tide maritime museum – on 'The Sea in Legend and Tradition'. Having seen the call for papers, I decided that a talk on lost islands (connected to my 2008 book from Heart of Albion Press) would be appropriate – I proposed it and was accepted. I set off Friday after lunch, taking my usual route back to the old town across the Cotswolds. About half-way I had a pit-stop at Delapre Abbey – my old haunt in Northampton – before arriving in Great Yarmouth, the other side of the country, at 8pm.

I dumped my stuff in the B&B and hit the town, following the gaudy neon seafront in search of sustenance. The vegetarian options were limited, to say the least. Why British seasides have to be so tacky, I don't know; can't they raise the bar and try for a Mediterranean ambience? We may not have the climate, but that doesn't mean it has to be always so naff. Does the modern holidaymaker actually want deafening amusement arcades, tatty piers, crazy golf, Noddy trains, and Z-list cabaret?

I met up with some of the fellow delegates in the Old White Lion, apparently Great Yarmouth's oldest building and pub – shame one has to run the gauntlet of the dodgy backstreets to find it. It was easy to spot the conference crowd, as one of them was in the middle of a sea ballad. The convener, Jeremy, identified by his purple balloon, was friendly enough and I got chatting with a chap called Mark, who was there to talk about lighthouses. My greeting to my fellow delegates ('Ya-haa ship mates!') failed to elicit a response. The pub's pooch was friendlier, a cheeky fellow called Spider, who delighted in jumping up on the seats next to the customers. At least the beer was alright, but I was too tired from my long ride to have more than one.

On the way back to the B&B, I made a detour onto the beach and enjoyed the full moon glittering upon the dark sea, gleaming through the mother-of-pearl cloud – a touch of sublime beauty amidst the kitsch seaside 'attractions', going some way to redeeming the 'set-your-teeth-on-edge' aesthetic of the place.

Wandering those moon-drenched shores, I started to have strange hallucinatory thoughts about werewolf mermaids, so I thought it was time I went to bed…

The next day, I arrived at the museum and signed in, getting my badge. There followed a number of papers on diverse subjects: sea beans, oysters, cannibalism(!), selkies, ghosts, shanties & ballads…

My turn came around 3pm – I started by declaring my interest (passion) for islands. I shared an extract of Oisín and Niamh – a classic lost island myth, which I used as a framing narrative in my book. And then I went into the Call, the Crossing, Arrival and Return. It was all over rather quickly (30 minutes, including questions). I felt drained, nodding off in the next talk, but seemed to do okay, because I sold a modest six books, and at least two delegates said it was down to my style of talk, my approach.

After the day's proceedings, I went to check out the Maritime Festival with my new friend, the lighthouse chap, Mark. There were a couple of impressive tall ships, but the rest was under-whelming – perhaps because it was winding down for the day.

Worn out by the day of talks, I went back to the B&B and crashed out, soothed by Mendhelsson's Scottish Symphony on the Proms. Went out to eat – reading Austen whilst dining alone in a cheap 'taverna' with the most awful table wine. After fresh-ening up, I made my way back over to the Old White Lion, hoping to bump into some of the conference crowd, but they had all gone off to some restaurant. Quaffing a lonely pint of Spitfire, I headed back to the digs, resigning myself to a rather dismal night in. An excellent Beatles documentary and, appropriately, *Pirates of the Caribbean* (yo-ho!) offered some mild compensation for the lack of company, but not my most exciting Saturday night!

Next morning I awoke early, looking forward to hitting the road. I packed and polished off a large breakfast, before taking the bike down to the seafront, where I sat and enjoyed the view, waiting for things to start. The morning was a 'light' one, with a story, a documentary and a talk. Once things had finished, I dropped some of my books off at A Novel Idea and headed west, relieved to be leaving but not altogether dissatisfied with my weekend: the book sales had helped to cover my costs and it was good to see the sea and imbibe the obscure maritime arcana, which whetted my appetite for my imminent pilgrimage to Iona with Anthony later this week.

Stopped off to see my Mum for a cuppa (which also made it worthwhile) before gratefully heading back across the Cotswolds – the landscape getting increasingly beautiful the further west my wheels took me. As always, it was with huge relief that I returned to the oasis of *Aquae Sulis*. It was good to be back in Bath.

Sleepwalking on the Isle of Dreams
Iona Hostel, Lagandorain
11ᵗʰ September

Anthony and I arrived yesterday early evening on the ferry from Oban (via Mull). Beautiful golden light – the skies clearing as we approached the island. Smooth crossing after a bumpy ride on the Mull bus with a grumpy driver. The night before we had stayed in Glasgow at Anthony's friend's place – Peter, an old university friend, who was most hospitable – offering us a beer from his fine collection (I had a bottle of 'Ossian'). His wife made a lovely meal, and the company was pleasant (another of Anthony's old college friends happened to be staying as well –

Andrew), but I was too tired to really enjoy things and went to bed as soon as dinner was over. It had been a tiring few days, with the preparation for the trip and the launch of Mary's book at Waterstone's the night before we departed – which was a big event for us.

Our trip to Iona is, in a way, a pilgrimage for Mary: last year I published her book *Iona* and this year we are taking copies of her new book (*Tidal Shift*) to the island – to the Iona Community Shop. Anthony has managed to arrange a reading on Tuesday night, so it feels like we will be honouring our friend's memory in a meaningful way – it marks the end of the journey that began earlier this year. In January, I suggested to Mary a collection. In June she died of cancer. Three months after her death, we published *Tidal Shift*, and now here we are. We were asked to bring up a twenty to thirty books for the shop – we couldn't quite manage that(!), but still ten books each on top of all our kit made for a heavy load, and with the provisions we bought in Glasgow, even heavier. The worst bit – in terms of effort and endurance – was the hike from the quayside in Iona to the hostel, right up the north end of the island. Yet the evening was beautiful and it was euphoric to have finally arrived on an island I have been meaning to visit for a number of years. I feel it was clearly not meant to happen until this year – in the wake of Mary's death and the launch of her book it is especially resonant. What with my publishing Mary's *Iona* collection last year and her Selected Poems this year, and our planned reading on Tuesday, it feels like we are participating and even contributing to the island – not just being 'consumers'. Regardless of these connotations and plans, I wish to experience the island as itself and let it work its own magic on me. I come with no agenda or script. I want to open and receive, savour and relish. The island waits to be explored, discovered. It is like a present waiting to be opened.

May it also open me.

Evening

Stunning day of glorious sunshine. Walked with Anthony to south end of the island, via the Iona Community Shop, where we dropped off the copies of Mary's book for Tuesday. We lazily ambled along the coves, stopping often to soak up the sun. We had no map or itinerary. It felt wonderful, after days of intense, time-conscious activity, meeting deadlines, etc.

We stopped at a high bluff overlooking the sea around the southern end of Iona and had our lunch of soup and sandwiches, relaxing in the sun. Then we wended our way towards what turned out to be Columba's Bay, where he apparently had landed. Here, we stopped to write on separate outcrops and ended up having siestas. Afterwards, we made our way back north, stopping on the Hill of the Lamb to talk about woundings – our conversation had turned in this direction after I mentioned how Columba was probably suffering Post-Traumatic Stress Disorder when he arrived in Iona, and guilt, having been the cause of a massacre of 3000 warriors in a calamitous battle back in Erin. He had chosen the white martyrdom – never to see his homeland again – as the 'bay of the back of Ireland' suggests. Perhaps he hoped that the isle of druids – the first place he made landfall – would purge him of his sins. He arrived, a man wanting to be shriven. The island worked its magic and turned him into the legend he is. Finally finding a track (we'd spent most of the day absent-mindedly bog-trotting, lost in conversation) we headed back to 'civilisation' – the tiny hamlet where a bar and a cold beer awaited. We couldn't resist, as we passed one by the quayside, where we sat on the terrace enjoying the Mediterranean climate and vista: turquoise sea, brightly coloured boats, dramatic mountainous backdrop. We were truly blessed on our first full day in Iona with one of the best days of the year here. We returned to the hostel in the 'hollow of the otter', satisfied and pleasantly weary. Tea and 'Tiffin' awaited. As Anthony prepared dinner (taking his turn), I watched the full disc of the sun slip over the horizon – the end of a perfect day on Iona.

Bay of the Woman of the Dislocated Shoulder
12th September

We both slept well and so were in better shape the next day, which was just as well. After a relaxing start to the day – no timetable, no rush – we packed some lunch and headed up to Dun I, the tallest peak on the island. Here, we sat against the walnut whip-shaped cairn and read and wrote in silent contentment. Anthony read to me the first draft of a new poem, composed on the spot. I shared some musings and we discussed various literary arcana. Then we descended, following the north-west coast of the island around – wild and unvisited – a rocky terrain interspersed with spongy bogs across which we trotted. It was satisfying to just strike out into wild country, with no map, following no path. Of course, we had the reassurance that on a small island you can't get lost. We stopped in a cove for lunch, lying back against a perfectly sloping rock by some 'flotsam art'.

I got up and walked to a rock ledge, where I sat, enjoying the crashing waves, when something caught my eye – it was a stoat of some kind (a pine marten?) popping up its head from behind a ridge of rocks to my right, thirty foot away. I froze and it deliberated whether I posed a threat or not. Thinking better of it, it retreated, but I felt blessed by the wild. We finally made it to Ban Bay mid-afternoon – a beautiful wide beach, the sand made of 'granules' of shells. Here, we took off our boots and socks and bathed our hot feet in the chilly Atlantic waters. We bumped into a Dutch lady staying at the hostel. Anthony had had a good chat with her and her friend Yvonne the night before. She wandered off as we went for a paddle. Then we saw her waving from the rocks. At first, I thought she wanted to take a photo. We went closer; still I couldn't make out what she was saying. Then we were within earshot. She had hurt her arm in a fall. I inspected it and it felt like something was sticking out, but not breaking the skin – a dislocated shoulder or a bad sprain, I couldn't tell. I fashioned a sling from her scarf and appraised the situation. We had to extricate her from the awkward rock pool area she had trapped herself in, which took some doing. I went in front, Anthony behind. We had to wade through a slimy pit of seaweed. Fortunately, nothing nibbled our toes and we made it to the sand. We sat her down on my fleece and tried to call – no signal. I ran up to the rise and tried again, to no avail. So we quickly decided that Anthony should stay with her while I went for help. Taking a swig of water, off I ran. Ali had left her hire bike by the gate back by the road; I leapt on this and pedalled furiously in search of help. I came to a house on the left and ran up to the front, where an old lady was sitting outside – a local I ascertained. She was unfazed by my news (perhaps it was a common occurrence, or it was something to do with living on a small island that makes you unflappable), and was very helpful, ringing round. First she rang the hostel, figuring John there would have first aid: no luck. Fire Station – no response! She tried various friends – there was a nurse, but 'she wasn't in the first flush of youth', as she put it. So we decided to try and collect her the casualty in their car. Douglas, her husband, turned up and accepted the situation without the bat of an eyelid. He drove his family car back to the beach. I opened and closed the gates. He managed to get his car along the sandy track all the way to the top of Ban Bay. We helped Ali up to the car, and she was whisked off to the nurse, who it turned out had broken her arm recently as well! She couldn't do much to help. The doctor on Mull was called and they advised that Ali should be taken over on the ferry. Douglas instantly agreed to do this – bless him – and Anthony went with them, as Ali didn't want to be alone. I took Ali's bike back to the bike hire and caught my breath, writing a couple of postcards by the quayside. What an afternoon! So much for a relaxing siesta on the beach...but it was good to be there to help Ali. I wearily walked back to the hostel, and informed John, who was going to the ferry. He didn't see Douglas or Anthony there, so we assumed that Ali was stuck on Mull. Fortunately, he had got an earlier one back and was rendezvousing with Ali's friend, Yvonne, breaking the news to her. Meanwhile, I recovered over a cuppa. A new guest, a German guy living on 'an island' in Switzerland', offered me the rest of his spaghetti for which I was grateful, being ravenous and too tired to cook anything by that point. Angels appear when you need them.

Wild-sleeping
13th September

One day, when St Columba was living on Iona, he set off into the wilder parts of the island to find a place secluded from other people where he could pray alone. (III, I)

Yesterday Anthony and I decided to 'do our own thing' – not through any fall-out, just to take it easy. As with all our decisions so far, we came to it quite quickly and effortlessly. One of the joys of this holiday has been the spontaneity and commonality of feeling. We've decided to do things in the moment and with ease. Having had three days together, the preparation and long journey up, on top of the book launch, made for a tiring schedule we've slowed to an island pace of doing things – the Iona groove. Although we usually wake around 8, and begin the day with a solo walk along the beach – as today (enjoying the glorious morning along an unspoilt stretch of sand) – we haven't been leaving the hostel till 10ish, often being the last. Today, I was even later, deciding to have a crack at my novel, *The Wounded Kingdom*, which has a section set on versions of Iona and Staffa. I sat in our dorm room and read through some of it on the laptop, tweaking and enhancing my description of the island. It was difficult to get into the zone with all the comings and goings (three older American ladies who had stayed in our dorm – one in the top bunk above each of us, Anthony, myself and the Glaswegian geologist – who turned out to be nature writers, were in a flurry of leaving to continue their three week tour of Britain and Ireland), but at least I made a start. That morning, before breakfast (porridge, honey and apricots), I walked to the 'White Strand of the Monks', its beautiful name and appearance belying its bloody past: here in 806CE Viking raiders massacred 63 monks. As I went to urinate amid the dunes (the hostel toilets taken over by the morning rush), I noticed a white stone in the sand and picked it up. It was a smooth pebble of quartz – it seemed an apt souvenir of Iona, an island of 'white peace'. I walked along the pale sand, taking in the vista of mountains and sea, slowly waking. I spotted some tracks that I speculated could have been those of the kind of stoat I saw yesterday. I tracked them as they wove along the beach, between the rocks. I reached a buttress of rocks where I recited my morning praise, glad to be alive. The weather here has been fair for three days now, and I feel truly blessed by it. Reaching the far point, I walked back through the long, dew-soaked grass, silvering in the waves of wind and sunlight.

Finally extricating myself from the hostel – it was a glorious day and it would be a shame to waste, though it was nice to indulge in some finger-tapping – I walked along the road to the Iona Community Shop opposite the Abbey, and waited contentedly for it to open at noon, it being a Sunday. Inside, I noticed with pleasure the lovely poster they had done for the reading Anthony and I are giving there on Tuesday. I purchased the excellent map of the island with all the fabulous place names on. I scrutinised it over a cup of coffee ('cheaper than Starbucks!' I had joked to another customer). With this in hand, I headed back along the lane to the start of the footpath up to Dun I; from there I took a bearing to the Big Hill of the Querns, where I hoped to find the legendary Well of the North Wind. It was satisfying to strike out with a compass and a map by myself. Away from the main attractions, Iona quickly becomes wild. I didn't see anyone for the next two or three hours as I made my way across the boggy landscape to the rocky outcrop of the Big Hill. Here, at the far end, I discovered (what I thought was) the Well – a circular enclosure beneath the far western cliff. It could easily be mistaken for a sheep-fold. Perhaps it was, but I couldn't see anything else that fitted the description. After enjoying my packed lunch, I descended to it and made my 'offering' – a length of plaited material I had found. I asked for a blessing on *The Windsmith Elegy* (my series of Bardic novels), then I found myself singing a melody that rose up with conscious thought – two parts, alternating, interweaving. It would have probably sounded painful to the casual listener, but it felt good to do it, to give voice to the wind.

Feeling I had honoured Boreas, I went to the 'Hermit's Cell', the remains of a roundhouse nearby: a low circular enclosure of stones, with a doorway facing South West (for maximum light). I entered and immediately lay down on the soft grass opposite the entrance and nodded off, feeling deep peace in this secluded spot. It seems I have spent the last few days having naps in beautiful places – it could be a new outdoor fad like wild-swimming: wild-sleeping! Could I get a book deal for a book about sleeping my way across Britain, as the late Roger Deakin did with *Water Log* and swimming, I whimsied? I could see why a hermit chose this spot – it lacks a decent view, hemmed in on three sides by rocky outcrops, but is sheltered and feels miles from anywhere, when in fact, it's only a kilometre from the Abbey. Yet it might as well be in another world; for the whole hour I was there, in the middle of the day; I saw no one, even though its meant to be on the 'Pilgrim Route', the trail that loops around the island which I was trying to follow, but without clear signs, I soon lost it and found myself once more bog-trotting (another new Olympic sport?) as I headed southwest towards the Bay at the Back of the Ocean through dramatically rugged country.

Somewhat anti-climactically, I emerged from this wilderness onto, of all things, a golf course. Half the island seems to be taken up by its manicured fields – God's fairway (the Devil's rough?). I reached the glittering bay and flopped into a sandy hollow. By this point, it was hot enough to go for a swim but it was too exposed and frequented to consider skinny dipping. Having run out of water, I was forced to head back to the village, retracing my steps from yesterday at a rather more leisurely pace. On the way, I ended up chatting to a lovely old couple from Ayrshire, up with a party of fellow Christians. We talked amicably about how lovely it all was. I bid farewell to them at the quayside and bought myself an ice-cream, which somewhat restored me – enough to get me back to the hostel in good time to cook (my turn – curry) before the daily feeding frenzy started.

Of Stars and Toads

After our 'Wetherspoon's special' (as I nicknamed it) of veg curry and lager, I freshened up and decided to accompany Anthony to the Abbey for the evening 'quiet space' service. As we left, the sky was a dramatic sandwich of dark cloud, orange horizon and dark sea, which reminded me, somewhat prosaically, of a Jaffa Cake. When we arrived, just before 9pm, the Abbey was lit up with candles and looked beautiful. It had been fashioned with local stone had a wonderful 'rough-edged' quality to it, no doubt partly due to its destruction and reconstruction. It was a painless ecumenical service, with little in the way of liturgy, the focus being on (mostly) silent prayer – although the reverent peace was challenged by my spectacular sneeze at the start (I imagined a collective 'bless you!') then further coughs and fidgeting from the congregation. I enjoyed the ambience, the chance to taste a little of Iona's sacred heritage and tradition, and also the extract of Thoreau read out by the American reader, which seemed uncanny considering our encounter earlier that day with the nature writers (they had claimed the US had given the world nature writing, something A & I amusingly debunked). The service was short and sweet – a nice end to the week – and as we stepped outside into the night, we were greeted by the most spectacular star-field, which we gazed at in awe. It felt like the interior of the Abbey, with its rows of candles, turned inside out and magnified beyond comprehension – and now we worshipped in the cathedral of the stars. We walked along the lane and passed St Oran's Chapel, glowing in the night, from which emanated haunting plainsong in some Eastern European tongue. A large ghostly image of a saint could be seen, projected onto the back wall, eerily luminous, framed in the dark doorway.

We decided, on a whim, to go for a beer – Ali, having returned, arm in truss, from Mull, had given me back the deposit for the bike she had hired. So I bought us drinks with it in the third place we tried (the rest were closed), Martyrs Bay Bar, which was lively for a late Sunday. After a local ale, I sampled a shot of the local malt, 'Iona', hoping its medicinal properties would help the cold I felt coming on. We wandered back merrily to the hostel, talking about, of all things, *Star Trek*. I spotted a shooting star and thought of a loved one back home. We came across two toads in the road – feigning Kirk's unique cadence, I asked 'Spock' to attempt a mind-meld. Alas, this devil in the dark remained taciturn. We also stopped to admire a long-horned snail with our torches. At last, we were back in the 'hollow of the otter'. Contentedly, but clumsily, I returned to our dorm while Anthony read in the common room. In the darkness, I became the cartoon drunk, trying to clamber into my bunk, before falling effortlessly to sleep; even Anthony's anti-snoring device of an umbrella prod failed to disturb me from my slumber.

Fingal's Cave, Staffa
14th September
This morning, we decided to go to the world famous Fingal's

Cave on Staffa. The weather was overcast for the first time in four days, but the sea-state was fine and visibility was okay and, despite feeling a bit grotty, I decided to go, accepting that the forlorn weather created a suitably melancholic air for visiting such a Romantic iconic landmark, immortalized by Keats, Wordsworth, Tennyson and Mendelssohn. We parked and walked down to the quayside to catch the 'Iolaire', which happened to have two spaces spare. The skipper was a charismatic Scotsman with a line in yarn-spinning, engaging in his West coast brogue. He had a good local knowledge, which he was happy to share as he worked his way around the boat. I was feeling 'under the weather', which I was worried would impair my enjoyment of the place, but as we raised anchor and put out into the Sound of Iona, my spirits raised. It was great to be sailing to a magical island. Along the way, we spotted baby seals on the rocks. Anthony, a keen twitcher, scanned the waters for the sea-birds: the shags and cormorants. Before I realised, we were there. I stood up and was greeted with a full view of the island and it was breathtaking!

From a wave-smoothed granite base rose the basaltic columns to a 'head' like a giant stone muffin, an island with elephantitus. It was weird – a mixture of the organic and artificial, like some alien spaceship. And the famous cave was enticingly dark and, well, sexual.

The sun had broken through at this point and created a dramatic play of light and shadow, revealing the variegated delineations of colour – black to ochre to rust, indigo to slate blue to grey.

The formation by the jetty (known as the Herdsman) was weirdly beautiful – the columns bent in every direction, like polyps on coral frozen in motion. It looked like a piece of modern art, the Guggenheim in Bilbao transplanted into the Atlantic, an Atlantis of art.

We alighted and made a beeline to the cave. Visitors

nervously edged along the side of a narrow ledge that hugged the cliff and led a little way in. A token handrail had been provided. An orange power boat took other visitors right to the back – I half-expected a giant eye to flick open and then a vast maw to open and devour them, but it was me who was nearly gobbled up! As I made my way along the line and stood looking in awe at the sight out of legend, one of the day-trippers brusquely pushed past me and nearly tipped me into the dark waters below with not a word of apology – completely unaware of his clumsy actions, it seems. I teetered on the brink, but the Cailleach didn't claim me this time!

When the crowd thinned, Anthony and I tried an Awen. Our voices reverberated amongst the cathedral-like columns of the cave. It was a magical moment, spine-tingling. The rocks seemed to respond and come alive.

Afterwards, we picked our way back along the columnar stepping stones, stopping to make three wishes in the wishing chair. An old fella sat in it, looking content. Further on, I'd asked him if his wishes had come true yet. He said he had been coming here for thirty years, so maybe they had – at that age (he looked ninety) another year of life might be all the wish he needed. Then we ascended the steps up to the 'roof' of the island, covered with squelchy grass, but our time was running out. An hour isn't enough to do the island justice, and reluctantly we made our way back to the boat. We were the last to return and I was the last to step aboard just as the engine grumbled to life.

Our skipper put out and we left Staffa, admiring its stern flanks one last time. It had certainly been worth it, a dream come true.

Returning to Iona, we had tea at the Argyl hotel, being persuaded into pricey brownies and shortbread by the Aussie waitress. Yet the pots of tea were capacious and it was pleasant to sit by the shore and reflect on our experiences, although serious writing was rather hampered by the chatty Lancashire ladies on the adjacent bench (A was able to pinpoint their accent – fifteen miles from his hometown). Anthony bought a couple of stamps from the tin-shack post office – a wonderfully ramshackle affair – and posted my postcards, hoping they will arrive. Then to the Spar for essentials, before checking out the Iona bookshop, as elusive as Brigadoon to catch open. I wasn't feeling up to serious browsing by this point and headed back for lemon and honey and the soothing tones of Jennifer Crook, a Bath musician, on my laptop.

Man Flu
15th September
Down with a cold so took it easy today, staying in, nursing myself and feeling sorry for myself (I imagined the headline in the Argyll Gazette: 'Outbreak of Man Flu on Iona – island in quarantine. Vaccine of malt whisky and DVDs flown in. Girlfriends on round-the-clock breakfast and massage duties'). Wrote this morning – well, worked on book. The weather had turned and was wet and miserable so felt quite happy to stay in. It brightened up later, so managed go for a little walk around the headland after lunch and practised the poems I was going to read later for Mary – at the Iona Community Shop. I tried to save myself for this, having a very lazy afternoon. I cooked with our dwindling supplies. Then we set off. It went well; we had twenty folk there, which for Iona is a crowd.

It felt well received and very poignant to do – the end of a journey for us, in terms of the book's creative arc, but hopefully the beginning of the book's journey. We shifted eighteen (10 stock, 8 sor), so our bags will be a lot lighter going back! Leaving the shop in the gathering dusk, I felt unburdened. It is done.

All's Well that Ends Well
16th September
Today we went on a final walk around the island. I was feeling a lot better – my head was clear and it felt like I had some life in my limbs. And so, in our usual way, we bimbled about and

finally left about 11 – but made a full day of it, not getting back until gone 9pm. We started off heading back up Dun I, to visit the Well of Eternal Youth, which is lodged in a gap in the north-ernmost crag. The setting is spectacular. We both drank a draught – Anthony, being the eldest, went first. We both took three sips – I for youth, maturity and age. The idea of being young forever is not appealing. I think each age of a person's life has appeal, like the seasons – we should experience them all fully. What is spring or summer without autumn and winter?

Two women from the hostel turned up. I said: 'Do you want to drink from the Well of Eternal Youth?' One of them replied, (the youngest and prettiest): 'I don't need to! 'From one well, we walked to another. I lead Anthony to the Well of the North Wind by the Big Hill of Querns, or at least to what I thought it was! But closer inspection of the map revealed it was slightly further north. We managed to find it after a bit of scrambling around – a boggy corner under a rock – and were disappointed. Preferred my first choice, but it was still satisfying to locate it. We sat in the Hermit's Cell for a while as well. Very peaceful – we imagined living there a hermit life.

Headed on to the Machair – the stretch of common land abutting the Bay of the Back of the Ocean, glittering in the sun. The tide was out. We sat and took a sip of water, then pressed on to the Bay of the White Stones, to have our lunch on a little grassy knoll in the lee of the wind, watching the spectral spumes of water from Spouting Cave.

We stayed here for a while, writing and reading. Anthony was clearly inspired and could have stayed all afternoon! But we had an island to circumnavigate, so onwards we went, ascending to the southern plateau where we navigated to the Cairn of the Back to Ireland, where St Columba was said to have done just that, turn his back on his homeland, taking the 'white martyrdom'. Here we were content to sit in the sun, enjoying the dramatic views over the south-eastern end of Iona and the shimmering sea beyond. Here we found peace and wisdom.

As the afternoon was pressing on, we headed east to the Marble Quarry in the south-eastern quarter – a strange post-industrial site of Heath Robinson-like machinery, rusting and broken, and gigantic piles of marble blocks, cut and abandoned, like some Maui-esque Easter Island cult.

Summoning our last reserves of energy, we headed north across the Plain of Wine, dreaming of our evening meal, which we enjoyed at St Columba's Hotel – courtesy of my fine companion – a treat to end our fantastic week on the island. Tomorrow, we sail back to the mainland, and our lives – but we take a little bit of Iona back with us, inside.

The journey home was a long one – eighteen hours – but it was made agreeable with Anthony's company (we jokingly modulated our accents the further south we went – from hammy Scots to Brummie!) and gave us a chance to reflect on our time on Iona. I arrived at Bath Spa station – after two ferries, two buses and four trains – at midnight. Wearily, I lugged my pack home, knowing that at 5am I had to be up to get to Stonehenge to run a ceremony for Jamie George of Gothic Image tours (no rest for the Bardic should be my motto)!

Although it was an effort, the morning was cold, clear and beautiful and to return to England in such a manner, from Iona to Stonehenge, felt a privilege and gentle reintroduction to the wheel – from one sacred site to another, from the Island of Stones, to the Great Circle of Stones. I blatted back along the virtually empty pre-rush hour roads, had a long soak to thaw out the chill of the dawn and then dived into my delightful bed to blissful oblivion, glad to be finally back home.

Summer's Wake
Solsbury Hill
21st – 27th September
This week I have been catching up with myself after the week on

Iona. There's been a lot to sort out as new terms start, etc, but amidst it all I've launched my new novel and been involved with other literary events. It's really felt like 'back to school' and a shift of emphasis – from the outward to the inward spiral. At the time of the autumn equinox, it is perhaps not surprising that it has felt both light and dark/good and bad – my week certainly has reflected that duality.

Monday, I spent mainly ploughing through my inbox and replying to messages. In the evening, I was due to start my new evening class in creative writing at Chew Valley School, but it was aborted due to low enrolment (apparently a fate several of the arts classes suffered, no doubt a by-product of the tough economic climate). Instead, I went to the Bath Storytelling Circle at the Raven, though I didn't feel very dynamic, still struggling with a cold. Numbers were down there so I forced myself to share a story in the second half to help out David, the host; I told a Scottish tale, the Well at the World's End.

Tuesday was the launch of my new novel, *The Well Under the Sea*. The plan was to launch it with a river cruise, but a phone call in the morning kaiboshed that idea; the Pulteney Princess's lights were on the blink (and the dim-witted staff seemed to be equally in the dark). Suddenly, I had to find a new venue. I looked at a couple of boats, but it was rather late in the day, to say the least. Fortunately, the Rising Sun pub came to the rescue, which just so happens to have a boat in the beer garden! So, this served as an agreeable substitute – the place has been tastefully done up since the days when the storytelling circle used to be housed there and the staff were friendly and helpful. The skittles alley provided a wet weather option, which turned out useful, as it started to drizzle – talking about raining on my parade! Still, despite the setbacks, it turned out to be a good night – I gathered guests in the garden to toast the book with a glass of mead as I stood on the prow of the boat, so at least I could say I launched the book on a boat! Then we repaired inside where I did a reading and answered questions. The atmosphere was pleasant; it was nice to see my friends there. It was a small event, but I felt like it had served its purpose – The Well was well and truly launched!

Wednesday was a busy day for Bath Writers' Workshop (David Lassman and I): we both had events in the Jane Austen Festival – I ran a writing workshop (Writing Jane) and David gave a talk (Adapting Austen); both were very popular events (sold out). Straight after, we had to go and host the fourth Wednesday event at the New Inn – Guest Writers in Conversation, once again a Bath Writers' Workshop production – with Jay Ramsay and Anthony Nanson down from Stroud. This was a superb evening; both authors gave excellent readings/performances and talked eloquently and insightfully about their work with each other: a high calibre event that could easily have been in the Bath Literature Festival and certainly deserves decent funding.

Friday was my first class of the term with the Community Learning Service, with a lovely group of older learners at Saltford Library. Afterwards, I helped my Finnish friends, Mika and Maarit, to move (they are moving to Helsinki). Fortunately, there were a few of us to shift the many boxes and bits of furniture out of the house and into the car park, where they piled up, awaiting the men with the van who got lost in Bath's one-way system (turning up two hours late!). In the evening, I went down to Glastonbury to do a second launch event for The Well... at the Cat & Cauldron. This one didn't go so well – only my dear friend Ola turned up, bless her! I cut my losses and headed home.

Saturday morning, I ran one-to-one writer consultations in Bath Central Library. In the evening, I went to Amy and Tim's joint birthday bash – a wild wild west party in Wookey – which was great fun (much needed after a tiring week). On Sunday morning, I rode back in the sun, glad to be a bard on a bike!

OCTOBER

A Typical Day (in Bath)
I discipline myself to write every morning, my best time: a
cafetière of strong coffee and I'm off. I like to write a thousand
words a day when I'm working on a book – often it's more (3-5000
on a good day). As long as I've done something creative – written
a poem, as I did yesterday for National Poetry Day; edited some
of my work; made notes about an idea – I feel I've 'scratched that
itch'! Then, after lunch, when I usually have to pop into town to
the Post Office (always things to post off) or do some other chore,
maybe bumping into a friend for a chat, I will attend to other
tasks, e.g. catching up with my Open University students online,
marking assignments, preparing for a workshop or a performance. Evenings, after dinner, it's usually off to an event, such as
Bath Storytelling Circle, Bath Writers' Workshop (which I co-run
with David Lassman), a gig (where I'm performing) or the
Garden of Awen (my monthly spoken word showcase and small
press platform). Occasionally, I have been known to have a night
off, which normally involves meeting friends for a beer, or
watching a movie if I can't stir myself from my sofa, getting in
touch with my inner-sloth. The day begins and ends with reading
then it's off to the Land of Dreams for more ideas...

Time Flies
25ᵗʰ – 26ᵗʰ October
I went time-travelling on two wheels yesterday – six thousand
years into the past – and early this morning we were all time-
travellers, briefly, as the clocks went back (as a nation, the UK
travelled one hour into the past – a country-sized time-machine).
Imagine the Good Ship Great Britain slipping through the Vortex,
in a kind of update of *The Philadelphia Experiment* (in which a US
Navy vessel travels through time, with disastrous consequences).

Sounds like a plot for *Dr Who*...

Apart from the Gallifreyan time-lord's stubbornly retro police box, there have been steam trains and De Loreans (both *Back to the Future*), battleships, starships (in *Star Trek IV: The Journey Home*, and many of the TV series episodes) and countless other plot devices, including some which do away with hardware (*The Time Traveler's Wife*). The pioneer of time-travel, HG Wells (author of *The Time Machine*, originally called *The Chronic Argonauts*, until he wisely changed it) who stayed briefly in Wookey, which I visited today on a ride-out, had a more modest chrono-conveyance – a bicycle. He once said: 'When I see an adult on a bicycle, I do not despair of the human race'. Wells clearly *did* despair, going by his gloomy prognostications, which he saw come true with dread inevitability – tanks, war in the air, genetic engineering, atomic bombs. On his grave he wished to have the epitaph: 'I told you so, you damned fools!' Wells spent an autumn at Wookey (he attended the National School there as a pupil-tutor in 1897, at the impressionable age of 13). In the long and winding road to becoming a novelist, he endured various jobs, including that of a draper in London – the experience of which fed into his cycling idyll, *The Wheels of Chance*, in which he wrote: 'You ride through Dreamland on wonderful dream bicycles that change and grow.' It tickles me to think of the young Wells cycling about Somerset, dreaming of time machines. I speculate that his time at Wookey, however brief, fired his imagination – the underworld of the Morlocks seems to have been inspired by the famous caves at Wookey Hole and Cheddar, where Neolithic remains had been found: to the Victorian mind, sub-human cavemen living below ground...

Hart Leap Point
(From field journal)
Awens of light break through the cloud, spotlights cast upon the Levels – I watch the drama of light and darkness unfold. A kestrel hovers,

poised in the hollow of the wind – he's come up here, to this high place,
for his lunch, like I. In the car park a cluster of vehicles – people having
their lunch inside. [I eat my sandwiches on a bench in a bracing wind.]
A pair of frilly knickers by my bike – cast off in the throes of passion –
a quicky in a layby – and left, a tawdry memento. Orange peel scattered
by the bench I sit on – spelling whose initial? A glider arcs high
overhead, beyond the wheeling birds. A black bird (a raven?) flips itself
as it flies along, marking an odd cry. A swathe of rain rakes the dark line
of the Quantocks on the opposing side of the Levels – gloominess passes.
The sun breaches the cloud and the Levels are flooded with light.

Wind dances around me, light and shadow. Peace and stillness. Blue
skies after the gloom. Rising above it all. Finding the centre amidst the
maelstrom. Heights from the depths. Warm sun on my face, balancing
the chill in the air. Memorial trees and benches – the phantom of other
lives linger, here, on these Hills of Peace.

After, I descended, past Ebbor Gorge, taking some notes from the
interpretation board (Pre-10,000BC: remains of Ice Age animals –
cave bear, cave lion, hyena, reindeer, wild ox, steppe pika: 3000
BC: Neolithic people sheltered in caves and under rocky ledges)
down into Wookey itself, and then through the traffic lights of
Wells to Glastonbury. I took the back lanes to the Tor – up
through Wick Hollow – parked up and climbed, making heavy
weather of it in my leathers, feeling ancient in my bones! On top,
I let the wind scour away any remaining cobwebs as I surveyed
the vista. Here is (supposedly) another great circle of time, the
wheel of the stars of the Glastonbury Zodiac, the local field
patterns providing a Rorschach Test for Katherine Maltwood in
the Twenties. We see what we wish to. Maltwood is not unique in
inventing secret or 'lost' knowledge to make herself feel special.
Glastonbury is full of such types. I'm sure some would accuse me
of being of the same ilk! But what 'mystery' do I offer, except
'stand and stare', be fully present, cherish each moment and find
your creative self?

Finally, I rode on to Shapwick, after a friend had mentioned the starlings which gather in stunning swirling clusters at this time of year. They seemed camera shy when I was there, although I did see countless flocks on the telegraph wires on the way there, as though waiting in the wings for the cue of dusk. I still enjoyed visiting the site of the Sweet Track and the Post Track – the earliest known trackways in the UK. Raised wooden walkways, they provided passage across the reedswamp between Polden Ridge and the 'island' of Westhay, a distance of 2km (1.3 miles). I love the fact that the Sweet Track was named after Ray Sweet, who discovered it while ditch cleaning in 1970. The timbers had been preserved in peat and hidden from humanity for nearly six thousand years. Radio-carbon dating has enabled the creation of the trackways to be pinpointed precisely, the Sweet Track 3806BC, and the Post Track 3838 BC. Various offerings (to the 'Gods of the Wetlands' as the interpretation board speculates) or lost items have been found alongside the tracks – flint arrowheads, a jadeite axe from the Alps, yew pins, a child's toy wooden axe – giving us a tantalising window into the people of the Levels. In that quiet place, sitting on a bench dedicated to a Gladys Hill (1903-1996), on that dark autumn day near dusk, it was easy to imagine the ancestors passing by.

Happy Halloween
31st October

Festive celebrations are a way of marking sacred time and tonight, on All Hallows' Eve, there will be countless parties of the most secular kind to mark Hallowe'en. Many think it is an American festival, and indeed its popular accoutrements have been largely imported from the across the pond – the pumpkin 'jack o' lanterns', the trick or treating, the fancy dress... the way it has been merchandised and turned into something tacky. Fall in New England, however, is beautiful to behold – in 2000 I was invited to perform at a Sacred Arts Festival on Rhode Island at the time of Samhain by my friend Debbi Mcinteer. I stayed with her in Maine by a beautiful lake surrounded by woodland, like Walden Pond itself (which was not so far away). The pumpkins on the porches, the wagon rides, the trees ablaze with colour – there, it is not tacky. But in the mainstream, Death is laughed away by crass commercialism, reduced to a skit on the Simpsons, Scooby Doo or Snoopy. The irony is that Hallowe'en, ostensibly a Christian calendrical event (the eve of All Hallows, aka All Saints, which is followed the next day by All Souls), is the ghost of a pre-Christian Celtic festival, Samhain, which marked the end of summer, the midnight of the year, and the Celtic New Year (the Celts saw midnight as the middle of the day). This was a time when livestock were moved from summer to winter pasture, passed between the bone-fires to rid them of evil spirits (on a practical level, parasites). It was a nervously critical time when tough decisions had to be made. What was to be culled, what was to be kept? It was a matter of life and death and whatever choices made had to be lived with all winter. Cattle were butchered, beef salted and stored. A 'carnival' putting away of flesh occurred – the last feast of the year before the austerity ahead. Tribes gathered to share stories, songs, genes. Celts believed that at such times – perhaps at Samhain most of all – the veil was thin. It was a time for looking forward (with divination) and looking back (with ancestor worship). The skulls of loved ones were sometimes brought out and lit with candles – the first jack o' lanterns – by followers of the Cult of the Severed Head. They were honoured, talked with, remembered, welcomed back into the circle of the living for a day outside time (or days – often the festival lasted for three days, if not longer). Divinatory games occurred (apple bobbing has survived). Apple peel was cast over ones' shoulder to discover the initial of a future lover. Forfeits and foolery helped to ward off the gloom as winter set in and nature hunkered down for a few months. There was much drinking, toasting, oath-taking, re-forging of the bonds that would protect the clan through the hard times to come... Hangovers are the same now as they were then – one way we connect with our ancestors! Indeed, it seems that if you were to strip back the plastic and the pop songs, you'll see that not much has changed. In essence, the festival remains the same, especially if combined with Bonfire Night and Remembrance Sunday. It feels Samhain has been split into these three events – it is interesting that although Remembrance Sunday commemorates the Armistice, signed on the 'the eleventh hour of the eleventh day of the eleventh month', 11th November, 1918, it falls on what would have been the original Samhain, when the twelve day shift in the calendar is taken into consideration, as Twelfth Night (5/6th January) is the original Christmas, and is still celebrated as such in some countries (e.g. Iceland). The madness of modern life is that we don't *acknowledge* these roots – large sections of the populace go crazy at Hallowe'en without really knowing why: dressing up, getting drunk, acting the fool. A similar thing occurs at Christmas, but at least most people have some inkling why it is being celebrated; this is rarely the case, however, with Hallowe'en. It is one of many instances of cultural amnesia. We enact these traditional patterns without real awareness. They are ingrained into society, but risk becoming mindless rituals, devoid of their original meaning. Here are two sharply contrasting experiences of the festival:

Samhain at Stanton Drew

I rode to Stanton Drew, my local stone circle – only twenty miles away – to take part in the OBOD (Order of Bards, Ovates and Druids) Samhain ceremony, run by the Dobunni Grove. I have been to one of theirs before, a few years ago now, and they seemed a friendly bunch. I know a handful of people who go and Ronald and Anna who run it. According to The Druid Network website, they hold an 'open public ritual' meeting at 11am on a Saturday near to IMBOLC, BELTANE, LUGHNASADH and

SAMHUINN. The DOBUNNI GROVE of OBOD hold a celebration of each Fire Festival at this Sacred Site. These are 'suitable for Pagans and friends/children of Pagans'. It was a sunny autumn day as I rode the winding undulating lanes down Chew Valley way – which was flooded to provide the reservoir for Bristol – towards Stanton Drew. Arrival at the village is heralded by a charming mushroom-shaped house. I pulled into the small car park, squeezing in next to a giant 4WD and got into 'costume', wearing my Bardic cloak and wielding my wolf-bodhran to blend in. Wearing special clothes is a universal way people enter into sacred time; it signals to the self and to others, 'I am no longer in normal time'. In some ways, it felt a disguise, although I was as much a pagan as anyone else there, though I feel less and less the need to wear such outfits these days. And yet 'disguise' is an intrinsic part of the festival, as Ana Adnoch mentioned in her introduction – it was a way of tricking the 'Good Folk', who were more present at such times, when the veil is thinner than normal. One had to take special precautions – and so the costume is a kind of psychic prophylactic! It's wise to stay 'covered up' when entering into sacred space...

As I entered the field, following behind a couple of mothers and their young children, I went to pass a rickety old kissing gate that stood by itself, no longer attached to any fence.

'You have to go through the gate!' one of the women insisted. Amused and fascinated by this ritual hokery, I obliged – it being all part of the 'tradition' created that I was willing to play along with for the duration of the ceremony. When entering sacred space, one has to oblige by the rules of those who have created it/controlling – otherwise one runs the risk of some kind of faux pas, offending the participants if not 'Invisible Ones'. It reminds me of the scene at the end of Antonioni's *Blow Up*, when the group of hippies play tennis with invisible rackets and balls. It's all a game of make believe – but isn't reality an act of consensus?

A ritual is an obvious manifestation of this, but it happens in more subtle ways in society at large: the 'invisible barriers' created by the unwritten rules.

I walked over to the stones in the far corner of the field, where quite a crowd had gathered, carefully avoiding the cow-pats. I said hello to Ronald (the last time I had seen him was at these same stones for a photo-shoot for Bard on a Bike, and now we were doing it for real) and Ana. Ana called us all down to the bottom of the field, where the remains of an avenue marked the processional route into the circle (there are in fact three stone circles – one large and two smaller). She introduced it in an engaging intuitive and intelligent way, admitting straight away that we don't actually know what the druids did, but this is what *we do*, what it means *to us now*.

Hallowe'en was taken over with the Irish to America in the nineteenth century and has now been exported to the rest of the world, through the wheels of commercialism – Guinness for the masses. She asked for ideas about Samhain from those gathered – about eighty people of varying background. There would be no easy demographic pigeonhole for those gathered – colourfully diverse, robed, unrobed, Goth, biker, folkie, hippie, greenie... The replies trickled back: 'Honouring the ancestors'; 'Death and transformation'; 'Trickery'; 'The end of the old year'; 'The Celtic New Year'; 'Bonfire'... When it felt like everyone had had a chance to pitch in (gauging these things is a subtle art), Ana performed a spine-tingling version of WB Yeats', *The Hosting of the Sidhe*, which more than anything helped to create a sense of sacred space/time. Poetry is often a neglected but is an incredibly effective way of raising energy and demarcating ritual space – for it insists on a deeper level of listening and, done well, can be spell-binding. The quality of silence and presence shifted, we were then asked to process towards the stands, but our way was soon blocked by the guardian of the threshold, a grey-haired man in magnificent green and gold hard leather armour (he had made it himself *and* forged his beautiful sword, he told me when I chatted to him just before the ceremony commenced). A ritual dialogue took place, as our entry was negotiated. Suitably appeased, we were allowed to enter the sacred place, passing beneath a veil held by a couple. We were asked to take a stone from a basket on the way in, gathered from the Worm's Head on the Gower (and to be returned there when collected later). I picked up a hag stone, with a hole in it – very apt for the time of year – but I was more than happy to let go of it when the time came. We circled deosil, sunwise, until we made a full circle. Then another woman introduced the circle and its intent. She cast a circle with her 'athame' – in this instance, a wooden wand carved like a unicorn's horn. Then my friend Kirsten Manley blessed us all with water, and a man blessed us with fire, via incense. The quarters were called – for once, with gusto (so many times I have been in circles where this is done in an anaemic way). Finally, we chanted the Awen three times and the sacred space was well and truly established (the latter is my favourite and, I find, the most effective method of all).

'Who here will speak for the ancestors?' asked the Mistress of Ceremonies. An old man stepped forward and began talking – unfortunately, he had a lisp, which, after the threshold guardian with the stutter, gave me a fit of the giggles. At times, such ceremonies slip easily into *Monty Python* territory as my dearly missed friend Tim Sebastian knew too well (he called his order, the Secular Order of Druids, SOD, with a tongue-in-cheek nod to the OBODs. The GODs, CODs , etc, followed).

We were given a sprig of yew, the tree of the underworld, which I put in my cloak. Then we were asked to call the Crone. Veiled in black, she sauntered into the circle and talked power-fully about her place in our lives. She has many guises, but cannot be ignored. She becomes our shadow, and yet we crawl to her when we our hurt or afraid, to hide amongst her skirts. She asked us to put into the stone we each held whatever we wanted to let go off this year – I thought of the friends I had lost, and also my recent misery. Grief, sorrow, anger, disappointment – I placed it all in the stone. Being the first into the circle, I was the last for the crone to meet. I threw my hag stone into the crone's basket, glad to be shot of it, and kissed her, by accident, upon the lips! My Lady Ragnall took it with grace. Then the dark lord appeared, played by Ronald Hutton, who used his usual verve and wonderful voice to bring the part to life. He gave us a basket of rosemary 'for remembrance' to take with us as we left the circle. But first, there was a feast of the dead – bread and cider was passed around. As I chewed on the bread, I thought of how an ear of wheat is a symbol of the Eleusinian Mysteries, sacred to Demeter and Persephone. The staff of life grows from the dark soil – life comes from the Underworld, as Persephone re-emerges every year. It is sign of reassurance, the covenant of the Goddess – trust in her darkness and light will come. The quarters were 'banished' (behold the gate of the west is closed, etc,) and the circle tidied away.

We left the way we came. I had to sit and be by myself for a while to digest all that had happened. I chatted with Mark, a fellow storyteller from the Bath Storytelling Circle, about how it is difficult to just switch back into normal mode, how it is good to 'hold' the feeling and carry it for a while, to let it sink in. He was going off to Chalice Well to reflect on things. He too had found the long wait for the crone painful – to be trapped in the circle with those feelings can make one feel raw and vulnerable, which is its purpose, I suppose. Such ceremonies are a kind of group therapy.

I wandered back across the field with him in the warm winter sunlight. The day felt benign, and less of a death than a rebirth. It is important to ground oneself after such an event; such experiences can often make one feel light-headed and clumsy. Accidents can happen if not careful. There is no better way of 'landing' than a bite to eat and a pint. And that's exactly what many enjoyed (eventually) at The Druids Arms. I took my bike to the car park by the Cove, another stone monument, the remains of a cromlech (a Neolithic burial chamber). I joined my friend Kirsten for a drink and snack, circulated flyers about Garden of Awen, chatted to a guy called Jim from Bristol who uses story-telling with people with disabilities, a couple from Manchester who were getting hand-fasted later that day, and some of the other ritual celebrants, now all 'normalised' by the pub setting.

When I was inside the sacred circle, looking out at the fields beyond – where cows chewed, looking at us with mild curiosity; as did the odd onlooker – I felt like Eithne in the Irish myth, looking across the veil to the otherworld. I was looking out from the inside of sacred time. My consciousness had been altered by the numerous ritual actions. We were no longer in the 'Apparent Reality', as the MC put it, because our awareness had been shifted.

Sacred time is a state of mind.

Halloween Party

Last night I went to a Halloween party – one of countless such gatherings across the Western hemisphere – and joined in the kind of celebration experienced by the masses. This is how the mainstream celebrates 'sacred time'.

There were elements of the **ceremonial ingredients** I had experienced earlier at Stanton Drew: The **wearing of costume**: the theme of the evening was 'Halloween Chic'. I know three of my friends who were planning their costumes weeks in advance. I didn't decide until the evening, but then I probably have more than my fair share of 'Halloween Chic' in my wardrobe! I passed many revellers in fancy dress (my own getting little attention) as I made the **ritual procession** – walking all the way up Lansdown Hill. There was the **ritual of arrival** – I bumped into a group of friends as I arrived, who had turned up at exactly the same time. We shook hands or kissed. Amongst them was A and her ex, G.

This was the moment of truth. Samhain is certainly the time to face hard truths. It all happened so quickly that we were perhaps all caught off guard. We shook hands and that was that. At the door – we couldn't remember which one and joked that 'any would do' (in our fancy dress we felt like a bunch of sniggering trick-or-treaters) – we were greeted by the **threshold guardian**, a tall horned man (Phil, the man of the house). But he turned out to be a hospitable demon and let us all in without much fuss – a placatory bottle of wine sufficed (our **offering**)! The party was in full swing downstairs, with a lively array of costumes. The usual banter took place – a **ritual exchange of insults**. Having just walked up a very steep hill, I was in need of a cold beer and so I made a bee-line for the kitchen, which predictably became the place to hang out – it serves as a **ritual space**, an inner sanctum, a comfort zone. My friend and I Svanur joked about this – why does this always happen? – as we sat in the empty living room, watching everyone squeezed into the small kitchen. Of course, booze was imbibed in copious amounts and occasionally spilled – this was our **libation**. Food was nibbled in a collective **'breaking of bread'**. Some gathered in the garden for a fag – **the sharing of tobacco**. The general intention was an **altered state of consciousness**, via intoxication – whether as a social lubricant, to mask nervousness, to help people to relax, or perhaps, as I suspect, to anaesthetize themselves from the psychic onslaught of the party, it was *de rigueur* – a **social norm**. Such celebrations, with their **codes of behaviour**, appearance and activity, are part of creating a **group identity** (the breaking down of the self/other divide – the former subsumed by the latter). Those who participate fully are accepted into the tribe. Those who do not are ostracised. The party got predictably livelier – a kind of **permissive insanity** occurs, a collective acting out of the Id. For a brief while we are allowed to go wild. And the wilder you go, the saner you are perceived to be. If one does not 'go crazy' then it is taken as a sign of mental sub-normality. One is stigmatised for not being extrovert – the wallflower becomes pariah. Despite all of this subconscious ceremonialism, the party lacked the meaningful connection of the Stanton Drew experience. We make the appearance of connecting – forced to rub up close in a packed kitchen – without actually making genuine connections. Our excessive intake of alcohol desensitizes us and makes us emotionally unavailable. It is a depressant, not a stimulant, and switches off the psychic receptors. We become meat machines. Partygoers came and went – made social noises, some pleasant, some unpleasant. There seemed to be little love present (from my subjective and probably skewed perspective). There was no heart connection occurring.

A simple 'ritual' I like to do at my gatherings is to get everybody to sit in a circle at a certain stage of the evening – when folk have let off some steam and are ready to settle down – and pass around my mead horn, asking each person to make a toast – to a loved one, an ancestor or 'whatever is in their heart'. Time and time again, this has created a special quality of connection, as people, for once, act sincere and speak from the heart and are *actively listened to by all*. This simple ceremony of remembrance and honouring creates a special atmosphere, which often leads into poetry, story and song.

There was no possibility of such a thing occurring at this very secular party – unless I took the risk of prompting it, but one does not want to impose on anyone. Not everyone would feel comfortable with such a hippyish sharing of feelings. But it is a shame – a missed opportunity. Despite the best efforts of the hosts, I left feeling a lack of warmth from this particular social group. Maybe it was the space I was in, but the event itself – this mainstream celebration of sacred time – did not facilitate such connection. We go through the motions, but miss the point completely. This is a time for sorrow and silence but we drown it out with noisy intoxication, afraid of what the dark might reveal to us, of what the night might say to our hearts. This is the schism in society – a head/heart split or mind/soul. How can this be healed? Are there places where healing occurs, or people who have healed the wound? I hope to find out on this journey. I clearly had to keep looking.

The crowds thinned out until only the hardcore were left, and some hysterical dancing took place (courtesy of a drunken Viking), but it was a futile endeavour to try and keep the party spirit going – fickle and heartless, it had moved on, a vampire of good vibes, glutting itself on the many pockets of revelry across the city. It would be bloated tonight, but ultimately would remain unfulfilled, always hungry, doomed to suffer the parasite's fate. We made our farewells and departed in a merry rabble, piling into a taxi, which hurtled down the hill, dropping us off at the bottom. I walked A back, but felt cold in my heart. The evening had left me somewhat empty. Bidding her goodnight, I walked home through the dark streets deep in decay, the leaves stripped from the trees, the moon two days from full, glaring like a skull through the naked branches. If the Wild Hunt was out tonight, they had given sleepy Bath a wide berth. It was as dead as a corpse.

November

Blazing Bright in the Year's Midnight
28th October – 2nd November

Now the light falls
Across the open field, leaving the deep lane
Shuttered with branches, dark in the afternoon
East Coker, TS Eliot

Finally have a chance to catch up after a hectic few days of Bardic busyness – it's that festival feeling again, as a flurry of events occur around Halloween, the deadline of the year (in Celtic Tradition, the festival was celebrated as Samhain, summer's ending, and Celtic New Year – for Celts, midnight was considered the middle of the day, and so the 'midnight of the year' – as I feel Samhain is, more than the Winter Solstice, which has a glimmer of light, as the sun is 'reborn' – would similarly be its negative axis – the dark pole around which the wheel of the year turns). As Mary Queen of Scots put it, stitching the shortening threads of her allotted time: 'In my end is my beginning', and as TS Eliot added in *The Four Quartets*, 'In my beginning is my end.' It is an Alpha/Omega time of year (although, in truth, things are always ending and beginning – it just depends on the level of our awareness). With the nights drawing in, it feels like a shift of focus, a turning inward – nature hunkers down – but life, alas, has other plans for us human animals! Hibernation is not an option!

Wednesday saw another 'Guest Writers in Conversation' with fabulous female poets, Helen Moore and Rose Flint talking at Bath Writers' Workshop, the event I co-run with screenwriter David Lassman. Helen and Rose's work and ethos shared some common ground, but also had interesting differences – teased out through the insightful talk and critical response they gave. They both performed a selection of their work and answered questions from the audience. Another superb evening – it was fascinating to hear the poets talk about the evolution of their work and themselves as writers. Lesser know writers rarely get a chance to discuss their work in such depth and have a fellow writer interview them and offer an insightful response.

Thursday I went to Bristol with David for the Cafe of Ideas, a monthly forum. I was invited to be on a panel discussing narrative with a bank manager, professor and BBC presenter. Held at Co-exist, an arts collective based at Hamilton House, the space was transformed with performance poetry, music and a buffet.

Friday, I was a guest performer at What a Performance! – a monthly open mic held at St James Wine Vaults, Bath, MCed by Richard Selby, keeping the spirit of Dave Angus (it's founder and original host) alive and kicking. The evening was dedicated to the writer Moyra Caldecott, now in her eighties and unable to perform her work due to a stroke. Moyra has been a great influence and inspiration to me – she has supported my work for the last ten years – so it was a pleasure to participate in this event to honour her. I read out three of her poems as well as my own fourteen page epic, *Dragon Dance* (from memory). My fellow guest performer, Kirsty, was on form with her three fabulous tales – and there were many other great contributions.

Following the OBOD ceremony at Stanton Drew and the 'Halloween Chic' party on Saturday, Sunday looked like it was going to be a washout, but the skies miraculously brightened after midday and I went for a quick ride-out to Stoney Littleton long barrow, travelling back five thousand years as I crawled into the narrow Neolithic burial chamber to remember my ancestors at the time of Samhain.

Later, I hosted the first Garden of Awen at Chapel Arts Centre, Bath – an event I put on with Svanur Gisli Thorkelsson, whose Icepax Productions did the business once again. A guest, Rosie, said she had never seen the venue look so good. A Bath Spa art student, Jennifer, painted two great backdrops to help create an Arcadian feel. Foliage was festooned on screens. Green candles and poem flowers decorated the tables. Chapel technician Jonathan provided some snazzy lighting. Svanur brilliantly choreographed the acts: Anthony Nanson, storyteller, got things going with a gripping and stylish start with an atmospheric tale about a vampire. Nikki Bennett launched her new poetry collection, *Love Shines Beyond Grief*, with a bang (or a pop and a fizz – as we wet the baby's head with flutes of Cava). David Metcalfe ended the first half with a powerful set of British death ballads and his spine-tingling poem, *The Last Wolf*. The second half started with a tune from Marko Gallaidhe, just back from Bampton Festival, but still with enough puff in him for a song. Richard Austin shared his poetry with aplomb. Marion Fawlk, also from Stroud, looked regal on the stage in her lovely velvet dress, sharing her deeply felt goddess poetry. The evening ended with a blistering set from guitar-shaman and sublime songsmith, James Hollingsworth. He was 'resurrected' for a stunning encore of Led Zep's classic *In My Time of Dying* – a suitable way to end our evening themed on 'Death & Rebirth'. And so, the 1st November, Celtic New Year, saw the birth of a sparkling addition to Bath's literary firmament – a professional spoken word showcase on the first Sunday of the month. Writer Crysse Morrison, in her blog, said: 'Great to see such an atmospheric venue join the local network of alternative entertainment.' The Garden will return – I've planned six of them with my 'partner in rhyme', Svanur, each with a seasonal theme. Meanwhile, I'm going to get me some quality zeds...

Remember, Remember...
(Bonfire Night to Remembrance Sunday

Bonfire Night
5th November

Bonfire Night is a strange festival when one thinks of its origins. It is even more divorced than most, and yet it continues to maintain a primal power. As we all may remember from school history lessons, in 1605, Guy (Guido) Fawkes and his Catholic co-conspirators tried and failed to blow up a Parliament that was persecuting their faith. A stack of gunpowder was placed beneath the seat of British Government but the fuse failed to be lit as Fawkes was discovered at the eleventh hour. He suffered a painful death, as did the others, when their identities came to light. The rest is history. What has helped generations of school children to remember this more than anything is the immortal mnemonic: 'Remember, remember, the Fifth of November, gunpowder, treason and plot; whatever the season, there is always a reason why it should never be forgot.' In my own old town of Northampton (Northamptonshire has Tresham Lodge, a remarkable building built on the principal of three, by Thomas Tresham, one of the gunpowder plotters, to symbolise the Holy Trinity of his faith) there is a brutal street-rhyme that local children (including my mother) used to chant as they went round, a penny-for-a-guying, which you don't see at all these days (not in Bath anyway, my current home town):

Guy, guy,
hit him in the eye,
hang him from the lamp-post
and there let him die.
Umbrella, down the cellar,
there I saw a naked fella.
Burn his body,

save his soul.
Please give us a lump of coal.
If a lump of coal
won't do,
please give us a ha'penny.
All round the Market Square
and up and down the Drapery.

How times have changed when kids used to be happy with a lump of coal! Of course, there are other nursery rhymes that commemorate historical events (London's Burning – the Great Fire of London; Ring-a-ring-roses – the Black Death; Little Jack Horner – the title deeds of Mells). The rhymes are remembered long after the event it commemorates is forgotten and, like many traditions, they are repeated without knowledge of what it means. It is just force of habit.

Sometimes festive celebrations are like this, becoming hollow repetitions, stripped of real meaning. We pay lip service.

Tonight I went to a Bonfire Night fireworks display in Bath where there wasn't even a bonfire. On the news earlier today I heard of a Rugby Club in Ilfracombe which had decided, due to health and safety, to have a big plasma screen showing a fire instead, with smoke machines and the sound of crackling fire piped through the PA! This is another example of our Nanny State gone mad, and how removed people can become from something authentic. There is something primal and satisfying about a real fire. A bonfire allows a large group of people to gather round. It brings the community together. The frisson of danger is all part of it: the loud bangs that make your jump; the fireworks howling like demons; the mildly Promethean buzz of twirling a sparkling; stumbling around in the dark; shadowy figures looming out of the night; cackles and screams; the flickering fire keeping the dark at bay. In Ottery St Mary tonight, burning barrels are rolled down the streets, traditionally carried on the back, with different races for men, women and even children. Barrels weigh up to thirty kilos and 'generations of the same families have carried them, taking great pride in doing so.' ('Rolling Out the Burning Barrels', Geoff Ward, Mysterious Planet, *Western Daily Press*, 4th November 2005). The narrow streets of the small Devon town are crowded with thousands of townsfolk and visitors, which has caused health and safety concerns and insurance headaches for the organisers. Near Okehampton is Hatherleigh, where a week later blazing fifty gallon barrels are pulled on sleds, the first at 5am and the last at 8.30-9pm, as part of the carnival now in its 107th year (in 2010). One of the members of the carnival and tar-barrel committee expressed his concerns of the event's survival in the face of rising costs and increasing crowds: 'The tradition is a very important part of our lives, and local people are very proud of their carnival.'

Lewes, in East Sussex, lays claim to the most 'hardcore' celebration, in memory of the seventeen Protestant martyrs burnt at the stake in the town in the Sixteenth Century, here described by Emma Tucker, a *Times* journalist:

It is an awesome sight: black sky, rammed streets, and burning crosses and torches snaking into the distance. There are prayers in honour of Lewes's 17 Protestant martyrs, burnt at the stake in the 16th century, after which 'bonfire boys' run with burning tar barrels to Cliffe Bridge, where they toss them, flaming, into the River Ouse. The processions include fabulous, towering effigies – the Pope of 1605 is always there, along with whoever the societies choose to lampoon. Later these elaborate 'enemies of bonfire' are blown up on the Downs surrounding Lewes at one of the giant firework displays and bonfires that see the night out. I have seen royals, politicians (local and international), sportsmen and celebrities go up in flames; I have seen NCP parking wardens explode in smithereens and in the 1980s I lost count of how many Thatchers I watched erupt in a blaze of rockets, sparkles and flashes. *The Times 05.11.09*

In the far North of the British Isles, there is the obscure winter light festival known as the Burning of the Clavie, which takes place in Burghead, Moray on January 11th (Old New Year, the original Hogmanay); and then there's Up-Helly-Aa in Shetland in January, when hundreds of locals in fancy dress, led by a formidable-looking band of Vikings, calling themselves Guizer Jarl's Squad, ritually parade through the town with flaming torches, before setting fire to a 'galley', a colourfully painted mock up of a long ship, in recreation of a traditional Viking burial. The festivities then continue with eleven hours of visiting different homes to perform, bless the hearth, and receive hospitality.

Yet even this is tame compared to Chinese New Year, where fireworks are left off in the street, as I witnessed in Kuala Lumpur. As with most festivals, it's a collective letting off of steam – temporary anarchy – that actually allows the status quo to continue. At one time, in the Thatcher Years, Bonfire Nights became politicised as effigies of 'Maggie' and even a large facade of the Houses of Parliament were burnt – pyrotechnic piñata. During the second Gulf War, I remember going to a 'tow-path party' along the Kennet and Avon canal just south of Bath, which had a reputation for being a little wild (a lot of the travelling community moved onto the canal when forced off the road by the Criminal Justice Act and other draconian legislation in the early Nineties), where a wicker man had been prepared (the burning of wicker men has become popular among the pagan community – an 'ancient' tradition inspired by the 1970s cult movie, *The Wicker Man* – and has spawned the massive Burning Man festival in the Nevada Desert, a steampunk Temporary Autonomous Zone). The Samhain Fair at the Peat Moors Visitor Centre on the Somerset Levels, 'climaxes' in the burning of a mini-wicker man. Already vertically challenged, placed in a watery ditch it comes to head height, if that: another victim of the Risk Assessment culture. The tow path party wicker man was an altogether different beast – at least twenty foot high, with a working TV in its chest. It was set alight just as *News at Ten* came on – and as George W. Bush's face appeared on the screen, the TV exploded to whoops and cheers! In comparison, the fireworks display in central Bath was tame, but the fireworks still looked beautiful and elicited the usual 'ooh's and 'aah's from the crowd. In the absence of a bonfire, the fireworks provided a hearth in the sky – lighting the darkness – for us to gather round. Briefly, and noisily, the tribe came together.

The following night, I went to see the new Jane Campion film, *Bright Star*, about John Keats – a beautiful and deeply moving masterpiece. It reminded me, as if I needed reminding, of why I write poetry. Although we know the hero's fate (like *Morte D'arthur* – the clue is in the title), it is nevertheless devastating when it happens. It brings to the surface one's own personal grief or griefs. The function of drama, unchanging since Greek theatre – the masks of tragedy and comedy are worn to elicit catharsis in the audience: a public venting of emotion.

Bright Star made me look back at Keats' poetry, but also other 'star' poets, including John Masefield, who wrote an untitled poem that begins:

So in the empty sky the stars appear,
Are bright in heaven marching through the sky,
Spinning their planets, each one to his year,
Tossing their fiery hair until they die...

And ends with the dramatic and affirming lines:

From dead things striking fire a new sun springs,

New fire, new life, new planets with new wings.

Ancestral Whispers – Dyrham Hill Fort
8th November

(Field Notes)

Standing here above Dyrham Park at the site of the battle of Deoram – a devastating battle that took place on this windswept hill overlooking the Severn, on 577 CE, as recorded in the Anglo-Saxon Chronicles:

> *Cuthwine and Ceawlin fought the Britons, and killed three kings, Conmail, Condidand and Farinmail, in the place called Dyrham. They took three cities, Gloucester, Cirencester and Bath.*

I came here in July 2007, on 05.07.07 (5/7/7) to enact a ceremony of healing to the fallen of both sides from that fateful conflict – celebrating Britain's 'melting pot', the diverse influences that gifted us such an incredible language ('all the jewels of Europe have washed up on our shore', as I once wrote) – and it seems resonant to come here today to remember those fallen in all the conflicts throughout history – all the victims of the folly of war. As Pete Seeger's haunting song goes, 'Where have all the flowers gone ...When will they ever learn?'

I came here with my friend A on the bike (on a whim) – a cold grey winter's day, though the sun tried to break through as I penned these words. A break in the light. I remember my Dad, who experienced the cruelty of the Civilian Internment Camp in Kowloon, Hong Kong harbour, in WW2; and my Pap, who fought in Dunkirk; my father's step-brothers, Joseph and Edward, who also endured the camps; and all my family throughout history touched by conflict. Oxleys (mother's father's side) might have fought on the Saxon side; the Manwarings, a name long associated with the services, came over with William the Conqueror (Warin); and on my grandmother's (mother's mother's) side, there were the Majors, who had a Major in the family – Major Major (all very Heller-esque)!

May they all Rest in Peace.

I read out 'Ancestor Worship' poem, which elicited a tear from A, thinking of all those who had gone before her.

I walked with my friend, A, on the Hill of the Seven Healing Winds, as I called it after discovering from a local that it had a reputation for its 'medicinal location' – local children were taken up there to be cured of whooping cough and other ailments. Today, it was 'hangover and sorehearts', and it didn't disappoint. Standing on the brow, overlooking the sweeping view of the Severn Vale, it was hard not to be uplifted. The sun broke through in spectacular fashion in what I like to refer to as a 'God-Cloud' – a Cloud of *Knowing*, perhaps, rather than Unknowing (*Cumulus Gnosis*?). From up high we get a perspective on things. Problems diminish. The order of things, and our place in it, is restored. The world still turns.

We rode a back lane to the village a mile off, passed the picture postcard houses, parking up by the Cotswold Way, then walked to the pond where two years ago a group of us had ritually deposited a broken sword – a bronze age replica made by a Glastonbury blacksmith, Tim – to make peace with the ancestors and between the ancestors of the land (I had imagined a mortally wounded warrior dragging himself to the pond to breathe his last, his sword dropping into the water, his blood draining away). I asked: 'May swords be turned to ploughshares still. May the world grow to peace, maturing like the oak that marks the Way.'

After its brief glory, the light was slipping away. A took a photograph of a cluster of bare birches reflected in the pond that reminded her of a Russian landscape. It was time to go. In contemplative silence, we made our way back through the shadow-wet fields to the bike, and rode back to Bath, dusk on our tail.

Inauspicious Days
Friday 13th November

Today, Friday 13th, is perceived in popular culture to be the antithesis of sacred time – an unlucky day. The air is filled with supposed bad luck and any endeavour is doomed to ill-fortune if the instigator has been foolish enough to attempt it on such an obviously unfavourable day. The calendrical equivalent of walking under ladders, it is just asking for trouble. Best to stay in, such superstitions would have us believe, because just walking out the door is tempting fate.

Of course, this is a hangover of Christian belief. Thirteen became an unpopular number because, in the Christian story, Judas Iscariot was the thirteenth guest at the Last Supper. However, thirteen has been symbolically significant for a long time. It is associated with the lunar cycles (thirteen in a year) and pagan practises the Church wished to quell. In the same way that all things to do with the feminine (Eve became synonymous with evil, for she had 'caused' the fall of Man) and the left-handed became tainted, so too did the number thirteen. A conjunction of the number thirteen (a moon number) on Friday – Freya's day, Norse goddess of love – was deemed especially auspicious, in pagan belief, and thus it became the opposite in Christian times. What was once deemed holy becomes unholy. This can be seen very visually in Hellenic temples, where earlier deities, notably Hera, are relegated by newer, more fashionable, or politically useful, gods. They become *chthonic* – often literally forced under-ground – as with the Tuatha de Danaan, the Lordly Ones of Erin, ancient Ireland, who retreated to the hills and dwindled in stature, as Christianity conquered the land, to become the Little People. This cultural pygmification is only one consequence of a

62

paradigm shift. Yet such beliefs are stubborn, and persist, albeit in a perverted form. In the Isle of Man, for example, there is the Fairy Bridge; whenever crossing it, one is supposed to hail the Little Folk, 'Good Morning!' otherwise it is deemed bad luck.

Returning to the notion that Friday the Thirteenth is an especially unlucky day, this is surely something that becomes a self-fulfilling prophecy, as jittery paranoid people bump into ladders, drop favourite mugs, burn the dinner, cut themselves shaving, get a parking ticket, prang their bumper, etc. In other words, these things happen to us all the time, but we notice them more on such days, seeing them as confirmation of its ill-fortune, a reciprocal loop of belief. It is avoiding-the-cracks-on-the-pavement mentality – a mild form of Obsessive Compulsive Disorder. For sure, stepping outside your front door *is* a risky business. Being alive is not good for your health. The world is a dangerous place. But such an attitude can make every action a possible influence of one's 'luck', when it's more likely to be a measure of your neurosis. It is a very solipsistic attitude to believe one's slightest action, or even mental state can influence the universe in this way. Surely, our actions and beliefs *do* count, but not in such a nervy, symbiotic way. 'God' isn't just waiting for us to slip up, poised with his thunderbolt in case we put out hat on at the wrong angle, or wear an unlucky colour. The natural world is always a healthy benchmark. Animals do not consider such things. They simply act. Luck is a human invention – an interesting one – and perhaps if it didn't exist, we would have to invent it anyway. It is a useful consoling fiction, telling us we don't have control over everything that happens to us, that (perchance) 'some people have all the luck'. It is one of the ways we demarcate what is 'good/special/sacred' from what is not. It would be interesting to look further at the tradition of 'bad luck days'.

Dismal Days

Etymologically, *dismal* means 'bad day' and it came to us via Anglo-Norman or Old French *dis mal*, from Latin *dies mali*, literally 'evil days', a term used to denote the two days in each month that, according to ancient superstition, were supposed to be unlucky. There were two days of each month which the Romans deemed to be unfavourable – usually anniversaries of great disasters – and it was felt unwise to begin any venture of importance on any of those days. This belief continued into the Middle Ages, and the days were actually marked on medieval calendars. Such days were said to have been computed by Egyptian astrologers, and were therefore also called *Egyptian days* or *dies Aegyptiaci*.

By the Fifteenth Century, *dismal* was often being used attributively. A 'dismal day' was one of the twenty-four that belonged to the *dismal*. It was not long before the word was reinterpreted as an adjective, meaning at first 'unlucky' but eventually 'gloomy' or 'miserable'. Since the term *dismal* acquired connotations of 'gloom' and 'calamity'; it has now progressed to be defined as 'depressing to the spirit or outlook; showing a lack or failure of hope,' and 'very poor or inadequate;' as in a 'dismal performance'. The word dismal, by extension, may also include a mental state of depressed mood characterised by feelings of sadness, despair, and discouragement; since it is natural to feel dejected and depressed about a 'dismal situation'.

It was considered unlucky to begin a new enterprise on any of the two days of 'misfortune' indicated on the medieval calendar:

- January 1 and 25
- February 4 and 26
- March 1 and 28
- April 10 and 20
- May 3 and 25
- June 10 and 16

- July 13 and 22
- August 1 and 30
- September 3 and 21
- October 3 and 22
- November 5 and 28
- December 7 and 22

But what of the opposite of 'dismal days'? Let us consider the day most considered sacred in the West, at least up until the end of the Twentieth Century.

Sundays

Sundays have long been set aside as 'sacred days', ever since, according to Genesis, God took a day off after knocking out the world and all that lives upon it in six days. Rather than go into the social history of the Western mainstream Sabbath, which has been chartered in detail by other authors, I will focus on my personal experience of the 'Lord's Day' as one example of how this day is spent in the early Twenty First Century – not that I could be perceived as typical in my lifestyle and career, although I am confident that there are commonalities with most folks' experience of this special day, which makes the beginning or end of the week, depending on your point of view (I have always seen it as the week's end – that's why it's called a weekend!). For me, an ideal Sunday consists of a lazy lie-in (more so than usual, one feels justified on a Sunday) with breakfast in bed with a loved one, preceding or following a healthy bout of sex.

When ablutions and dressing has finally been done, it's time to go for a pre-lunch walk – to blow away the cobwebs of the previous night (Saturday's saturnalia). A walk somewhere highish – a windswept hillside – normally does the trick. It's good to step off the wheel on a Sunday, get a perspective of things. Even though things wait to be done, they can wait for a day. Nothing much can get done on a Sunday anyway, businesswise, which is just as well. I remember a time when shops rarely opened on a Sunday. Now we have the big shed cult – the ritual of going to B&Q, Homebase, Ikea, sundry garden centres ad nauseam. This seems like the worst way to spend a Sunday, but I guess people who work full-time don't get a chance otherwise. Anyway, back to my walk... Frosty under foot, a crispness in the air, winter sun... an amiable tramp to an ancient site, e.g. a hillfort through the woods, followed by a pint of real ale at an out-of-the-way pub: old-fashioned, thick-beams, real fire, friendly dog. Maybe a bite to eat, if we haven't eaten already – a picnic or a packed lunch on the hill. Then the slow walk back. Relaxing back home in front of the fire over a pot of tea and some cake or crumpets, listening to Radio 4's 'literature hour' (Open Book and Poetry Please). Then perhaps a siesta, nodding off, book on my lap. Waking to the aroma of dinner on the go, sounds of activity from the kitchen. Helping out a bit! Laying the table. A lovely Sunday dinner – vegetarian roast with all the trimmings – a glass of dark wine or two, and snuggling up to watch a film. Finally turning in, feeling peacefully content – the velocity of the week brought to a point of stillness, a hiatus. In a way, Sunday is the week's solstice; there is a feeling of cessation, a break from the norm.

So, a completely hedonistic Sunday on one level, but the secular becomes the sacred, as everything is done slowly, for pleasure, but without pressure. The accelerator is eased off on a Sunday. Slow time. There's a movement for 'Slow Sundays' – as promoted by *Resurgence* magazine – but they seem to be hard-wired this way anyway.

This is an example of a perfect Sunday, mine at least, but often its discreet elements are not always present – they can be dislodged by returning from a gig, being at a festival, or travelling in the summer, and in the winter, by the eco-arts showcase I run called Garden of Awen. I started to have an open house in the summer on a Sunday afternoon, as often it's easy to miss people. This was an artificial way of creating something that should be second nature in a healthy community – folk just dropping by. But sometimes we have to plan informality – encourage spontaneity, by making space for it.

Long live Sundays!

Heavy Weather – Bath
14th November

A contrasting weekend. Yesterday, went to the Big Transition Bath Event at the Bath Royal Literary & Scientific Institute (BRLSI) – a day of talks, workshops, networking and inspiration organised by Transition Bath. Mark Lynas, author of *Six Degrees*, opened the event with a sobering but galvanising talk about the effects of climate change and how we can respond to its challenges (as the Maldives is doing, becoming the world's first carbon neutral country). There followed a triple programme of interesting and empowering talks. Oh, and some nice cake.

The weather was suitably ominous, like the start of some disaster movie. This particular 'pathetic fallacy' was simply a pain in the arse for most of storm-battered Britain. Unfortunately, it will probably take some extreme weather event (London flooding, a la New Orleans) to shock the majority of people, including the government, into action. Most people are still in the denial stage, preferring to see Climate Change as a myth (a morally outrageous and unscientific stance perpetuated largely by the Oil Industry), in itself a consoling fiction for those who wish to stick their heads in the sand and continue their carbon-emitting lifestyles. Yet, it is difficult for even the greenest person to lead a completely carbon-neutral lifestyle; from the day we are born we become a burden to the planet. In this 'new paradigm' the sin of carbon can be absolved by the purchase of carbon credits – the modern equivalent of medieval 'indulgences'. Carbon-traders are the modern Pardoners, giving people the odour of sanctity with their invisible benedictions.

Climate Change gurus are the new priests – the greener you are, the 'holier' you are – as people try to outdo each other in what could be called 'hair-shirt-man-ship' (e.g. 'I turned green twenty years ago'; 'I went green twenty *five* years ago…') and there's even a happy-clappy song to go with it: at the end of the day, a guy called Chris got everyone to join in his 'Climate Change' anthem, which had the lyrics: 'Energy … Descent … Plan – Transition Culture!' I don't think they're going to win over many people with that – they need to work on their song-writing! Green art doesn't have to be bad art, and the last talk I went to (and the most interesting for me) was a session on Imagineering led by eco-poet, Helen Moore, where we discussed such matters, and the 'spectre of the preacher' as I put it: people don't respond to a hectoring tone (I certainly don't – and I'm sympathetic). You have to enchant people by sheer quality – entertain, impress, *then* you have their attention. Ask tough questions, but don't spoon-feed answers. Light a candle, don't fill a pail (although a few buckets today – when the heavens opened – wouldn't have gone amiss).

Afterwards, went to Bristol for something completely different – ostensibly – a critically-acclaimed Tobacco Factory production of *Uncle Vanya* at the marvellous Old Vic, but as it turned out, it had a strong ecological subplot, as advocated by the Doctor, with his forests, his love of trees, his vegetarianism. And in its stark depiction of how we have to keep on living – even through depression and despair – Chekov perhaps hints at how we might also 'keep going'. It was surprisingly funny and shows how much humour is an essential for life on Earth also (the probes being sent out across the Solar System should be scanning planets for it as well as water).

Grey Wethers – Avebury Musings
15th November

Today, the skies miraculously cleared, so I made the most of the window in the weather to take my shiny new steed out on a long run to Avebury. I'd been working hard. After two weeks of marking OU papers, I needed to blow away the cobwebs (all work and no play makes Jack a dull boy – and I didn't want to do a *Shining*: 'Here's Johnny!')

I first went to Silbury Hill (Europe's largest manmade mound, dating from 2400 BCE), then walked up to West Kennet long barrow (3650 BCE), enjoying the glorious light, the wind, the space. Hardly a soul around.

Good to get away from computers, etc, in this vast sacred landscape temple – ancient technology that has stood the test of time. The incredible West Kennet is still standing after nearly six millennia – how many things these days would last so long?

Then I rode the short distance to the massive main circle and had my packed lunch in a copse of beech trees, enjoying being back in this magnificent sacred space where I have been coming for twenty years ('I've been coming for twenty *five* years!').

The standing stones are made up of what are known locally as 'grey wethers' (because they resemble, in poor light, sheep – many of which were manically munching away amidst the megaliths, bulging-eyed grass addicts). I walked all the way around the henge, stopping occasionally to scribble in my field journal . Out in the sun on my shiny new steed, working on my new book – life is good.

Silbury Hill (Field Notes)

The circle of the sun is shining down as I sit on my 'time machine' (Triumph Legend, 2001) looking at Silbury Hill (2400 BCE), sipping a cup of coffee from my silver flask. It's midday; the sky is blue – scrubbed clean after the storms of the last couple of days that have ravaged the country. A bird sings, over the roar of the traffic from the A4, the old Roman road (a few minutes later the traffic dies down, to be replaced by tranquil silence). It feels good to be alive. Silbury Hill is the motherlode, the node at the heart of this vast sacred landscape – a landscape temple constructed over millennia, with many facets. I hope to explore those over a number of visits. I have been coming to Avebury for two decades and it still has secrets to reveal to me – and that is as it should be. Silbury Hill, the largest manmade mound in Europe took many thousands of man hours to complete, so it is only right that one spends time to appreciate it, to learn from it.

An exhilarating ride here on my new wheels – took it easy, but still a real thrill! A sense of freedom, of unmitigated pleasure – turning the wheel, shifting the gear of the week – out on the open road, cobwebs blown, a Legend between my legs! Even riding a motorbike can be a way of creating sacred time – it makes you focus on the moment, wipes your mind clean of all concerns – there is ritual garb involved, a ritual of preparation, and when riding one has to enter a state of alert relaxation, of calm. Lose that state of grace and accidents will occur. Lose that state of grace, and accidents can occur. It is about being 'in the zone', in the Awen even.

There's 'the nod', the wave of a fellow biker – a salute of respect. Two horse riders, crossing by Cherhill white horse – and me on my 'black horse' (the pub opposite is called that – they have a 'bikers' night'). Opening it out on Labour-in-Vain Hill. Power! The torque of chieftainship. King Sil was said to have been buried under the hill of Silbury on a horse with buried treasure... Excavations have proven otherwise; it has a more secret, less obvious treasure – the golden hoard of memory. I think of all the times I've been here – the wild and crazy times with friends! Sleeping on it, dancing on it, seeing sunrise, dawn, full moon or solstice. The hub of a great wheel. Personal gold. Once slept on it with an American woman I met in the circle at Avebury while I picnicked, walking along the henge; she wore red, white and blue. We got talking. Both on our 'quests'. We broke bread. I cut my finger and she bought some plasters for me in Marlborough. We made respective beds on the summit. Nothing happened – it wasn't like that – we lay wrapped in our bivvies and watched the stars. Talked until we fell asleep. We awoke to a damp dawn and bid each other a warm farewell.

Inside West Kennet long barrow, in the dripping gloom. Writing this under the shaft of light in the end chamber. An unknown bird sings. The thing that strikes one about West Kennet is the scale – I can walk straight in here without stooping – and there's plenty of head room, even in the end chamber. Compared to the barrow of Stoney Littleton, it's a palace. And it's the age: 3650 BC – how many things these days would still be standing after so long? This extraordinary structure has survived five and a half millennia of human history. It has weathered countless storms. And still it silently endures. I honour my father here; I say 'Dad', a word as monosyllabic as death. Then his full name... Declaring to the silence I will not forget. A couple of weeks ago, over the Samhain weekend, this would have been heaving. Now I have it to myself... (Just then a woman entered – I left her in peace.)

Outside – light. Wind. Colour. Life. Blocking the entrance – a massive slab of rock, lichen-mottled mustard, green, grey – dividing the quick from the dead. The ultimate full stop. It faces east to the Sanctuary – the palisade enclosures that mark the terminus of the Ridgeway: a ritual dialogue between sacred sites.

Clumps of dark beeches on a rolling chalk landscape, fields of stubble – canvas for cloud paintings, slow shadows moving across the Downs, God's radar. A dome of blue, marbled with low cloud. A bird shrieks – a plaintive wintry sound – calling for its mate, seeking its kindred spirit, to answer death with life.

The exclamation mark of my shadow stretches out across the winter fields. It's peaceful here today – the calm after the storms. Perhaps it feels more peaceful because I am peaceful within myself. Content to be who I am, what I am, where I am – following my path, living in sacred time, fully alive.

Avebury (Later)

Sitting under a copse of beeches overlooking the Great Circle. The sound of beeches in the winter wind is different to the sound of the oak down from West Kennet (adorned with rags and fetishes) – or small boys (who barrel in nearby – full of noisy excitement). Lots more people here and traffic droning past. It is sad that this great wheel is impaired by the tyranny of the tyre! They should reroute the road around Avebury – with enough will this would be achievable. If they can do it at Stonehenge, as planned, why not here? Families, young parents with children, carried and held, amble by on their day out – the wheel of life turns. The vast circle would have surely been at the centre of the various communities that used it – as it does today. A couple of weeks ago there would have been several groups here (covens, groves, gorseddau) performing their ceremonies here for Samhain, although in fact today is the eve of the Samhain dark moon, the true dark point of the year. Muted browns and greens, robust-looking sheep, and me in my flying jacket, kept warm by a fleece or two. Light breaks through the clouds.

Walking full circle around Avebury in honour of my ancestors, but also to release all pain, all grief, all anger, all sadness – thus I walked it, for once, widdershins, anti-clockwise, at Samhain dark moon, to banish all that I've been carrying these last 365 days (and 5 years...). Now I sit on the 'throne stone', facing the Avenue, where I remember Ian and Sarah parked up in their big blue van, offering a cuppa. Rest in peace, Sarah (committed suicide on 1ˢᵗ May this year). Rest in peace, Mary (died of cancer in June). Rest in peace, Richard (suicide, November 2004). Rest in peace, Simon (deep vein thrombosis, 2005). Rest in peace, Tim (cirrhosis, Imbolc, 2007), who came here many times, leading ceremonies, opening up the mysteries and the magic of these places for all. And rest in peace, Dad (chronic pneumonia, 2008). And all my ancestors. So may it be.

A sheep genuflects, nibbling grass. A rook struggles in the wind, as though dangled on a string – a child's special effect. White dog's private bits like the rain-holes of the stones. Sheep shit everywhere. Hot columns of ewe piss. The sky changing its mood – the circle turning still. Smoothed wood of the gate, oiled by many pilgrim hands. The click of the lock. The rasping of crows. White paths, slippery around the stones. The bone path. Once, a halo of gleaming white, a beacon seen for miles around – like the white mound of Silbury.

I pass a tall woman in dark clothing. She looks at me as I approach, but I avoid her eye. Her presence lingers in me as I walk to the bike and prepare to leave. When I turn to find her, she has gone.

December

Mistletoe the Line
5th – 6th December

Yesterday, decided to visit Tenbury Mistlefest – Britain's only mistletoe festival. This event came about when the old mistletoe auctions were under threat. They had taken place in Tenbury for a hundred years. Tenbury mistletoe is exported all over the country and is renowned for its quality.

I waited to see what the weather was like before committing to going. I checked the BBC weather on my laptop and the forecast looked good – at least for the first half of the day. I decided to risk it and seized the day – I chucked what I needed in a daysac, togged up and set off. The run up to Tenbury, through the Welsh Marches, was beautiful in the winter sun. I felt glad to be alive and living in such a lovely country. This part of the land feels very special – an artery of quintessential 'Englishness', deep England, ironically on the border of Wales (and originally of course belonging to Wales). I can see why Tolkien was so inspired by it; it does have a Tolkienesque quality to it. Deep wooded vales, timber-framed houses, mysterious knolls, brooding hills like old Brythonic bears, licking their wounds.

I made good time on my Triumph Legend; the roads were clear and it was sunny and dry. The eighty five miles passed in a pleasant couple of hours. It was only when I reached the Rose and Crown, just outside Tenbury – where the druids were gathering for the procession – that I realised I had left without my wallet! No cards, no license, nothing. I had about a seven pounds worth of change in my pocket – enough for lunch and not much else. I put this problem to one side – there wasn't much I could do about it – as the procession was about to start. There was a brief briefing in the pub and I was designated 'hop carrier' in the ceremony; my role was to pass around a bottle of beer!

About twenty of us set off from the Rose and Crown car park, some in full robes. Suzanne from Cransfield Bardic Arts led the way, leading us in a chant, which we sang in a half-hearted slightly embarrassed English way as we crossed the bridge from Shropshire to Worcestershire into the town. The high street was lined with stalls – a Christmas market to coincide with this, the biggest day in Tenbury's calendar. It wasn't exactly buzzing, but the atmosphere was congenial. We passed a couple playing medieval instruments, all dressed up. They attempted to join our procession, but we were walking too fast (as they told me later)! In previous years, the mistletoe ceremony had taken place in the heart of the town, but this year it took place in the gardens, under a lime-bearing mistletoe overlooking the river Teme, flowing vigorously after the heavy rains recently.

The previous Tuesday a small contingent of the local druids (Cornovii Tribe) went to the Mistletoe Auctions and performed a discreet ceremony incognito (in plain clothes – undercover druids). In other years this has been more visual – in full regalia – to varying degrees of reception. Some traders claimed the blessed mistletoe did especially well, while others disagreed! My old friend Tim Sebastian used to do cheese-blessing: 'Blessed are the cheese-makers'!

We gathered in a circle by the Mistletoe Foundation banner, as a small crowd of curious and amused public looked on. Suzanne had a gentle touch and conducted the ceremony with grace and humour. Although the celebrants had to read from scripts, it was done from the heart, albeit in a slightly ramshackle way. I did my bit; the ale is normally passed in a horn, but because of health and safety they were forced to use plastic cups, but they were forgotten! And so I had to simply pass around the bottle of local ale (Hobson's Town Crier), saying to people to drink at their own risk – all the druids did! Folk were asked if they wished to say anything about mistletoe; I said: 'Our ancestors called this All Heal – may it bring healing to all who need it, especially to the planet – and may it bring wisdom to those in Copenhagen who are deciding the fate of the planet.' After we blessed the mistletoe with water, fire, hops and apple, everyone was offered a sprig of mistletoe. At the climax of the ceremony, the mistletoe was cast into the Teme.

We then wended our back to the Rose and Crown for lunch. It was nice to chat to the celebrants. I then went back into the town to look around. By now it was grey and miserable. It was about 2.30pm; the crowning of the mistletoe queen wasn't until 4pm. I didn't fancy hanging around for a couple of hours in the rain, so I decided to head back and make the most of the remaining light.

It wasn't as pleasurable going back – I was constantly aware of the petrol level, and went as slow as I could. It was getting dark and it had started to rain – conditions were getting worse. I stopped briefly to take a photo of an amazing silver tree – the silver branch, quite literally – then carried on, hoping my reserve tank would last. It got me about forty miles before it finally gave up the ghost outside Hartpury. I rolled into a bus stop and tried to resurrect it. Dead. No juice left. So I had to walk a long two or three miles back to the nearest petrol station. All I had was a couple of quid. I explained my situation and asked the attendant if I could fill up my water bottle; she said fine, so I started to do that until a guy came up, complaining. He was owner and was concerned with losing his license, so I had to stop and left with only 61 pence worth of petrol! I trudged back through the rain, sweating profusely under all my biker gear. By the time I got back to the bike I was exhausted. I drank some coffee, scoffed some chocolate and tried to recover a little before heading off. I got as far as Gloucester before it ran out again – my hopes of reaching the next petrol station dashed. I was now in a fix. And so I reluctantly rang my friend Miranda, whom I was hoping to visit on the way home as my route passes the top of her road. From an impromptu visit, I was forced to impose on her. I asked if she could come out with a can of gas. She kindly agreed, but it took a while for her to find me. I stood in the driving rain, looking out anxiously for my friend's car... lights in the darkness.

Finally a car pulled up – my saviour had arrived! I took the can of gas and tried to pour it into the tank, but the wind blew half of it away. So I had to fashion a funnel from the ceremony script – it came in useful! With sufficient gas, I followed M back to her place, a lovely cottage on the Edge, between Gloucester and Stroud. A couple of big mugs of steaming tea later, my gear drying out in front of the range, and I was starting to feel human again. God bless her!

I had to get back to Bath to meet my friend Paul, who was arriving from Paris. He was due to headline the following night at the Garden of Awen and I had offered to put him up. It was foul night and I was exhausted – I would have preferred to have stayed (M hospitably offered me her spare room), but I didn't have his number and wasn't able to get through to Marko, who did. And so, somewhat reluctantly, I headed off into the night. But the cuppa did the trick and I was able to get back to Bath, through the driving rain. The A46 is a notorious traffic black spot, so I took it real easy. I arrived at the bus station at 10pm; my friend had been due in at 21.50 hrs, but there was no sign of him. It turns out the London coach had got in early and he had gone to meet Marko and friends in the pub. Relieved he had arrived and wasn't wandering the streets, I headed back to mine to thaw out in a bath, have some hot food and prepare for my guest. Friendship had saved me and friendship had made me slog back through the dismal night. It had been a powerful experience; leaving home with my wallet (and watch), I had run out of petrol, money and time, and discovered that ultimately we don't need the first two, only time for our friends.

Lighting the Darkness
6th December

Garden of Awen on Sunday at Chapel Arts Centre was a magical banquet of Bardism in the heart of Bath. To celebrate the solstice theme of 'Lighting the Darkness' I had gathered a constellation of shining talent: sublime wordsmiths from Stroud, a jazz duo and a Bard of Bath, a troubadour from Paris and a Russian ballet dancer/poet from Australia.

This was the second Garden I had organised with playwright, novelist and all round Mr Fix it, Svanur Gisli Thorkelsson, whose Icepax Productions made it look so professional.

After a much needed lazy Sunday chilling out at home with my guest Paul, we made our way to the venue laden with musical instruments, books, CDs and stuff! Svanur was there, co-ordinating the sound checks and attending to final details – he's a wizard!

I MCed the night, introducing each act, assisted by 'the lady with the satin larynx', Anna D, who recited the odd Arcadian quote to punctuate the proceedings. First up was Jay Ramsay, poet of the heart, and Hereward on percussion – performing a deeply felt set of beautiful poems. Next was fellow Fire Springer, Kirsty Hartsiotis, who did a riveting version of Pandora's Box. Master Duncan, 13th Bard of Bath, followed with an impressive triptych of poetry and song. We ended the first half with jazz duo Venus Eleven – Tracey Kelly's ethereal vocals, accompanied by some mellow guitar enchanted the audience.

After the break, we had the extraordinary American-born poet, Gabriel Bradford Millar – our third guest from Stroud. She delivered a wise and spell-binding set of poetry. And then we had Irina Kuzminsky, the Russian-émigré Australia ballet dancer/poet, who performed her blistering *Dancing with Dark Goddesses* set: a performance of complete commitment, passion and technical brilliance. Herewood and Jay came back on for some drumming to warm us up for the final act, Paul Francis, Le

Troubadour, who ended the evening with a splendid set of songs that took the audience to an absinthe-soaked Left Bank for an all but brief time. Paul ended with a personal request – his magnificent song, *The Sailor and the Magician*, which has a chorus of fine sentiment: '*May there be Peace in the East, Peace in the South, Peace in the West by the river's mouth, Peace in the North, Peace across the Land, Peace, Love and Harmony...*' I'll drink to that – and we did!

Such nights show how the Bardic arts can create sacred space and time in an accessible, engaging way that can be enjoyed by anyone; it is a very informal kind of ceremony, but with its own structure, intention and etiquette. For myself, as a bard, this is my preference. Let the words and the music work their own magic. Create the right framework and the Awen will flow.

Cutting the Thorn
8th December

Today I attended the annual cutting of the Glastonbury Thorn at St John's, on the High Street of the legend-soaked Somerset town. The Glastonbury Thorn is said to be a cutting from the very tree that apocryphally sprouted from the staff of Joseph of Arimathea – Jesus' uncle or *brother* (according to the vicar of St John's, David) – plunged into the good soil of Somerset (traditionally on Wearyall Hill – appropriately named, at his journey's end) when he made landfall here after his long voyage from the Holy Land, with or without a certain young messiah under his care (a new film is coming out exploring this: *Did Those Feet in Ancient Times?*) All rather dubious, but a wonderful notion – Glastonbury is obviously very proud of its famous roots: a headline on a High Street newsstand read 'Did Glastonbury Druids Teach the Young Jesus?'! And the brush with fame, albeit on a merely national level, continues. Every year a sprig of this tree is sent to the Queen, who has it on her Xmas table at Sandringham (apparently it is sometimes spotted in the background of her Christmas Day broadcast).

I was caught up in the 'crocodile' as hundreds of pupils from St John's, St Benedict's and St Dunstan's converged in the grounds of the church, lining up in ranks of descending size in front of the Thorn. Local worthies were gathered in their finery. The town crier started proceedings in a typically stentorian manner, then Rev. David MCed the event, with contributions of cute songs from the local schools before the moment we had all been waiting for occurred. The 'oldest pupil' of St John's cut the thorn, with a little assistance from the Town Crier and a helper from the school. As the thorn sprig was held up, they were cheers, and the little girl, looking like a wee brownie in her pink woolly hat, beamed.

It was a heart-warming community event – a lovely way to mark the 'first shoots' of the festive season.

Changing of the Bards
20th December

On Sunday night, I went along to the annual contest for the Bardic Chair, this year held at 'Back to Mine', a nightclub – another first! Each bard gets to stamp their identity on it. Master Duncan, 13th Bard of Bath, being our youngest to date (until tonight!) has appealed to a younger demographic with his hip-hop style and topical lyrics. Tonight, he pulled out all the stops to create an entertaining night blending poetry, music and dance.

The dance floor 'well' was transformed into a grove with Christmas trees from the farm of one of Duncan's contacts. Birdsong was piped through the PA, creating an effect very similar to my Garden of Awen, started two months before... Ah, well – a sign of flattery I suppose. The first half consisted of a cabaret of various acts: a powerful singer-guitarist; a rapper; a flamenco guitarist; and a rather raunchy dance troupe called Nice-as-Pie.

After the break, MC Duncan performed a couple of his poems as his final performance as Bard of Bath, before the contestants were called up. A coin was tossed and called. 'Tails never fails,' said Jack Dean, and sure enough it was, though Duncan thought it was 'heads'! Perhaps he had a suspicion that it would have been easier on Dave S., the other act, because Jack's blistering tour-de-force was a hard act to follow. Not wanting in ambition, he interpreted the theme, 'The Last B— —', in a Biblical sense, telling us he was going to do a version of the Bible! Although this wasn't strictly the case, he did cover the history of the universe up until 2012, ending in a kind of Armageddon – the finale being an *8 Mile* rap battle between Jesus and Jack! It was funny and technically impressive, as he performed over his backing track in perfect time, miming scratching the records on the turntables, giving a new spin to the music of the spheres.

In contrast, Dave S. – who had been drinking all day (so he claimed) and turned up on stage with three drinks in his hands – played it completely for laughs, obviously not taking it seriously. This is a classic coping strategy for nerves and to save face – 'Oh, I didn't want to win it anyway.' His story was a modern fairy tale, but he read it out and sometimes couldn't even do that. It was mildly amusing in places – and might have worked, had he recited it. He had a comic touch, and might find his niche as a stand up comedian (or a sit down one in his case). But at least he entered, and helped to create a contest. A few more would, of course, have been even better, but few are willing to step up to the mark.

Throughout the performances, Richard Carder, chief druid, held his hands over his ears, sitting next to the other two judges, like one of the three wise monkeys (hear no evil).

While the judges deliberated, the dancers came on – like a pared down Pan's People – doing very well in such a small space!

Then, finally, the judges returned and Master Duncan announced the winner, milking it for dramatic effect, X-Factor style – no surprise to hear it was Jack! He was called up, stumbling over a stool. Duncan handed over the robes and Jack performed a poem, receiving a warm round of applause. He was clearly a popular choice.

Then the Bards of Bath present were called up, which I wasn't keen to do, being 'off duty' and because the ceremony is so naff. We stood in a circle, held hands and Richard half-heartedly took us through the Druid Vow (x2) and an Awen (x1). It seemed ludicrous in that setting, but has become 'tradition'. The day after, we perform a proper inauguration ceremony at the Circus – this is the time for ritual, not a night-club. It was a very poor attempt to create sacred space, and I suggested to Richard the next day that we skip this element in future.

Miranda said it had 'lost its spirit' – no mention of the solstice, or what it all means. Richard, as Chief Druid, should have gone up at the start and introduced things, put it into context, but he was late arriving. I wonder how many people who came along that night realised what it was all about?

As I left it started to snow – the only real magic of the whole evening, and effortlessly natural.

The following day – the 'official' solstice – a small group of us gathered in the Circus in the centre of Bath to hold our traditional winter solstice ceremony and inauguration of the new bard. It was freezing and icy underfoot as I made my way (carefully) to the Circus, through the crowds of Christmas shoppers. I got there at noon to find Richard the druid and the two bards, outgoing and new. That was it. We were joined by Thommie Gillow, the twelfth Bard, her wee baby and a couple of her friends from Cardiff. So, our small and merry band set to work. Richard led the ceremony of 'Alban Arthuan', as modern druids like to call it, and kept it mercifully brief. We used scripts, which aren't my preference, but they helped since most of the participants had little experience in such things, and they all joined in, in good spirits. We called the quarters: I had to call the east, my 'usual' (Richard didn't even ask, knowing that's my preference –

although on such a chilly day, calling the fire in the south would have been a better option!). We recited the Gorsedd Prayer and raised the Awen. Jack was welcomed to the Gorsedd and asked to perform a poem. Master Duncan also shared one. Halfway through the ceremony, Thommie suddenly dashed off, as though filled too full of Awen – a traffic warden had spotted her car! She caught him just in time, but had to move it. All the while, her little toddler never made a sound but just stood there, with enormous gloves on, looking astonished (the default look of toddlers). Richard brought the ceremony to a brisk end. I suggested three cheers for the new bard (although in the cold, it came out as 'three chairs'!). I took a couple of photographs for the press release and archives and then we separated, leaving only Richard and I to decamp to the Chequers for some much-needed refuelling. It had been a Bard Day's Night!

And the Bardism does not end there; tonight is the tenth anniversary of the Bath Storytelling Circle, which should be a special evening. I am going to be one of the three hosts, as one of the organisers of the circle (along with Anthony, its founder, and David, its current 'chair'). There should be a feast of fine story-telling, poetry and song – what better way to spend the longest night of the year?

The oral tradition is very much alive in Bath, but don't tell anyone I told you so!

Yuletide Gathering
19th December

Although I am not a Christian (but not un- or anti-) and Christmas means little to me in terms of its specific religious symbolism, I can appreciate the wider mythic meta-tropes at work in narratives about the return of the light in the depths of winter – be it in the form of an avatar, sun king, solar deity, or simply the sun itself – and I enjoy Yuletide with all its festive trimmings. I love the holly and the ivy, the mistletoe, the tree, the candles, the wassailing, the rosy-cheeks of the carol singers, the shining eyes of the children and, most of all, the gathering around the hearth and connecting with loved ones. Beyond all the consumerism and emotional blackmail (the Scrooge story hauled out every year to make curmudgeonly humbugs like me buckle), this is ultimately what the season is all about, as encoded in the message that is often forgotten in the stressful run-up to the big day: Peace on Earth and Goodwill to all Mankind – a universal positive message often drowned out in the endless partying, the booze-ups and bust-ups, the relentless television and shopping frenzy. Yet, I decided to try and 'do my bit' and acquit myself socially by opening my doors to friends last night for my Yuletide Gathering.

I spent the day preparing the house – cleaning, decorating (with holly and ivy I had gathered outside), making food, sorting out music and so forth. It was quite relaxing, especially the cooking: nothing elaborate; just a vegetable winter stew, mulled wine and mince pies. Once the fairy lights were up and I had hung the mistletoe and lit the candles and some frankincense and myrrh, I felt I had created a lovely Christmassy ambience. All I needed now were some guests... I guess I shouldn't have expected anyone to turn up on time, but when it was 7.30pm and still no one had arrived I was starting to feel a little anxious, the nasty goblin in my head telling me 'you don't have any friends, nobody likes you!' Then I heard footsteps and they all started to arrive. Suddenly, the party was happening!

I served up goblets of mulled wine as folk arrived, wrapped up on a chilly night (it did try to snow earlier; and the country is beset with 'wintry conditions' – flurries of flakes on the tracks!) and offered them some stew. Folk brought their own tasty offerings and soon the kitchen surfaces were overflowing. After the majority of the guests had arrived and made themselves comfortable, I asked for some peace to start a session of sharing –

beginning with a poem about stillness, to tie in with the time of year. I talked briefly about how the solstice means stillness: the atmosphere changed, became 'sacred', just through the simple act of going round in a circle and sharing. People offered poems, songs, anecdotes. There was a poem in Icelandic by my friend Svanur and a song in Korean by Jin (a government-censored protest song about 'dew'). I ended the first session by getting everyone to read out a verse of Carol Anne Duffy's poem, *The Twelve Days of Christmas*, from the *Radio Times* – very topical and amusing in places. It allowed those who didn't have a chance to join in.

Later, I asked people to sit round once more to share the mead horn – an 'old tradition' of mine, which actually has precedents dating back to the Dark Ages. It's mentioned in *Beowulf*, and in the thirteenth century a custom was observed that involved toasting 'Wassail!' and replying 'drink hail!' before passing on the wassail bowl/mead horn – with a kiss. Everyone joined in this with gusto; the first time, folk were a little embarrassed and came out with relatively trivial toasts, a little glib or silly. The second time, it got a little bit more authentic; and the third time, folk were being far more genuine. It worked its simple magic – a powerful but effective way to create sacred space.

And then the partying started in earnest. I'm not sure whether it was the mead, or the tension release, but suddenly, dramatically the atmosphere changed to something far merrier than before. Songs were sung and everyone joined in – corny Christmas carols, but good fun. There was some Icelandic blues(!) from Svanur and other 'campfire classics' like the Pete Seeger song, Where *Have All the Flowers Gone?* It turned out to be truly great night. There was the perfect amount of people there, and a good mix. Everyone seemed to get on and didn't seem to want to leave...

The best sign of a good night is the atmosphere of the room afterwards. There was a lovely warm glow. Good vibes.

Everyone said goodbye with hugs and kisses. There wasn't too much to clear up – the worst was tidied away, the washing up left until morning. It was late. I went to bed in good spirits and awoke with fond memories, and a head not too fuzzy, considering. A good fry-up and a walk in the winter sun and I was feeling on top of the world.

Winter Solstice Walk
22nd December

Wanting to celebrate the winter solstice in a physical way, I decided to go for a midwinter walk. I have a storytelling friend, Peter Please, who every winter solstice goes on a walk – a personal tradition. Well, in December 2004, I lost a friend, Richard Wilde – we had gone for a walk together one midwinter's day. In his memory, I re-walked the route we had taken on 22nd December that year, (up St Catherine's Valley towards Cold Ashton, then down the Swainswick Valley - about ten miles) and it was a very tough walk to make. And so doing it a third time, albeit in a different location, has made it my own personal tradition. Richard's birthday is 23rd December (today, as I write this), so it seems like a poignant thing to do – to walk with Richard and remember him on the eve of his birthday. I wrote a poem about the experience, and read it out at his memorial, when we planted a tree for him. And now I write about this new experience – a walk with ghosts, but an affirmation of rebirth. Remembrance and renewal. Strong solstice themes.

So, to the walk.

After the tenth anniversary celebration of the Bath Storytelling Circle, my mortal frame wasn't quite up to getting up at the crack of dawn and heading for the hills. Instead, I set off just after nine, as the sun breached the top of Bathwick Hill, piercing shards penetrating down its length, photons passing over the Georgian sundial in the front garden, a thin shadow marking the light dusting of snow on its face. I made a flask of coffee, got kitted up to withstand the frosty clime, and set off.

I first had to run the gauntlet of the city centre, to get some money out, buy something to break the note, and catch the Park and Ride to Odd Down, to the start of the walk. Wellow is about three miles from here, and Stoney Littleton Long Barrow a mile or two after that – making it a ten to twelve mile round trip with all the winding footpaths, quite enough for a winter's day. I've only ever ridden it, although I seem to recall getting a flat once, cycling down the lovely long hill from Odd Down into Wellow, and having to push my bike all the way home (taking the Combe Hay/Midford route). It was nice to experience it on foot and notice all the details I would normally miss. The tracks were fascinating – a runic code I could hardly read – various birds; a fox, perhaps; boot-prints; a four-wheel drive, which looked like it had skidded off the road into a hedge.

I soon left the road, taking a steep footpath along a hollow lane of beech, picture postcard perfect in their covering of frost. I descended to a hidden vale, with beautiful houses, golden oolitic limestone catching the precious rays of winter sun. I hailed the horse and mule, standing stoic on the hill in their winter covers; a slobbering St Bernard guarding Fortnight Farm.

At the Combe-Hay crossroads, in the canopy of a copse, a murder of crows seemed to be engaged in dogfights with a rival clan. They would take off as one, see off the enemy, then settle back down again, only to repel another onslaught, making an inordinate din as they did so. It was dramatic to watch, a Corvine Troy – night-feathered Hector and Achilles having it out, amidst the melee of Myrmidons. Further on, feathers on the snow, which I tried to identify – brown, striped – a pheasant, perhaps, savaged by a dog; or simply a road kill? Or maybe a victim of the crows, who have a tendency to harass birds of prey.

I slogged on, walking along the road, facing the traffic. In forty five minutes, I had reached the brow of the hill looking down into Wellow, and on the other side of the valley I saw the distinct outline of the barrow. Cheered by this visual fix, I set off along a bridleway, which cut out the village and took me straight to the lane leading to the barrow.

I grunted at a farmer going about his business, carrying on down the lane covered with snow. My bike certainly couldn't have coped with this! I soon came to the footbridge, passing over Wellow Brook, running deep and clear – and no doubt, close to freezing. I crossed over and climbed to the barrow, cutting across a field.

As I approached the barrow, I noticed a couple of people there, taking photographs. I thought one of them looked familiar. I walked around the barrow and appeared at the entrance. Yes, it was Helen Moore, fellow Bard of Bath! We greeted each other warmly. Helen had walked there from Radstock with a small group of her friends. They had celebrated the longest night with poems and songs around a fire. We were both tickled to bump into one another. Helen said she wasn't altogether surprised to see me there. On the same ley line, today anyway!

She explained that some guys had spent the night in the barrow – most impressive! After we had a photograph in front of the entrance, which used to be gated over (the key collected from the local farmer) one of them emerged from the chamber, a little shaggy and bleary-eyed, like Neolithic man! I asked if he'd been there for thousands of years! His name was Steven, a very nice chap from the nearby village (well, his grandmother lived there – he is currently based in Sheffield). Helen and I talked easily with him, as he described the experience of the solstice dawn.

Bidding farewell to my Bardic friend, the group of women left. I carried on chatting to Steven. He suggested I check out their den at the back of the chamber. They had lined the floor with straw, then a groundsheet, then mats and sleeping bags – very snug. I lay there in the darkness and imagined what it must have been like. I did three Awens and then crawled to the light – rebirth!

With all the fields covered in a white blanket, the effect of emerging into the sunlight was even more dazzling. I felt the rebirth of the light.

Steven's fellow chamber-dwellers appeared from across the rutted frosted fields – his brother, James, and friend, Jack. They all wore their hair long and had hippyish clothes. They were a nice trio of guys – a pleasant energy about them. They were clearly mellow from their all-night vigil and possibly other reasons. James told me that the Beatles had stayed in Wellow once, with the artist Peter Blake, who had the old chapel there (I had gone to a NYE party there once, hosted by his daughter, Daisy). Apparently Ringo said Wellow was a 'good place to get stoned'. We joked that this would make a good tourist sign.

I made some field-notes and shared some coffee. I was offered a segment of tangerine and a crunchy russet apple, grown close by. The guys packed up their kit; they had a lot to carry back so I offered to help and walked back with them, taking a different route, across a field and along (what sounded like) Gurtz Lane. We crossed at the ford – the water low for once – and came out by their cottages. I bid farewell to these three interesting fellows, and pushed on, back up the hill out of the village and crossing country passed the former Robertson estate (stopping to look at a monument dedicated to the family who had lived in the valley for sixty years).

A final yomp up the hill, past yapping dogs and silent horses, and I was back at the park and ride, soon back to 'civilisation', satisfied and scruffy, walking home passed the Christmas shoppers in my grubby gear, savouring my priceless solstice gift.

The Point of the Solstice

I returned home for a nice long soak – another way of creating sacred time! Candles, bubbles, a glass of something nice, maybe some ambient music – bliss! I emerged and, wrapped up in warm clothes, I sat by my fire and enjoyed a mince pie, feeling a warm solsticey glow from my day out; a winter's walk seems to justify any amount of indulgence! It certainly sharpens your appetite. I was just settling down into an afternoon nap when the gate went and someone came down the steps. I recognised the bright red spiky hair. It was my friend Sheila, delivering a Yule card. I invited her in for a cuppa and a mince pie, but she couldn't stay – her sister was in the car. I mentioned I had just been on a winter solstice walk and had bumped into fellow Bard of Bath, Helen Moore. Unfortunately, this triggered one of Sheila's hobby horses about *when* to celebrate the solstice.

According to her – and she is categorical about these things – it's not until the 28th or something, according to her friend, Rae Beth, the hedgewitch. I told her that it was from today that the days start getting longer – infinitesimally at first (the sun seeming to stand still at its southern nadir until the 24th) and that for me is the reason to celebrate. She wouldn't accept this and pointed out the card she had given me – a lovely image of a double spiral, created apparently by the path of the sun as recorded by New York artist, Charles Ross, over the course of a year, using a lens to burn the sun's passage onto a piece of wood on his studio roof ('Sunlight Convergence, Solar Burn: The Year Shape', Ross 1972). This for her was evidence; although, has it been tested and validated? Because it was art it 'must be true' and because I cited the science of the Met Office, that must be false. Such is the reasoning of many pagans I meet, who distrust anything that comes from an authoritative source, but have a default credulity for any spurious theory they happen to like the sound of. I could not help but smile at Sheila's fundamentalism, as it mirrored that of the lady at the Story Circle the night before, who insisted the solstice was *that* night, when the sun went into Capricorn. 'All pagans believe that!' she insisted. Since when did pagans agree on anything? It's amazing that groups of them manage to organise themselves. Perhaps this is the universe's way of avoiding bottlenecks at sacred sites, since every group seems to have its preferred time for conducting their rites. A feature on the BBC talked of record numbers of pagans celebrating winter solstice in UK: 'There's been a rapid increase in the number of pagans in the UK, according to experts. Robert Pigott reports on the phenomenon. (*Record numbers of British people have celebrated the winter solstice festival*, BBC News, 21 December 2009). In this feature, the Dolmen Grove, based down in Dorset, were shown celebrating the dying of the old year at sunset on solstice eve, in their ceremonial site (indeed, Stonehenge is actually aligned to the winter solstice sunset, as well as the summer solstice sunrise). Nobody is 'right' and I am suspicious of anyone who claims to know The Truth – and is unable to listen to anyone else's point of view. The truth is, Paganism is a 'broad church' and it contains many different belief systems, some of which make uncomfortable bedfellows – although most are a pretty harmless bunch. The fact, as the BBC feature attests, that more people than ever are feeling compelled to celebrate the 'turning of the wheel', as it's often referred to, is very telling. Whatever the authenticity of the various Traditions these people follow, there's no doubting that they feel compelled to celebrate these sacred times in the present day – no one is forcing them to. I feel it is an urge to restore some connection between the individual and the greater cycles; to synchronise; to harmonise; to feel connected to the past, to the 'Old Ones' here and now in the present. There's something reassuring about this sense of continuity; whether it's genuine or imagined, it still has the desired placebo effect. Whether druids worshipped at places like Stonehenge or not is perhaps academic. The fact is that modern druids, and other 'neo-pagans' (as the academic like to call them), feel drawn to worship in them *now* – and that is what matters. It is not 're-enactment' or 'revivalism', but perhaps a re-sanctifying of modern lives.

We are pulverised by secular time – always rushing; always trying to squeeze everything in; giving away our time in exchange for money seldom to the true value of precious moments of our life span; we kill time; wish time away; wanting it to be the weekend, or our holiday, or home time; one minute it's flying by, the next it's crawling – but get mocked when we try to create meaningful time: qualitative, rather than quantitative time. Ritual is largely about slowing or stopping time, about altering consciousness, our perception of time, of space, of one another, of the Earth and the heavens, of the elements and elementals, animals and spirits, Gods and ancestors. It is about becoming conscious of the time locked in our own bodies, our DNA. We are the result of millions of years of evolution, of generations of challenge, love and destiny. At many of the festivals, we remember those who have gone before and those yet to be. We connect, consciously, with the wheel of time, while stepping off it. We gain chronological perspective. Like the workings of an expensive watch, there are different dials – wheels within wheels: cycles of varying sizes, from the diurnal to the cosmic. All time can be mapped upon this chart. No time is too insignificant to register, to be not worth marking in some way. But the point, of course, is not the time itself, but simply to connect on a human level with the 'tribe', the community, with kindred spirits across the world, with one's immediate circle and with oneself. The rest is just splitting hairs.

Tom Bawcock's Eve
23rd December

West Cornwall has a unique Christmas celebration on the 23rd December, known as Tom Bawcock's Eve. There is a lantern procession and the world-renowned harbour lights illumina-tions. The celebration has got so popular that neighbouring Newlyn and Penzance have joined in, sharing in the good catch of grockles it brings in. This is the story behind it (if you like, imagine it told on a dark and stormy night in some low-beamed pub, fire crackling in the hearth, by some ancient mariner over his foaming tankard):

Mousehole man, Tom Bawcock, lived about two centuries ago. During a bad winter of storms with Christmas coming up, the fishermen of Mousehole had not managed to gather in any fish being too afraid to take their boats out. Folk were starting to starve. On the Eve of Christmas Eve, with the gale still blowing, Tom gathered his crew together; 'Come on, me sons, let's see if we can get us some Christmas dinner.' They were the only boat to set sail into the storm. They managed to land a good catch but, heading back, Tom's ship was lost in the storm – the coast was obscured by the lashing gale. Wearily, they struggled to make it back to safe harbour. Locals put candles and lanterns in their windows to guide the crew home. The boat made it – men and fish all. Tom and his crew had a good catch and bought back seven different types of fish, lifting the famine. This is celebrated on Tom Bawcock's Eve by the baking of Starry Gazy Pie, which has seven types of fish baked under a crust, with the heads sticking out a hole in the middle. And villagers light their windows in the way those former residents had done, to guide home all.

Such a custom seems a way of remembering all souls lost at sea. There are many comparable traditions around the coast of the British Isles. On the Isle of Wight, at St Catherine's Point, there stands a curiously shaped tower, looking like a stone rocket, known locally as the Pepper pot (since Tennyson Down was used for rocket-testing by the MOD, this ancient monument seems an uncanny precursor). It is St Catherine's Oratory, the remains of a church built around 1328. It was built by Lord of Chale Walter de Godeton (sometimes spelled "Goditon") as an act of penance for plundering wine from the wreck of St. Marie of Bayonne in Chale Bay on April 20, 1313 AD. There was already an oratory on the top of the hill, dedicated to St. Catherine of Alexandria (home of the famous Lighthouse of Pharos, one of the Seven Wonders of the World). It seemed fitting that this was augmented by the construction of the lighthouse, so there would be a chantry to accommodate a priest tending the light. The priest would also say Mass for those lost at sea. Used as a beacon, both metaphysical and practical it seems to have served a similar purpose to the lights of Mousehole. It stands next to a Bronze Age barrows: clear evidence that the hill had been regarded as sacred for a long time.

In Thailand, around Halloween, there is the festival of Loi Krathong, when lanterns are floated onto water in remembrance of the ancestors. Water is commonly seen as a gateway to the Otherworld; ships of the dead abound in many cultures, from Arthur being taken to Avalon, to the spirit canoes, preserved in an underground river in the Philippines.

As is often the case, such traditions are preserved in story, ritual or song. Back in Mousehole, there is a local song which is sung, capturing the tale of Tom Bawcock's Eve – written in 1927 by Robert Morton Nance to a traditional tune called the *Wedding March*. Nance apparently witnessed the celebrations at the dawn of the twentieth century. The 'tradition' might have been a relatively recent invention, although Nance believed it relates back to ancient pagan practices, the word 'Bawcock' coming from the French 'beau coc', the rooster said to herald the rebirth of the light. However, Bawcock seems also to be a Middle English term for a 'fine or worthy fellow'. With its symbolism of fish and light, it chimes well with the Christian tradition as well: Tom Bawcock, a kind of local Christ figure, feeding the multitude with a few fish on the cusp of Christmas. Whatever its origins, it is charming custom which brings a touch of magic (and wealth) to a corner of Cornwall in the depths of winter.

Tom Bawcocks' Eve

A merry place you may believe
Was Mouzel on Tom Bawcocks' Eve.
To be there then who wulden wesh

To sup o sibm soorts o fesh.

When morgy brath had cleared the path,
Come scences for a fry,
And we had a bit o scad
And starry gazy pie.

Next came fairmaids
Bra thusty jandes
As maade our oozles dry.
And ling and haake
Enough to make
A raunin' shark to sigh.

An aich we'd clunk
As health were drunk,
And when up came Tom Bawcocks name
We pris'd un to the sky.
(Traditional Rhyme)

Christmas Eve
24th December

Yesterday, I celebrated Christmas Eve in the same way as many of my countrymen (and possibly across the Western Hemisphere), rushing into town to buy some last minutes essentials (because the shops are going to close for a whole day – gosh, how will we survive? – and, not even that these days: somewhere a corner shop or garage will open for at least half the day); squeezing in another 'mince pie and mulled wine' invite (in former days, the great and the good would open their houses and offer food and drink to the community, and it felt a little like this, visiting the rather nice new house of a doctor and an osteopath. I had to resist the urge to tug my furlock as I was offered a drink and a nibble; by the time I had dashed round town and hiked up to their house, I was starving!); going home to wrap up presents; listening to carols; sipping some sherry and finally feeling 'Christmassy'; nodding off by the fire listening to a spooky tale on the radio (maybe this is less common – the majority would be probably glued to the gogglebox). Then in the evening, I met up with some friends for a drink, before finally ending up at Midnight Mass – not alone in being slightly merry.

First though, I went to a lovely real ale pub on the sweeping Georgian terrace of the Paragon, called The Star, which has its own fine micro-brewery – Bath Ales. It was packed out and I could barely squeeze in to the bar. There was a real fire blazing away, an impressive smorgasbord of cheese on the bar, and some festive ale to savour. Later, Santa hats and antlers were handed round, along with carol sheets for a Christmas sing-along. Our snug was dominated by a group of boozy blokes and it turned into 'rugby carols' instead, as they murdered each carol in the same drunken yawp – 'carols', which included the Band Aid song and Slade's 70s classic! When they mercifully stopped, the sound of carols drifting in from the bar next door was far easier on the ears. It seems some people find it difficult to be sincere, to try their best. So instead, they do their worst. Yet, in pubs like the Blue Ball in Yorkshire, carol-singing in pubs is a passionately maintained tradition. If those guys had tried it there, they soon would have had an angry pub to deal with.

Christmas often leads to violence – on the news earlier there were reports that a snowball fight in Denbighshire had ended in a twenty-year-old man being stabbed to death. With so much alcohol going around – after weeks of stress – it's no wonder such incidents occur.

Around our table, a conversation with my girlfriend resulted in her dramatically walking off in tears – talk of her father had all got too much. To add to this, we were joined by someone who holds extreme views and isn't shy about sharing them – extremely anti-religious, to the point that you could call his 'fundamentalist atheism' a dogma. He dislikes any reference to Christianity or other religions, yet here he was celebrating Christmas Eve with us, wearing a silly Xmas hat, drinking seasonally named beer, and talking about what he's going to cook for Xmas day. I found his absolutism tedious and wished I could have been sharing this time with kindred spirits, rather than people I actually feel I have little in common with. I was the only one who wished to go along to Midnight Mass – many people who attend this aren't necessarily Christian, in the strictest sense, but like me, enjoy the aesthetic of it and the special atmosphere.

After the boozy dysfunction of The Star, it would prove to be a blessed contrast. Leaving the fug of the pub, into the freezing fog of the winter's night, I breathed a sigh of relief. Peace!

I arrived at Bath Abbey, its large windows glowing with warmth, making it look like an enormous Chinese lantern (it's known as the Lantern of the West, being made of seventy per cent glass), just in time, catching the end of the first hymn. I was given a hymn sheet and found a seat. The place was packed. The interior of the Abbey looked beautiful, the high forest-like vault glowing with the light of the chancel, where the white-robed choir stood in the stalls by their candle-lit readers. The sound of their high voices floating into the night was hauntingly beautiful. The organ resonated deeply through the stone of the building, through the soles of your feet, as though the whole place vibrated – a tuning fork of the soul. It seemed like an interesting echo of the effect of song and musical instruments in a Neolithic site like Stoney Littleton Long Barrow – where the three guys spent the night in song – and it felt no different to me. Here, we gathered to celebrate the return of the light, albeit in a more formalised, mainstream way, yet its roots go right back to those Stone Age ancestors, waiting for the sun, at places like Stonehenge and Newgrange. As the service progressed, there was a palpable sense of the numinous – especially after the

Communion, when the choir burst into the most beautiful song. There seemed present a real sense of immanence at that point. Something divine, the Awen I would call it, entered then, through the portal created by the sublime music. There is something very powerful about sharing such an experience collectively. The Bishop of Bath and Wells officiated over the service, providing a 'human touch' to all the esoteric proceedings – a good speaker, his sermon had the 'common touch', making reference to popular culture (*Gavin and Stacey*). There was just the right sense of ritual for Anglo-Saxon sensibilities – not too over-powering, no vulgar expressing of feeling(!), but rather a restraint of feeling, a certain dignified acceptance of Higher Powers and an Ineffable Mystery. For many, this would all seem too bloodless compared to, say, Catholic Mass or a Charismatic service (I heard of one held at a church in Combe Down, which used CS Lewis' classic Christian fantasy, *The Lion, The Witch and the Wardrobe*, to transform the church into Narnia – entering through a wardrobe, a winter wonderland inside with lamp-post, clips from the film between the hymns and sermon, etc. Full circle in a way, since Lewis was drawing upon Christian tropes in his tale). Funnily enough, in the Abbey, the effect of the music at times reminded me of Peter Jackson's version of *The Lord of the Rings* – the sublime music of Howard Shore, which is headily religious in places. And the whole story has, of course, mythic resonance, infused with Tolkien's own belief system, but stripped of any direct reference. For me, Tolkien's tale of the return of the king – overlaying the story of Christ's redemption of the world – had more resonance for me than the 'official version'. The story of Jesus retold that night had little direct meaning for me but, in a wider sense, I could relate to the return of the light, and the renewal of hope. The one thing that did cross-over for me was the reiteration by the Bishop of the traditional Christmas message – Peace on Earth and Goodwill to all Humanity. This has as much relevance today as ever and surely transcends all the artificial barriers of faith.

Whatever one's belief system, this ultimately humanitarian message surely has validity for us all. With this in mind, I left the Abbey and walked back through the freezing fog of midnight – the first hour of Christmas Day. I was tired and dehydrated, but glad I had made the effort to go to the service. It was rather long and rather too dry for me (I would have liked a few more carols) but it gave some meaning to this time of year, which is otherwise just a nauseating round of hedonism.

Yet, there was still plenty of time for that!

Christmas Day
25th December

Every family who celebrates it (Jehovah's Witnesses look away now) have their own Christmas traditions. Our family is not typical (although perhaps everyone feels that about their own family) but this is how we celebrated Christmas. We were never a religious family and so it meant more about a chance to be together, to have some treats, and to make merry. Never having much money, Christmas was the only time of year when we were allowed 'luxuries' that the rest of the year we could not afford. So this is a typical Christmas in the Manwaring household, circa mid-70s. Dad would always take responsibility for putting up the Christmas tree – an artificial thing that was in vogue back then. He would bury it in a landslide of tinsel and the same chipped plastic baubles – red or blue – that were preserved from year to year. He would enclose it in a barbed wire of fairy lights and this would sit, in a bucket full of soil from the garden, enclosed in crepe paper on a tall table out of reach of our ubiquitous canines (we always had three). Mum would hang the paper chains with our help as we grew older and taller and there would be a string or two of Christmas cards. All that would be lacking was the food. I recall waiting until late Christmas Eve afternoon for Dad to come home from the pub so we could dash to the supermarket before it closed to get all our Christmas shopping! There would be a bowl of walnuts, some bottles of sherry, port, ginger ale, maybe a Party 7, or small bottles of Schweppes drinks. There would be a big tin of Quality Street, which plainly we were not living on. There would be cheese and crackers aplenty. And of course the big joint – normally beef – and tonnes of vegetables to peel and cook. Earlier in the month I might have attended my mum's works Christmas do at Church's shoe factory or the one down Dad's working men's club, both of which involved children running wild while the 'responsible adults' got sloshed. Christmas Day would start early (4 – 5am?), with the three of us – my brother, sister and I – sitting at the top of the stairs while our parents did some last minute wrapping (presents were normally hidden in the wardrobe in my folks' room before this). When the all clear was finally sounded, we leapt down the stairs, taking several steps, if not all, in one leap. We burst through the door into the living room where our presents were piled on three respective chairs. Without further ado, we tore open our presents in a blizzard of wrapping paper. I remember one Christmas being particularly pleased with a toy steam train (I was about seven). My brother had an air fix model of the Apollo Moonlander (which took flight from his bedroom window, when a breeze caught it – it did not achieve orbit). My sister had some kind of hairdressing salon, but I wasn't interested in that because it was a girl's toy. From 1978, always included in the presents was the (for the Manwaring brothers, essential) 2000AD annual, which I spent the morning reading in front of the telly. We were indulged in little treats throughout the day. Our Nan would sometimes visit us then with further goodies. Before midday, Dad had gone down to the local, the Golden Horse, and then onto the Working Men's Club down Main Road, in the middle of a light industrial estate. We would have to wait, belts tightened, for him to return – on good years before 3pm – in time to sit down for Christmas dinner and the Queen. Mum spent the whole day in the kitchen, cooking mountains of food, but hardly eating or drinking anything herself. In contrast to Dad, she drunk nothing but tea, but smoked like a chimney. These two staples kept her going through every adversity. Dad finally back, we could begin. Crackers were pulled; hats were donned; jokes were groaned at; plastic toys lost. We were allowed a little glass of sherry. And a contented silence descended as we tucked into a splendid feast. This was a belt-buster by itself, but there was still Christmas pudding, mince pies, cheese and biscuits and chocolates to come – mercifully spaced throughout the rest of the evening. After dinner, we were allowed a lucky dip from the Santa on top of the telly – often a diary or some other stocking filler. We would then collapse incapacitated in front of some hoary Christmas classic like *The Wizard of Oz*. If movement was possible, then toys or games would be played with. We seldom sat round at a table to play something sophisticated like Monopoly. It was more likely to be Mousetrap, Connect 4, Battleships, Mastermind, Haunted House, Operation, or a similar plastic choke-hazard from Fisher Price. Lego or remote controlled vehicles, Action Men or Scalectrix would get under the feet or on the nerves of the adults, but all were generally content, gathered together around the one fire in the house – a gas fire in the living room. Winters were colder then and the house was never a warm house, and so the living room was the only option. The rest of the day passed away in a carb-coma or slightly drunken haze, falling asleep in front of the telly. I don't think Mum ever got much help with the scary piles of washing up, but we were never told to help – Dad certainly didn't set a good example. He would soon be snoring away in his favourite chair, surrounded by his devoted dogs, recently indulged in their own 'Xmas dinner' from the leftovers. Eyelids grew heavy and bedtime called. Christmas was over for another year.

Christmas on Solsbury

After ringing my mother, sister and brother and speaking briefly to A, I decided to go for a spin up to Solsbury Hill – it was a beautiful sunny day with a clear blue sky. It really felt the sun had been reborn today, as the guys in the barrow had predicted. The ice of recent days had melted away and I deemed it safe to go out on the bike for the first time in over a week. Getting out of the back lane was slightly tricky, but I took it easy on the patches of ice and gravel and was soon on the road. The streets were clear – if only it was like this all of the time.

I made it all the way up to the end of Solsbury Lane and parked up. There were various walkers around, but it wasn't crowded and it was easy enough to get away. I walked in a sunwise direction around the hill, enjoying the sense of light and space. The view today was spectacular – a cleansing radiance of sunlight, sharp shadows, hills of muted greens. There was a tangible sense of peace – hardly any traffic on the roads or in the air. Stillness.

I walked a full circle around Solsbury, considering how Yule means 'wheel'. I came to the turf maze cut by the road protesters, as part of the famous Batheaston Bypass Protest in the 90s, and walked it mindfully (not easy in motorbike boots!), ending with the affirmation: *May I walk with love.* Whatever happens, hold to your truth, keep centred. I had a hill-top epiphany – don't be turned by the wheel, be at the centre of the wheel. We can be spun about by all that happens, by the demands of life. At Christmas, the festivities themselves seem to be relentless and one gets swept along, sometimes forced to join in, it seems. It is good to step off the wheel sometimes, rather than repeat these cycles meaninglessly. Up there on the hill I felt such a sense of peace and space. Solsbury hill is so empty – devoid of trees, thanks to the cattle-grazing. Just an enormous sky, a bowl of light. The blank canvas of each moment. We fill our lives with so much clutter, with so much noise and business, but where does it truly get us? Better to live simply and in peace, not striving, not yearning, just being. Living in the now.

All this effort, all this money spent, energy used, goods consumed, carbon emitted, debt increased, stress and sorrow, when, in truth, it is just another day. We make it special – or try to – but in fact it is only what we have imposed on reality, like the turf maze carved into the hill. A pattern we give to things. And yet, knowing all that, it felt good to walk on the hill in the winter sun. After the craziness of the last few days, stillness at last.

Boxing Day Mummers
26th December

Picture the scene: it's a frosty Boxing Day morning. You feel the bite in the air, this high up, for you're on the Cotswolds in the village of Marshfield. Just along the road is the aptly-named village of Cold Ashton, said to be one of the coldest places in England. You stand on the High Street, hemmed in by stern looking dwellings, grey monoliths in the mist. Other die-hard visitors look on, wrapped up and huddled together for warmth, bleary-eyed and bulging from the Christmas Day indulgence. Locals look smugly out from their bedroom windows or doorways. This is their day and they have the best seats in the house. The conversation is subdued, frosted breath escapes with the odd laugh. The wise save their hot air. There's anticipation hanging in the mist. Something is about to happen – possibly – yet its slight uncertainty creates a mild frisson of tension. Small miracles cannot, after all, be time-tabled.

Then a bell can be heard, clanging in the distance, drawing closer, and suddenly, out of the wintry haze they appear – a curious procession of moochers – seven men draped in rags of paper, led by a figure clad like a pall-bearer, black from top hat to toe, ringing his bell in single chimes. He could easily be chanting 'bring out the dead'. The strange raggle-taggle figures 'mum' beneath their festooned hats, proceed in silence to the far end of the High Street where they gather in a circle and begin their play. It's difficult to catch as the men (Marshfield boys every one of them) are not professionals and can rarely project. A bite of wind, or facing the wrong way and you miss a part of their speech. You have to watch each of the five performances held along the High Street to patch together the whole script. Even then, the play seems to be hotch-potch, stitched together from fragments of memory. Most of it sounds like nonsense, or the result of Chinese whispers, yet there is something hypnotic about it – the incantatory effect of their introductory refrain, 'In comes I...' in the lilting Marshfield accent, the stiff ritual movements, as each character steps forward and speaks his part, engages in a bit of business, the hushed reverence of the crowd.

Something magical has broken through into the mundane and briefly we are held in its spell. A story is taking place – a very old story. In the dead of winter, a brightly clad hero appears. He wears the cross of St George and we are meant to cheer, for he England's patron paladin. Then a darker knight steps into the circle, Bold Slasher or the Turkish Knight. He plays the pantomime villain and we are meant to boo. There is an illicit pleasure in this as we realise we are temporarily outside the PC control zone of modern Britain. This is older than political correctness and more authentic because, beyond these labels, a simplistic moral dualism which seem ludicrous now, and perhaps makes us realise how the first decade of the twenty-first century, the so-called noughties, have seen the West demonise the 'Saracen' – a media- and government-fuelled Islamophobia. The dodgy stereotypes of the Mummers offer a comic reminder of how little we have progressed since the jingoistic Crusades. Yet beyond these cultural masks are older symbols – archetypes – of the light and dark halves of the year. In the combat-and-resur-rection, as the solar hero is slain and then brought back to life by the Doctor, we perhaps witness the death-and-rebirth of the sun itself as witnessed over the last few days, from the winter solstice to Christmas morn. And other curious figures step into the ring –

Grandfather Christmas, wishing us good cheer; a devil-figure, red-horned Beelzebub, with a large phallic club; Saucy Jack, 'with his family on his back'; and Ten-penny Nit, the fool – and we could be forgiven for mistaking what we are seeing as a fertility rite, one as old as the hills. It wouldn't take much of a leap of the imagination to picture this slapstick Mystery Play taking place in a forest clearing; the players covered in leaves; the watchers in the shadows; our ancestors witnessing a re-enactment of the inexplicable mystery of the sun's rebirth at its lowest ebb. Perhaps those gathered around this primal woodland clearing feel that if this rite is not performed the sun will not come back. Their existence hangs on a thread, connected to the great Web of Life. They will do all they can to ensure their survival. If a little bit of hocus pocus helps, all well and good. No point in tempting fate.

Yet, this scenario is a Victorian fantasy – what could be called the Frazer fallacy, after Sir James George Frazer, who believed that such customs, as exhaustively listed in his magnum opus, *The Golden Bough*, were the remnant of ancient fertility rituals. This theory was taken up by the Folklore Society and various writers and remained popular for half a century before scholars began to question it, and now it is largely rejected. The problem is that there is no firm evidence of mummers' plays before the early 1700s and many have been 'contaminated' by those who collected them, as is the case of the Marshfield mummers play, which was resurrected by Violet Alford, the sister of the vicar of Marshfield, in 1930. Alford was a keen folklorist and had firm ideas of how the play should be enacted – adding rituals elements that were not there, such as the standing in a circle. If there were authentic elements in the play, these have been lost in the Alford reinvention, which can be witnessed in Marshfield every Boxing Day. Pausing for the Second World War, the play has been performed ever since.

Regardless of its actual origins and 'authenticity', the fact is that the Marshfield Mummers is a strange, magical thing to behold and adds a richer dimension to Boxing Day. Considering the alternative – fox-hunting and sales madness, cold turkey and rubbish TV – the country would be impoverished without its eccentric charm.

Afterwards, many cram into one of the pubs along High Street, the Catherine's Wheel proving popular for a glass of something warming, and it is here I bumped into my old friend Niall Darroch, who's from an old Marshfield family. His grandfather used to be one of the Old Time Paper Boys and according to the local custom, he could follow in his footsteps as a blood-relative, but he has moved to Ireland. Yet, he remembers seeing the costume hanging in the house and the script they used to learn their lines. Niall was there with his wife, the Irish rose he met when he moved to Dingle, and their new child. The fertility rite certainly worked for them.

Christmas Boys

In contrast to the Marshfield Mummers, the Keynsham Mummers play is far more professional, but lacking in atmosphere, held in the centre, in what passes for the town square, in front of the ugly office block of Keynsham town council. Keynsham was possibly once a picturesque market town but it now looks like a bomb hit it – which it probably did in WW2 – and it has been patched up with hastily thrown up concrete carbuncles. It looks and feels rundown – one of Britain's many crap towns.

The Keynsham Mummers is a good attempt to restore some soul to the town. Revived in the Seventies by the Bristol Morris Men, it is based upon a transcript fortunately recorded by a folkloric collector, Hunter, in 1822 when it was originally performed by the 'Christmas Boys'. It has one of the most complete scripts available, but as a result feels slightly soulless. It is an artificial revival rather than the real thing – far better to have a completely modern mummers, as in the recently formed Widcombe Mummers, who perform on New Year's Day, and whose cast includes traffic wardens and other topical local figures, such as King Bladud, and the King of the Beggars of Holloway - elected every year by the homeless who converged on the rich pickings of Bath, as discovered by the late Tim Sebastian in his research into obscure folklore.

About two hundred people gathered outside Keynsham townhall in the sun – the cold snap had been replaced by milder weather. Still, the coffee and hot chocolate purchased over the road was welcome as we stood waiting. The players proceeded in from the car park, singing their 'theme song'. They entered the space and introduced themselves. On the whole, they knew their lines better and could project. There was a little bit of improvised business and the whole thing was good natured and mildly amusing – lacking the starker, more sinister edge of the Marshfield Mummers. Apart from the usual figures of Father Christmas, Saint or King George, the Saracen (here called the Valiant Knight), Saucy Jack and a 'village idiot' type in a shepherd's smock, there was the addition of a 'comely shepherdess', played by a man – complete with enormous boobs and pigtails – and another knight, who tries to woo her. There was also a bit of Morris dancing at the end – an obvious speciality of the Bristol Morris.

Weston Mummers at Southstoke

The third of Bath's Boxing Day Mummers is at the Pack Horse in Southstoke, a very pretty village just south of the city. This play is the most recent, with the least amount of information, but is in some ways, the most entertaining. It is performed by the Weston Mummers, who perform their 'seasonal play' in and around the village of Weston, on the western edge of Bath, usually on the Friday before Christmas, and then on Boxing Day outside the Pack Horse, Southstoke. The performers are not as competent as the Bristol Morris, being forced to read their often forgotten lines from the backs of their props – shields and bottles – and yet the rapport with the audience was better. Maybe it was because we were closer to them and they didn't have to compete with background traffic noise. The beer garden terrace of the Packhorse provided a perfect stage – south-facing, it was lit up by the winter sun. The setting is far more picturesque and romantic. This all adds to the effect.

What really made it stand out was the carol singing before the play begins. This allows for audience participation and warms-up the audience and the place itself. It was magical to hear such classics as *The Twelve Days of Christmas*, *Good King Wenceslas*, *The Boar's Head Carol* and *The Holly and the Ivy* sung out, full-voiced and sincerely by those gathered. At the chorus of the latter – *'The rising of the sun, and the running of the deer'* – it really felt wonderfully pagan and deeply representative of the midwinter magic, as though we really were taking part in an ancient fertility rite about the sun's rebirth.

It is definitely a more 'up-market' affair than the Keynsham or Marshfield plays – both in the performers and audience – which is ironic, since originally it was performed by working class amateurs. Now it seems to be an amusing distraction for the middle classes – a charming thing to watch on a Boxing Day, a refreshingly low-tech alternative to the virtual entertainment proffered on the plasma screen.

As a topical footnote, it is interesting to see how Russell T Davies' revamped *Dr Who* (Britain's longest running science fiction series) has become as intrinsic a part of Christmas as turkey, *The Snowman* and the Queen's Christmas Message – a 'tradition' since 2005. In thrilling, colourful adventures, the larger-than-life hero goes up against larger-than-life villains. From David Tennant's 2005 Christmas Day debut to his exit, New Year's Day, 2010 (regenerating from Christopher Eccleston's incarnation and then being regenerated himself into the newest and youngest Doctor, played by Matt Smith), we have a modern updating of The Death-and-Resurrection Show of the Mummers' Play. In Tennant's debut, he had a sword fight with an evil alien on a spaceship floating above London – an echo of the ritual combat between St George and the Turkish Knight. And in Tennant's two-parter exit, *The End of Time*, the Doctor's nemesis, the Master, plays the role of 'Bold Slasher' – someone we love to boo at. The supporting cast add an archetypal spectrum to the proceedings: here is a Mystery Play with flashy special effects, an analogy not too far-fetched, as the messianic subtext of the enigmatic 'Who' character is played up with each Earth-saving story. The Doctor is the one who heals all of us and mends the world, redeeming the planet from a dystopian fate. So, the Mummers' Play lives on – in unlikely but enduring forms.

But why does this all take place on Boxing Day?

To anyone but a Brit, Boxing Day remains a small mystery – something we have of our own, in the same way Americans have Thanksgiving. Christmas has become pretty much a global festival, but Boxing Day remains stubbornly and uniquely British. St Stephen's Day, or Boxing Day, as it is more commonly known in Britain, gained its nickname from the custom of giving servants and tradesmen Christmas Boxes, often in the form of money (an early form of Christmas bonus, but sometimes in victuals and good drink, as a reward for loyal or good service). It was common for the larger houses to have 'open house', when all could come and partake of the host and hostess's hospitality, but this became exploited and fell out of favour as well-meaning hosts found themselves eaten out of house and home, or sometimes burgled by guizers, or finding themselves having to cope with rowdy wassailers. These days, Boxing Day is more often celebrated in the larger retail outlets, as people go hunting for a bargain – shopping junkies keen to get a new fix after a whole day without – so it might be more accurately called 'Flat-pack Day'. If Christmas Day is dominated by Norwegian spruce,

Boxing Day belongs to Swedish pine.

New Year's Eve
31st December

There is so much anxiety and pressure over celebrating New Year's Eve. If it's not 'the best night ever' it feels like you've failed in some way. Where you celebrate it seems to be a measure of your success or social standing somehow. If you're not at the best party in town, in the country, or even in the world – for many travel far to celebrate NYE in far-flung places – then you're over the hill. With so much expectation, it's no wonder that it is often a terrible anti-climax. To avoid this – and all the social miasma of midnight, when if you're not snogging the love of your life, you end up swapping saliva with strangers – some react against it and hide away. Some deny its relevance, like the chap I met in the long barrow who said in an email: 'It's funny this thing we call New Year – it's really just a January thing – not really connected to sun cycles or owt!' It is, after all, only another day – an artificial demarcation of time. It is a largely Roman custom that the world has inherited along with its calendar. Quite a few hate NYE; it's not a tradition that you can have ambivalent feelings about.

After several days of uncertainty about exactly where and with whom I was going to celebrate the arrival of the New Year, I arranged to spend it with my storytelling friends, Anthony and Kirsty, at their place in Stroud. It turned out to be a low-key but pleasant evening with only a small group of us there. We shared a meal – a nice warming chilli (just what I needed after a chilly ride there). Then we shared stories and poems. Kirsty performed a Wiltshire story about a shepherd and his dog. We had *The Journey of the Magi*, and a couple of TS Eliot's cat poems; a Whitmanesque anaphora from Fred; Anthony read out Tolkien's obscure poem, *Immram*; and I read out my modern fairy story, *The Glimmering Girl*.

At midnight, we went out the front and toasted in the New

Year with a glass of mead another local friend Miranda had brought, watching the fireworks over Stroud. It was a cold, clear night and the blue moon shone brightly in the sky. It was a blue moon on the eve of the New Year and, according to some, the new decade. It seemed auspicious, although it is really what we make it. Any day can be equally as significant.

We went back into the warmth and did a terrible version of Auld Lang Syne; being sassenachs we didn't know more than the first verse. Miranda led on her whistle and Kirsty prompted us with the full lyrics, but it was a dismal effort. Yet, it was true that old acquaintances shouldn't be forgot. I thought of all those who I would have liked to be there, absent friends both living and dead. Yet, the company I had was most agreeable.

It wasn't the wildest NYE I've had, but it was a pleasant start to the year – quite civilised! Afterwards, I stayed up to about 3am chatting. The mead woke my fellow guest up, but I was nodding off and lay down on my air bed (which had provided some Carry On style hilarity trying to inflate). We talked until I couldn't keep my eyes open any longer – a gentle 'touchdown' to slumberland.

In the morning, we shared a nice breakfast together before M and I left our kind hosts to go on a walk up Haresfield Beacon, by Miranda's place. Anthony could not join us because he was still recovering from his hernia operation and had spent most of the night horizontal, lying there before us like the 'fisher king', as someone commented at one point.

It was a beautiful clear day on New Year's Day – cold and crisp underfoot. Frost still hung on the slopes of the beacon – the edge of the Cotswold escarpment overlooking the Severn valley. There were lots of walkers out enjoying the sun as well, and blowing away the cobwebs of the old year and the night's revelries, like us. A bracing walk on New Year's Day has become something of a tradition as well and for me is the most enjoyable part of the festival. It's great to be up high on a clear day and get a perspective on everything – thinking about the year ahead.

After a quick cuppa, I hit the road soon after our return to Miranda's charming cottage to make the most of the remaining light. It was pushing four, so it was starting to go already. I estimated I had about half an hour left, so could break the back of the thirty mile journey at least. Wrapped up like a Tellytubby, I bid farewell to my friend and set off through the gathering dusk, racing the dark, and the encroaching cold, inexorably numbing my extremities. I knew it was only so long before the frost would dangerously impair my dexterity and concentration and make the roads lethal. An hour is about all I can cope with, which is how long it takes; even then, by the time I got home, even a bath didn't thaw me out completely. I didn't get warm inside again until I'd had a big roast dinner, which had to wait until after the grand finale of *Doctor Who*, watched by ten million (the 'old' Doctor, played by the popular David Tennant, died and the new one, Matt Smith (of my old home town, Northampton) replaced him like Old Father Time being replaced by the infant year – symbolism not lost upon the makers of the programme, no doubt). Unable to do much else, I watched Sting's *If on a Winter's Night*, recorded at Durham Cathedral, which caught the mood and magic of the season perfectly. Sleepy from a heavy night, followed by a good walk and a freezing ride, I gladly went to bed before midnight and slept very soundly. The New Year could wait.

JANUARY

New Year
1st January 2010

Across the world last night, billions of people were celebrating
New Year's Eve – one of very few global celebrations. Although
several calendars coexist – Christian, Muslim, Hindu, Buddhist,
Mayan – the start of the new year, as is commonly accepted by
clocks, businesses, governments, computer systems, and so on, is
hard to ignore. Ten years ago, people were panicking about what
became known as the Millennium Bug, or Y2K, which vanished
like scotch mist on the 1st January 2000 – like so many WMDs.
This was tied in with millennial anxiety, whipped up by the
media and world religions. The world didn't end. Computers
didn't crash. Planes didn't fall out of the sky. Legions didn't die
in hospitals. The world carried on. Our millennium fears seemed
ill-founded. We can laugh at all the worry about Y2K – looking
back, ten years on, it seems so ludicrous (it shows how much we
swallow what the media dishes out – how much we buy into the
culture of fear). If only we knew what lay around the corner. The
charnel pyres of CJD or Mad Cow Disease, as it commonly
became known, were bad enough (with whole sections of the
countryside off-limits, like some awful *Quatermass Experiment*
scenario), but this was trumped by the inconceivable atrocity of
9/11. This earth-shattering event stamped its indelible mark on
the decade, and we're still feeling the shockwaves now. Yet, even
after such a moment – when the world seemed to stand still in
horror – life has gone on, and this decade, however dire it has
been at times (and it's hard to imagine it being any worse – wars
raging, global financial meltdown, climate change, peak oil), has
flown by. It's hard to believe it really; ten years ago, I was
standing on Glastonbury Tor, guiding people up and down the
spiral of light (777 lanterns dedicated to peace, spiralling around

the hill); and all over the world people were doing extraordinary things to celebrate the new millennium. Even then, however, there was dispute, some saying the new millennium didn't start until 2001. It's like those who don't like to celebrate NYE, because for them the winter solstice or samhain is the start of the new year. I know what they mean and intellectually I can agree, but surely, anything that brings people together in celebration – family and friends, old and new – has got to be good. Any excuse for a party, to step off the wheel, dance, make merry, watch fireworks, sing together, greet strangers warmly, re-forge connections is better than 'business as usual'. What the world certainly does not need right now is 'business as usual'. We need to stop, take stock, and resolve to lead better lives, create a better world. It is only a collective act of will. Twenty years ago, the will of those maintaining the Berlin Wall relented and it toppled. Two hundred years ago, slavery was abolished. All it takes is a change – a shift in the collective will. We are more powerful than we imagine – as Nelson Mandela once said, quoting Marianne Williamson (*'Our deepest fear is not that we are inadequate. Our deepest fear is that we are powerful beyond measure.'*) . We create time and we can bend it to our whims – create national holidays, two minute silences, and so forth. We can choose to create quality time for our loved ones and we can create quality time for the world.

We can make this new decade what we want it to be. We could stop the wars tomorrow. We could stop destroying the only planet we have. We could be kinder to each other, forgive old grudges, melt all the guns and decommission all the warheads and mines. We could make all transport run on green fuel; stop building nuclear power stations and start building more wind, wave and sun farms; create works of great beauty rather than that which makes a quick buck; favour the well-made and the meaningful rather than the shoddy and the trivial; consume less; love more; live well and die happy.

Millennium Grove and Time Capsule
3rd January

I decided, on a whim, to visit the Millennium Grove I planted with friends of the Bardic Chair of Bath on 22nd December, 1999. It was a beautiful cold clear day – deep blue skies and sunlight like cream – and I wanted to make the most of the precious few hours of daylight. I had originally planned to go up Solsbury Hill, but when I rode up Solsbury Lane my way was blocked by a van well and truly stuck, askew on the road, skidding on the ice, wedged in the narrow lane. The road was dicey – with the double-peril of gravel and patches of ice – and so I turned back, but at the bottom I decided to go left, rather than right, and follow the lane along St Catherine's Valley and come back along Bannerdown Hill. It was too beautiful a day to go home early.

It was a joy to be riding along the winding lane, through the deepening vale of St Catherine's, past cosy farmhouses, golden in the low sun. By the time I reached the bottom of Rocks East Woodland – my destination – the track was all but iced over and I had to be bold to traverse it on the bike. I took it real steady and only nearly lost it as I had to cross a whole sheet of ice going *up* a hill, which needed some revs and nerve! Heart in mouth, I kept the bike upright and made it to the tarmac on the other side. Relieved, I rode the couple of hundred yards to the car park of the Rocks East Woodland educational centre, which was empty for once (no one in their right mind would come out on a day like today...).

I have been coming here, to this '100 acre wood' at the head at St Catherine's Valley, where the three counties of Wiltshire, Somerset and Gloucestershire meet, since 1997 – after I read about it in the local newspaper in an article that compared it to something out of Tolkien's opus. And today just so happens to be Tolkien's birthday (last year I had a Tolkien Birthday party, getting my friends to read out my radio drama, *The Rabbit Room*). I fell in love with the place – the old man in the tree, the sculpture trail, the grotto, the witch in the woods, the valley of the rocks, the old coach road and billy goat bridge – and started to visit frequently. At the time, I was living in the centre of the city, and so it was a much needed sanctuary away from the madding crowd. I got to know the owner, Tony Philips OBE, an old soldier, local independent councillor of nearly sixty years' service, district president of the Wiltshire West Scouts, and a real-life Man who Planted Trees. Even then, in his seventies, he seemed ancient, weathered and tough like an old oak, but he would be down in the woods every day, working. He was a forester first and foremost – he loved his woods, practically lived in them – and for me he *was* the 'old man of the woods'. At first, I wanted to keep the place a secret, but it was too special not to share, and so I started to take friends up there and guide them around. I must have introduced hundreds of people to it. Over time, a trust was built up and I was allowed and then asked to put on events there and contribute to the wood creatively. I put on eco-arts events, like the Lost Forest Festival in 1998 or the WildWood Camp in 2003. In my year as Bard of Bath, 1998-99, I was 'in residence', running monthly events there – readings, gathering. I started a poetry trail, which still remains. I lived there for the summer in a tent, throughout one of the last beautiful summers for some time. I painted backdrops for the Rocks annual flower show display, which won prizes. And for the millennium, I decided to do something more permanent – a Celtic Tree Wheel, which was co-devised with artist and priestess Sheila Broun. We got different people to sponsor a tree and we planted thirteen native hardwoods in a circle with an apple tree in the middle. This was planted at the turn of the solstice, 22nd December, 1999, on the eve of the new millennium, so it became known as the Millennium Grove. The idea was to have a natural calendar – one tree per lunar month. Working with the appropriate tree each month, one could work one's way around the wheel. We had created, like our ancestors, a sacred space in which to mark sacred time. I initiated a series of 'moots' there on the Sunday nearest the full moon. We started promisingly with a large group at Imbolc, but by the late summer I was going up there by myself and I started to lose heart in it. I kept visiting when I could, seeing how the trees were getting on, occasionally organising working parties to do maintenance on the grove. A beech overshadowed the grove initially, which meant the trees in its shade didn't take, but when the offending limb was taken down, and the dead trees replanted, the grove became established, and has grown healthily ever since. The local druid, Tim Sebastion Woodman, suggested a turf-maze, which we created in a clearing just down from the grove, starting it on May Day. A mum and a young girl were present; the girl was called Fey, and so Tim called the miz-maze, 'Fey's Maze'. When Tim sadly died at Imbolc in 2007, we planted an oak tree for him, by the maze, putting in some of his ashes. We did the same for my poet friend Simon Miles, honorary Bard of Bath. Tony instigated an avenue of redwoods, each of which is dedicated to a loved one – more often than not, no longer around – and so the woodland has become increasingly a memorial woodland. A place to remember lost loved ones.

And so it was with bitter irony today that when I turned up and bumped into Philip, who was looking after the place, he informed me that Tony had passed away in the summer (while gardening on 22nd June – the start of the 'dark half' of the year, perhaps suitably for this real life Oak King). I knew he was old and half-expected to hear something each time I've been up over the last couple of years. He was in his eighties after all, but he was an old soldier and as tough as nails, working down in the woods every day – come rain or shine. Yet still it was a shock – horrible news on a bitter day. The sad thing was there had been a memorial service but we had not been notified. But he will not be forgotten. I will think of him every time I visit. He made these woods what they are – buying the place when it was in a mess and painstakingly restoring the gardens in the woods and sensitively managing it. Rocks East is a working wood – timber and firewood is the main income – but it has one of the best campsites around and some good trails and resources for school children. The centre is low, timbered and blends in the woodland well, nestled in a little amphitheatre, its roof covered in moss and lichen. The place isn't over-managed – the campsite doesn't have the usual eyesore plug-ins. The facilities are a little ramshackle, but that's part of its charm. It is a pretty unique place and we've held some pretty unique events there – a Druid/Maori camp, for instance – thanks to the open-mindedness and pioneering spirit of Tony Philips. He was one of a kind. I remember him saying he was instigating things, like the redwood avenue, that he would not see the culmination of. Unlike many around today, he did not leave the Earth impoverished by his impact, but enriched. He has left a legacy at Rocks East and at Broker's Wood (the other wood he owned) for future generations to enjoy. Through the beautiful green spaces he created, the 'old man of the woods' will live on.

One of the many glowing tributes that appeared on the local newspaper website, following the announcement, sums up the general feeling: '*Heaven's garden however will bloom just that little bit brighter now.*'

This sad news made my visit to the millennium grove even more poignant. It was touching to be there ten years on from when we planted it – some no longer with us, but the trees planted in their names provide a positive living memorial. Death is part of the natural cycle of things and, standing there in a 'naked' wood on a freezing winter's day, this hard truth was driven home. But there is the reassuring fact that... life goes on. There is the promise of spring, of rebirth. I noticed some trees even had buds on them, tiny slithers, like pen nibs dipped in ink, waiting to write the book of the year.

I walked back up; it was starting to get dark and I had to go while some light still remained, and before the roads froze over.

I passed the two yurts where the woodsman and his wife dwell. Smoke curled invitingly from the chimney of one. To most, living in such a place in winter would seem insane, but these picturesque but practical nomadic dwellings are designed for cold climates.

I talked briefly with Philip – shaking with Parkinson's, hand curled like a fern – who was incredibly looking after the place by himself. We discussed the possibility of doing something for Tony at the woods in the warmer months – planting a tree (although the whole wood is his memorial) or having a gathering of remembrance... something. I left determined to not let Tony fade away.

I set off, turning right at Hunter's Hall, where an infamous murder took place (caused by a nasty highwayman), onto the Fosseway, then stopped briefly at the Three Shire's Stone, the remains of a cromlech, moved from its original position – although that couldn't have been very far as the four stones (three uprights and a cap stone) are massive and must weigh several tonnes. Here, on a snowy day at the turn of the millennium (the same day I came up to collect the trees for the grove), I came and buried a time capsule. It was a comforting thought to know it was still there – some kind of continuity. The sun was setting in the west – a bloody yoke pierced on a pollarded stump, oozing its load over the horizon. I thought of Tim (who gave a talk here, at one of my events) and Tony, and wished them both peace in the Summerlands.

Twelfth Night Wassail
5th January

This evening, I held my annual Twelfth Night Wassail to thank the orchards for their fruits and to mark the end of Yuletide. This is a lot nicer than just taking down the decorations, as we are meant to do by the 6th (Epiphany). When so many Christmas trees lie discarded by the roadside, and the pavements are heaped with black bags destined for landfill sites, I think it is more important than ever to thank the Earth, rather than take from it. Certainly, the credit crunch has made people more circumspect in their consumerism, although the impact upon the environment of Christmas was probably just as devastating. Still, rather than get all preachy about it, I think it is far more positive just to thank the Earth, and that's literally what we do at my annual wassail – braving the freezing temperatures to gather round my apple tree at the bottom of the garden and wassailing it, that is toasting its health. I ushered my guests out into the darkness, equipped with the necessary wassailing regalia. I got the fire going dramatically with a little help from some petrol – not ideal, but it was a freezing night and the wood was damp. I asked people to imagine what dreams they wanted to bring through this year and to visualise them as apples on the branches. Then, taking up my old blackthorn shelaghley (formed from a Gloucestershire wodwose) with its gold knob, I rapped the trunk of the tree chosen to be our Apple Tree Man. I asked my guests to call out, 'Wake up, wake up, Apple Tree Man!' three times. Then I poured a whole bottle of 'Wurzel Me' Somerset cider onto the roots. Next, we toasted the tree, literally, with triangles of toasted bread dipped in the steaming wassail bowl impaled on the bare branches of the tree. These offerings were to thank the tree for its generous bounty and to welcome in the 'good spirits', i.e. the birds. They could have a feast too! To finish our ceremony, we scared away any 'bad spirits' with loud noises, using party poppers instead of the customary shotguns, the weapon of choice in some Somerset orchards (Carhampton being the most famous on 17th January, Old Twelfth Night)! My work done, I asked Richard (Sulyen Caradon, Druid of Bath) to lead us in a couple of wassail songs. It was so dark, it was hard to see the words, and the temperature was dropping as the fire petered out, but we valiantly carried on carolling. I performed Yeats' *Song of Wandering Aengus* in the interlude, and then we gratefully decamped inside, where we carried on the circle with more singing, poetry and merriment, fuelled by more mulled cider, baked pomme de terre (apples of the earth: potatoes!); and numerous other nibbles: the last of the Yuletide feasting. Chrissy Derbyshire, a budding Bard over from Cardiff, was eventually persuaded to sing, and what a lovely voice she had, offering something from Blackmore's Nights repertoire, before she had to dash to catch her train. Mairead led us in some rounds. Richard read out Rose Flint's specially commissioned Wassail poem. Peter Please offered a couple of excellent tales (the one about a wounded bird guiding a friend of his to its trapped mate was especially enthralling) before generously gifting me a copy of his new book *Clattinger: an alphabet of signs from nature*: a beautiful tome made with elfin craft. Sheila Broun, arriving late, sang a haunting song. Stephen Isaac read out his poem about birch trees from *Writing the Land*, and I recited the poem, *Wheel of the Rose*, fortunately remembering the words despite the intake of mulled cider and beer! The conversation flowed, but I was flagging after a sociable few days and was relieved when most departed by midnight. I felt I had done my 'bit' for the season – three gatherings around my place – and was looking forward to taking down the decorations the following day and getting stuck back into things. Time to strip away the frippery and knuckle down to some work. Yet my heart and my hearth had been warmed by friendship, merriment and Awen.

Epiphany
6ᵗʰ January

Heavy snow overnight across most of Britain has transformed Bath, at least, into a Brueghel-esque wonderland. I had to go into town and I'd never known it so quiet. There was hardly any traffic on the roads. Great Pulteney Street – Bath's longest and widest thoroughfare, featured in films such as *Vanity Fair* – was practically devoid of traffic, like a scene from a modern post-apocalyptic vision. It was interesting to reflect that recently I have finished adapting a version of Richard Jefferies' *After London* – in 1887, depicting a flooded England – when perhaps I should have chosen his chilling short story *The Great Snow*. Yet it felt benign. The thick blanket of snow – at least a couple of inches – unifies and purifies. It seems to give the world a blissful reprise – as we are forced to take a hiatus, with many schools and businesses closed – and a taste of grace. It makes us feel like children again. People forced off work join children in playing in the snow, making snow sculptures, sledging and having snowball fights. The Orange Grove, by Bath Abbey, became an impromptu snowball arena, the ring of thin birch trees affording psychological shelter at least. The indoor market was closed and so I trudged back home, still happy to be out in the snow. Once it settles, it doesn't feel so cold for some reason (a fringe benefit of the Albedo Effect, perhaps?). What makes today's snowfall especially resonant is the coincidence with the Christian festival of Epiphany, or *Dia de los Reyes* (Three Kings Day): The Epiphany is an ancient Christian feast day and is significant in a number of ways. It celebrates the baptism of Jesus by John the Baptist and also celebrates Jesus' birth (source: BBC website). It is the anniversary of the supposed time when the Three Kings arrive to hail the birth of the Christ, and the avatar makes his official appearance in the world – 'When God revealed himself to the world through the incarnation of Jesus'. The Word made flesh, as the Bible puts it. Humankind gets a second chance. Snow seems to wash the world of its 'sins' – blesses it. Yet for most people, the 6th of January is the time to take your Christmas decorations down. Consequently, the most common and saddest sight is that of Christmas trees cast out onto the street, most still with a healthy covering of needles. It seems such a waste and insult to the generous forces of nature. This is how we repay Her bounty. With the casting out of trees, it seems people cast out any vestiges of goodwill left of the season. It's 'back to work' or 'back to school' in most people's minds, concerned with trying to earn some money to balance the excesses of the previous month. Yet, Mother Nature won't let us, and she has maintained Peace on Earth for a little while longer at least (with many airports out of action, the effect on the global average temperature will be noticeable, as after 9/11 when all the planes flying in or out of America were grounded). Against the backdrop of this larger Epiphany are the countless little epiphanies that life is made up of – the unadulterated joy of a snowball fight, an exhilarating sled-run, an unexpected day off work, quality time with family, simple pleasures of hearth and home. The world breathes a sigh of relief.

Now, I might just go out and build that snowman.

Mari Llwyd
1st -17th January

Every year in the Welsh valleys, any time between New Year's Day to Old Twelfth Night, there is a weird and slightly unnerving spectacle to behold – the Mari Llwyd. A man wielding a horse skull on a pole, shrouded in a white sheet, proceeds through the town, calling on households in the guizing tradition. In its purest form (still to be seen at Llangynwyd, near Maesteg, every New Year's Day) the tradition involves the arrival of the horse and its party at the door of the house or pub, where they sing several introductory verses. Then comes a battle of wits (known as 'pwnco') in which the people inside the door and the Mari party outside exchange challenges and insults in rhyme. At the end of the battle, which can be as long as the creativity of the two parties holds out, the Mari party enters with another song.

I was planning to go to this today, but the weather has been so bad that it was completely rearranged; all the outdoor activities (the procession) were cancelled, as well as the ceilidh, and travelling to Chepstow in the forecast 'heavy rain' didn't seem so appealing.

So, from the comfort of my armchair, I discovered more about the origins of this strange custom.

The Mari Llwyd (in Welsh, Y Fari Lwyd) is one of the strangest and most ancient of a number of customs with which people in Glamorgan and Gwent used to mark the passing of the darkest days of midwinter.

It's no accident that Christmas, with its emphasis on fire, lights and decorations, is celebrated at this time of year. Before the arrival of Christianity, the Romans used to hold similar festivities at the same time. And before the Romans, these long, cold nights were the time of fire festivals in Wales and across the Celtic World.

From this time on, the days get longer as spring approaches. All these festivals and customs reflect man's awe at nature's annual miracle of death and rebirth. That's why evergreens, like the holly and the ivy, are such a feature of the season, and why a dead horse mysteriously comes back to life.

Customs involving animal skulls are widely known across the world. The Native Americans of Alaska use them, as do the Indonesian people of Java, and variations crop up at most points of the globe in between.

But the Mari Lwyd is unique to this part of Wales.

The industrial revolution and the rise of fire-and-brimstone chapel preaching had a serious effect on the Mari Lwyd. The parties had gained a bad reputation for drunkenness and vandalism as they roamed the villages. Many a sermon was preached against the continuance of such a pagan and barbaric practice, and the participants were urged to do something useful instead, such as taking part in eisteddfodau.

In some places, like Llantrisant, the pwnco disappeared and the Mari party sang only their arrival verses, adding Christmas carols to the repertoire. In other areas, such as Llanharry, Cowbridge and the Vale of Glamorgan, the parties interspersed English-language verses with Welsh-language rhymes.

The Mari could still be seen in many villages in the 1920s and 1930s. By the 1960s, only a few survived in places like Pentyrch and Pencoed.

Llantrisant's Mari Lwyd custom was revived nearly two and half decades ago by members of the Llantrisant Folk Club, very much in the style in which it was being performed when it originally died out, probably at the start of the Second World War.

Mr Vernon Rees, a freeman of Llantrisant, remembers that his father, Tom John Rees, was in charge of the Llantrisant Mari. The Llantrisant head was not a real skull but was made of wood, bandaged right down to the snout to make it look like a genuine horse's head. Mr Rees remembers the Mari being kept in the cupboard under the stairs and knows it was still around in 1937, when the family moved house. Tom John Rees was a miner at Ynysmaerdy Colliery, just north of Llantrisant, and died of pneumoconiosis in 1945, when he was only forty-five years old. Mr Rees does not know whether his mother gave the Mari Lwyd away or what became of it.

The 'new' Mari Lwyd is a genuine skull, which was prepared and mounted in the traditional fashion by Ian Jones of Pencoed, the last thatcher working in South Wales. Ian kindly donated the Mari to Llantrisant Folk Club, and today it is a regular and much-loved feature of Llantrisant and Pontyclun's Christmas and New Year festivities.

Yet even the uncanny totemic magic of the Mari Lwyd couldn't hold off the foul weather, and Chepstow at least will have to wait until next year for its 'blessing'.

Brean Down

A sunny Sunday is not to be wasted by staying in and working. After weeks of bad weather, I had itchy wheels, and so leapt at the opportunity of going on my first ride-out of the year. I packed some lunch, togged up and set off... after a false start. I was hoping to take the Legend out on its first spin of O Ten, but the battery in the Triumph was flat after nearly two months sitting on my drive, and so I fired up the Zuki, fresh from its MOT.

It felt great to finally escape the city, to turn the wheel and blow away those cobwebs! The run to Brean is very picturesque, if winding, along the A368 via Chew Valley. Parts of it, with chocolate box villages nestled amidst steep wooded hills remind me of 'little Switzerland'. With all the hairy bends its slow riding so you are forced to enjoy the view.

Leaving the Mendip ridge of hills, you then have to negotiate the big sheds of Weston Super Mare – dreary, but you soon pass these, heading south. The turn to Brean is easy to miss and the ride is, frankly, bizarre, zigzagging back and forth without any clear reason, and disconcertingly heading away from Brean towards Brent Knoll. Finally, it hits the coast road that takes you past dismal caravan parks and crazy golf type places. But it's all worthwhile in the end; the headland of Brean Down looms into sight, looking stunning on a sunny winter's day. I park up and grab a much needed cuppa, as my head had gone numb!

The sunlight on the sea was dazzling; it was so good to see the coast. Brean is the nearest decent stretch for me in Bath. I climbed the steep steps, sweating in my leathers, but the view was worth it: spectacular panorama over the Severn Estuary, looking glorious today in the sun. I sat and ate a sandwich; just as well, as my rumbling stomach must have been audible from Wales – 2.30pm being a bit late for lunch for me. A 'boost' on the way stopped my blood sugar levels from completely crashing.

I walked along the south side, topping up on Vitamin D in the sunlight. A notice in the cafe mentioned someone had lost an engagement ring on the Down, and so I couldn't help but scan the grass. It would've been nice to have found it for them. Imagine!

It gave the place a certain luminosity to know I was walking where Violet Firth, aka Glastonbury-based occult writer Dion Fortune, had walked. And also where they shot scenes for the

Shekhar Kapur movie, *Elizabeth: The Golden Age*, Brean Down providing an unlikely stand-in for the White Cliffs of Dover. To think of the delectable Cate Blanchett riding here, in full armour with a special effect false leg (so she could appear to be riding side-saddle), surrounded by hundreds of extras, cap-a-pie, also gave the place a certain layering of weird glamour.

Brean Down – a long finger of carboniferous limestone pointing out into the Severn – is a like a 3-D history lesson. From the 300 million year old rock (cousin of Gower Peninsular, on the Welsh side), forced up into its present ridge 230 million years ago; to the remains of animals from the end of the last Ice Age (auroch, giant deer, reindeer, arctic fox, bison, mammoth, wolves and lemmings), 14 to 10 thousand years back – and the first signs of human habitation; a worked giant deer antler from 10,000 BC; to Iron Age settlement – a hill fort from 300 BCE; to a Roman temple 370 CE (which must have inspired Fortune, who based the temple in her 1930s novel, *The Sea Priestess*, there); to the Napoleonic fort, Victorian follies and WW2 gun battery and secret weapons testing; right up to the National Trust primping of the present day – an amazing place.

Yet despite millennia of human activity on the headland, it still feels like nature's own, a wild place, if not true wilderness, with an impressive array of plants (including the lovely named White Rock Rose, growing in its most northerly European location), butterflies, birds and animals. A sign on the way up said 'Beware Steep Cliffs and Goats'. I didn't see any of the latter today, but there were plenty of walkers out enjoying the sun, and I did meet a couple of young 'rock monkeys', who started chatting to me as I stood on the site of the Roman temple, having a moment's connection with my personal spirituality.

I felt an edifying sense of peace and space. We get so hemmed in by life and forget to look outside of our respective boxes. Visiting a place like Brean Down gives you a perspective on things. The stoic longevity of such a place helps one to endure, to keep going, to weather all that life throws at you. You leave feeling 'lighter'.

I descended for a final coffee before I hit the road. I sat on the sea wall and watched a man trying to get his dog, a young Alsatian, to come back. The dog clearly wanted to keep on playing, gamely leaping back, head down to front paws, dropping a ball in front as if to say, 'Come play. The sun is out. It is a good day to be alive – work can wait!' This dog wanted to have its day. Alas, the chain awaits and we all get called back, eventually, but it was worth bearing the cold to blast away the winter blues.

Such an excursion – a walk somewhere beautiful – makes one feel like the end of the week has been 'marked' in some way, providing a break from the routine of the week. Stepping off the wheel briefly, creating a sense of hiatus. Sacred time, before mundane Monday kicks in again.

I enjoyed the fast ride home – taking the A38 and A4 – through the lengthening shadows and low golden light. Hitting the traffic lights of Bristol, the night swiftly fell and the temperature dropped. I was glad to get back. It is one of the pleasures of such an experience to return home to a long soak, warm fire, a big mug of Earl Grey, hot buttered crumpets with cinnamon, and a peaceful mind as one slides into Sunday night, with a good book or good film to ease the brain into blissful oblivion.

FEBRUARY

Imbolc in Avalon
1ˢᵗ – 2ⁿᵈ February

Monday evening, I rode down to Glastonbury on my Triumph Legend, on its first outing of the year. I really felt like turning the wheel – a shift of energy after the increasing stagnancy of winter. There's a subtle movement around this time of year, after the long dark nights and cold weather. It may not seem that much warmer or brighter, but it feels like the tide is turning. In my garden, snowdrops are starting to push through, impossibly frail, in the face of the iron grip of winter, but somehow they win through. Their bright hope is irrepressible.

The sunset over the Mendips on the way down was spectacular; the sky was aflame, the golden yoke of the sun oozing over the horizon as I passed Bronze Age round barrows, the Mendip Mast and descended towards Wells and the Somerset Levels. Upon seeing the Tor in the distance, I let out a whoop of delight. It felt like a long time since I'd visited. In fact, it was just under a couple of months (for the cutting of the thorn). It was good to be back on the road again, riding my Legend in my fortieth year. Life is good, I thought to myself. I am so lucky to be following my path, living my dreams.

I arrived at my friend Ola's new digs, a pleasant house on Manor House Road (owned by Amanda Gazidis, organiser of Poetry by Candlelight). We caught up as she cooked a fabulous spicy soup and I met her housemate Jason.

We set off for the Goddess Hall in Benedict Street. Ola told me the story of how it was funded and bought by the Goddess Temple from the Catholic Church. They did not read the small print; they discovered six months later that the contract specified that the building could not be used for any religious worship. This was something of a problem! By this point, it was already consecrated and active as a sacred space dedicated to the Goddess. Through delicate negotiations, an accord was mercifully reached and the Goddess Hall is now legitimate in the eyes of the law. The lesson received from this was a positive one; the legal entanglement had forced a dialogue between the respective faiths, which has got to be a good thing.

The building was glowing from within as we approached; it looked like a pretty unremarkable community centre: one level, utilitarian in design. It could have been a youth club. Indeed, as we approached up the path, two young lads clowned with us, pretending to be threatening, but in a playful pirate manner. We had to run the gauntlet of these diminutive threshold guardians to reach the door, where we were greeted by a pleasant 'Melissa' (their name for volunteers) who welcomed us and gave us the 'order of service'. We took off our boots and coats and entered. The inside of the building had been beautifully renovated – with love. Artworks were proudly displayed marking the eight directions. At the far end, five goddesses sat on the stage/shrine, the central one like a large wicker female Buddha. Most of the women and many of the men wore white. There was a healthy mix. The atmosphere was charged with pleasant anticipation. I wandered around, looking at the icons and imbibing the ambience. I recognised a couple of friends and greeted them.

Finally, it began. The lights were dimmed. The room was lit by candles. A woman with a crown of small white feathers called us to order. Most sat on the floor. In the centre, half a dozen priestesses in long white robes formed a circle. As the ceremony started, they parted to reveal a black robed figure, hunched and sitting between them.

The 'quarters' were called in (more 'eighths', as they diligently did *all* the mid-points). We started in the north-east with Bridie. As she was being invoked by one of the priestesses, a baby started crying in the background (this seemed rather apt – the end result of Bridie's journey from virgin to mother. It seemed to be a health warning: fertility magic can result in screaming babies – be warned!). I tried not to develop a fit of giggles.

We slowly worked our way around the circle. Eight times, the Goddess was invoked. Eight times, we were told to breathe in the energy of said Goddess in a voluble collection inhalation (like some Smokers' Self Help group, or Asthmatics Anonymous) and then return to the centre, by turning in a clockwise direction. Even if you were already facing the centre, it seemed the done thing to turn around, like some kind of daft game show (remember *Runaround*?). This may have been intended to be mildly trance-inducing, but was just plain annoying after a while. Why not just turn directly to the centre? Of course, "it's the spiral path that leads to wisdom", I can hear the reply. But sometimes, it's better to cut to the chase, to be direct. Sword energy – piercing to the core of the matter, rather than beating around the bush. Perhaps that's a male, or rather masculine, trait. Certainly, we were in the realm of Goddess Mysteries, which seems to involve taking as long as possible. I have already experienced something of these kinds of ceremony, which seem to take forever, normally ending up with endless chanting or toning. Basically, they make a song-and-dance out of it. This approach is nothing if not inclusive – many people had a part to play, their 'moment', young and old. A local choir leader, Sally, played the parted of Brighid; although, no doubt the faithful would say 'channelled'. She seemed to ham it up like a pantomime character, going more for the joyful and childlike than the demure grace I associate with the goddess, rightly or wrongly (perhaps my image of Cate Blanchett-type acting in elegant Galadriel fashion is just a male fantasy – a projection of the goddess, not the 'real thing', which no doubt most there would claim they knew and were authorities on, when in fact their version of her is just as much a projection). Who can know the 'Goddess'? We all have our own relationship with deity, and it's all valid. Sally clowned about in an entertaining way, and her enthusiasm was certainly infectious. Her god-dess within (*en theos* – where we get the word from) shone out.

The real stars of the show revealed themselves next. We were asked to call Bridie in. The door to the kitchen opened and out proceeded a charming line of children, holding candles, in diminishing stature (eleven in total, ending with a tiny tot). They made their way to each quarter, singing a lovely song.

Osha, a local woman renowned for her voice, sang a beautiful song. Then poems were offered by various people.

Next, we were given the opportunity to make Bridie Crosses. A local had cut hundreds of reeds. We were given a brief demonstration and then were left to get on with it. My first attempt fell apart, much to the amusement of my friend. It looked more like Bridie's Asterisk, than Cross. Elouise, another local starlet, played and sung, which was lovely but didn't help me to concentrate. The ceremony had put me in a different 'head space' and I couldn't focus on such a task easily. But I persisted and finally made something vaguely resembling the intended article.

Apparently, next there was a story from Koko, but I completely missed that if it did happen. Then there was a rather dull dance routine from the Sacred Goddess Dance Group – bring back Pan's People (a friend of mine in Bradford-on-Avon is actually attending a dance class run by a former member. So, I quipped to her, 'Does that make you a Pan's Person?').

We were all encouraged to become as seeds, slowly waking, pushing our way up through the thawing earth. I felt rather ridiculous, becoming 'a beautiful snow flower', when in fact I felt more like a groundhog, sniffing the air, and deciding it's not spring yet, and going back into his hole. Perhaps I was just a bit worn out. The ceremony lasted two hours and the room had become very hot, with no windows open, lots of bodies and candles and hot air.

It ended in a bit of a knees-up, although my heart wasn't really in it by that point. I was glad when the circle was closed and the ceremony was brought to an end. There was a sonic crescendo – an exhortation of sound – which would have been a good place to finish. I was dying for a pint! Unfortunately, 'Parish notices' were included and, being Glastonbury, there were a lot of them. Finally, we made our way to the George and Pilgrim, where I enjoyed a Cornish ale in the atmospheric six hundred year old bar, a real fire crackling in the grate.

We chatted about the ceremony – our Bridie's Crosses on the table before us – and I raised a glass to my friend, Tim Sebastion Woodman, the Arch-druid of Wiltshire, Chosen Chief of the Secular Order of Druids and Druid of the Gorsedd of Caer Badon. He passed away on the 1st February in 2007, on Imbolc, in what could be seen as impeccable druid timing. For me, the festival will be forever connected with this remarkable man. In keeping with his good humour, I tend to think of it these days as 'Timbolc'.

It would have been nice to have had that male balance and Tim's refreshing down-to-earth self-deprecation and ironic awareness. These things always run the risk of becoming pompous; priests and priestesses can easily come across as self-important and lost in their own ego trip. Saying that, I didn't feel that at the Goddess Hall. The whole ceremony was done with, generally, a lightness of touch, but also with absolute commitment and sincerity. They held the space very well and kept in the zone throughout. There was none of the drunken messiness and egomancy I have seen so often at other (largely druidic) ceremonies – no names mentioned! Ola informed me that the priestesses had met at the Hall at nine and had been building up to it all day – it showed. So much love had gone into creating the sacred space, the regalia, the ceremony itself.

I can't imagine a better place to experience an Imbolc ceremony than Glastonbury at the Goddess Hall. With its sacred wells, the town feels like a resonant place to celebrate this particular festival. As far as I have experienced, nobody does it better.

Nevertheless, I missed Tim and his Pythonesque clowning. He provided an essential ballast to the inflated egos out there. One of the last things he did, before ill health claimed him at the age of fifty-nine, was to lead a walk around his neighbourhood about the 'lost wells of Widcombe'. This was informative and entertaining – his style, in a nutshell. He knew his stuff, but didn't take himself too seriously. Of course, it ended up in his local 'watering hole', but we had connected with some special springs in the area, something I felt was lacking this evening. I feel Imbolc has to be connected with a real spring. In previous years, I had been involved in a spring dressing at Rocks East Woodland, where I had run various events and where we had created a miz-maze. Tim's legacy lives on there, and in the burgeoning English Bardic Chair scene. He was a true ambassador of the Awen.

Yet Imbolc has, side-by-side with this personal significance, a genuine sacred dimension for me.

Imbolc has always been a favourite festival of mine; I think of it as the poet's festival, because it is sacred to the Brighid, goddess of poetry, smithcraft and healing. These seem strange companions on the surface (perhaps less so than Athena/Minerva and her poetry, wisdom and warcraft), but I can see a metaphorical connection between them: good poetry requires craft, the chosen words need to be as strong and supple as iron to a blacksmith, and at its best can be healing. It is a good time to renew commitment to one's creative path, especially the poetic one, and this year my offering was a new collection of poetry, *The Immanent Moment,* sent to press this week in time for its launch at Garden of Awen next weekend. It was only after I had chosen the title, that I realised it spelled TIM.

Next day, we went up the Tor. When we left, the sun was trying to shine through, but by the time we started to ascend, it began to rain. In the time it took us to climb five hundred steps, it had become lashing rain. We huddled, breathless, in the tower, only to discover a curious package – a carrier bag with a note on:

If your heart has
a song it longs
to sing,
then take & enjoy
all you find within
with the blessing
of the Fisher King

with an amusing practical footnote (*'but the weather can be a pain,*
so keep the bag in case of rain'). Looking inside, I discovered first a
metronome, then, amazingly, a beautiful zither! There were also
a couple of Celtic music CDs and a collection of *Prayers from the*
Highlands and Islands (from the Carmina Gaedelica). Whoever left
this was very generous. We must have been the first people up
that day. It's unusual to find the Tor deserted, to have it to
oneself. I guess the weather must have put other visitors off. It
seemed theses gifts had our names on them. Ola wanted the CDs
but was happy for me to have the instrument – it seemed to be
an affirmation of my Bardic path ('as if you need it affirming!'
quipped my friend). I found a poem to St Brigit in Carmichael's
collection and recited it while strumming the zither:

Brigit of the white feet,
Brigit of calmness,
Brigit of the white palms
Brigit of the kine.

Uncannily, as we arrived at the tower, I pointed out to Ola the
relief of a milk-maid above the entrance to the tower: Brighid
herself (and a canny way of making the local farming community
feel included in the narrative of the church).

After our prayer of thanks to the White Goddess, I suggested we 'do an Awen' and I led Ola through my Sunrise Praise (optimistically titled on such an overcast day). She gave thanks in her own words. It was a small 'ceremony' but resonant, there on the Tor in the rain, two people making sacred time in a simple way. Carrying our gifts, we gladly descended, feeling 'cleansed' by the rain and wind.

We went to the newly opened White Spring and sat for a while in silence with the Goddess in a dark alcove. The place was mainly lit by candles (not many) and was dark and wet – very wet. Water cascaded over a series of pools and ran along the floor, following gravity. More often than not, you found yourself standing in running water. I was glad to be wearing my relatively waterproof motorbike boots!

As I looked at a shrine to Brighid, trying to read a poem in the gloom, a man came up to me and said they were going to be holding a Celtic Christian Candlemas ceremony in five minutes and we had to leave or stay for the Service. We decided to stay; it seemed the natural balance to the previous evening.

Half a dozen of us gathered on one side of the White Spring, the spring water pouring out of a pipe high in the corner, making it almost impossible to hear the Priestess – a woman with dreads in her ceremonial robes. It was just as well we had a liturgy to follow, although the 'vicar' kept skipping about and it was hard to know where we were. Her words were lost in the white noise of the water, although she at least accepted that it probably said more than she could express in words. It was dark, and cold and damp, not conducive to feeling spiritual. A distance voice issuing incomprehensible dictums in a large echoey, uninviting space seemed to sum up Christianity for me. It seemed to have little relevance. I could not feel it. I was there out of intellectual curiosity and a sense of fair play. But the tedious service (literally *Te Deum*) would have tested the patience of even a pagan saint. We were told it would last twenty to twenty-five minutes. An hour later, and the priest seemed no closer to completion (it was hard to tell from the Liturgy anyway). Since it was now noon and I still had to drop some books off before getting back to Bath for my evening class, we decided, guiltily, to leave. We got off the bench carefully – when we had been asked to stand before the worshipper on the end fell off onto the wet floor, as the bench flipped up. She wasn't hurt, but had a comical expression on her face, like a dog who had been dropped in cold water. I extinguished my candle (Candlemas is traditionally when candles are blessed for the year) and we went to leave, only to discover the doors were locked! Fortunately, the man came up and let us out without a hint of annoyance. He even blessed us. With relief, we stepped out into the light.

We decided to fill up our bottles with white spring water. Unfortunately, there was a woman there who looked like she was storing up for the apocalypse – a boot full of five litre bottles. She didn't seem keen to let me in to fill one, so we opted for the 'claret', filling up from the red spring. We carried our two containers, musical instruments, books, CDs and more books with us into town, feeling in need of a coffee! I managed to lighten the load by dropping some books off at Chalice Well (new titles from Awen). After we had restored ourselves in the 100 Monkeys Cafe, we went round some of the other bookstores and managed to get rid of most of them. I, at least, now had enough room in my tank bag for the treasures from the Tor! Feeling well and truly 'Imbolced' I togged up, thanked my hostess, and rode back through the rain, wearing my sunshine inside.

Early February

Today, I went to the Lunar New Year celebrations held by the Museum of East Asian Art in the elegant Bath Assembly Rooms opposite – the Regency splendour providing a surreal but splendid context for this Oriental 'Hogmanay'. Tables were arranged around the main hall, more used to Jane Austen-era glamour, offering a colourful assortment of activities: make your own money bag (used to gift money to family and friends); have a go at a tiger mask; origami; or paper cuts – a traditional Chinese New Year decoration. Before the afternoon programme got under way I had popped over the road to the Museum for free Chinese tea and saw many impressive examples of these paper cuts by Chinese artists. Apparently, at this time of year, the old ones would be taken down, to be replaced by the new ones, displayed fresh in windows and so on.

Last Sunday was the actual New Year. It fell auspiciously on St Valentine's Day, but according to the Chinese astrology website I viewed, Wayangtimes.com (found after a brief Google), years of the Tiger are often times of war, not love:

Drama, intensity, change and travel will be the keywords for 2010. Unfortunately, world conflicts and disasters tend to feature during Tiger years also, so it won't be a dull twelve months for anyone.

'Far reaching changes for everyone,' it predicts, rather broadly. Basically, the only certainty is uncertainty; the only constant – change.

Back in the Assembly Rooms, I pulled up a chair and watched a poetry reading by a Chinese poet, who read her work in English and Mandarin. It was fascinating listening to the soundscape of her poetry – a very different set of phonemes to English ones. It's great to see poetry being an important part of cultural life (over the Lunar New Year celebrations, homes are often decorated with paper cut-outs of Chinese auspicious phrases and couplets). The common theme to the poems she recited involved reflections on time and good fortune. She mentioned a great Chinese saying: *'An inch of time, an inch of gold, an inch of gold cannot buy an inch of time.'* A good message – time is infinitely more precious than gold, which is merely a naturally occurring ore. (Our time is priceless yet we sell it cheaply in the market place – a buyer's market). Yet Chinese, being shrewd in business, place great importance on it, praying for wealth and wearing red for luck. I recall in South East Asia – Thailand, Malaysia, Indonesia – the symbolic bank notes they would burn in the temples.

Next, there was a sample of Chinese opera. Two members of the London Chinese Opera Society, looking splendid in their costumes, performed a shy, gentle mating ritual on the stage, like two birds in the Springtime: the male boldly making his advances, the female coyly dismissing them. The man sang in a falsetto to symbolise the fact that he was on the cusp of adolescence! It was charming, but after a tiring ride back and a fitful night's sleep I struggled to keep my eyes open.

I went for a walk outside in the lovely spring sunlight to try and wake up, wandering to the Royal Crescent and back. Then I girded myself for the final events with a pot of lapsang souchong and a couple of stem ginger biscuits in the Assembly Rooms cafe. This helped to keep me going for the grand finale – the magnificent lion dance, followed by the letting off of fire crackers. There were two 'lions' on stage, operated by two guys each. Both were decorated by 'fur' and lots of gold; one was red, the other white, and they lively cavorting reminded me of the rival 'osses' of Padstow. They wove their way through the crowds, to the delight of the children, who followed them, Pied Piper-like, outside where gunpowder awaited! The event certainly ended with a bang; in fact, several leaving a strong Guy Fawkes-like odour in the air. Of course, the Chinese invented gunpowder, as they did paper, centuries before the West cottoned on. They are a remarkable civilisation; it's such a shame that their current regime has such a poor human rights record. I cannot forgive them for invading Tibet, but this was all forgotten today. It was a joyous occasion and quite rightly.

It made me think of my Chinese grandmother, Emilia Ku, who spoke Cantonese. Unfortunately, I never met her, and so all of that part of my family tree seems so remote to me, which is a shame. It would have been fascinating to have talked to her. And yet today I felt closer to her, watching the celebrations. My father seemed to reject his oriental heritage; he was completely blue collar and Anglo-Saxon in his behaviour and outlook. He never continued any of his mother's traditions, other than bringing back the odd Chinese takeaway! What would he, or his mother, have made of today? I send them both love, wherever they are, and I wish everyone a Lucky New Year!

St Valentine's Day

The 14th of February is a date that can chill the blood. Like Christmas and New Year's Eve, it is an emotionally sensitive time when, unless we are having a certain pattern and quality of experiences, we feel like we are 'failures' in some way. While Christmas and NYE are predominantly focused on family and friends respectively, St Valentine's Day has its gaze adoringly fixed on one's sweetheart, lover or partner. On one level, it is a just a way to boost sales in the post Yuletide slump – a stopgap between the January sales and Mothering Sunday in the commercial sales calendar. It shifts cards, chocolates, roses, booking at restaurants and romantic breaks. It's good for business. Despite conscious adults knowing this, if you don't play along with it you are branded as unromantic, and worse, you risk upsetting your loved one. The beloved must be placated, like some terrifying Kali-esque deity who must be propitiated with ritual offerings (unless you want to end up with your head on a necklace, joining the string of men who foolishly thought they could get away with ignoring St Valentines).

I jest.

In some ways, anything that honours our loved ones has got to be good, but we can do this any day of the year. Spontaneous gestures are far more romantic than ones co-ordinated by marketing companies. Acts of love have to come from the heart, otherwise they are meaningless. Legions go through the motions this time of year, sitting in an over-priced restaurant, gazing across the table decorated with the de rigueur candle and rose, holding hands, listening to gushy muzak, cooing appropriately, hoping that the real feeling will kick in, but the second sitting is due and the waiters are looking twitchy. Sometimes the magic does happen, despite all this. I've had some romantic Valentines, but they have often been the ones that are not so 'off the peg'. It is thrilling to receive a Valentines card (ideally made by a local artist). It is even better to share a Valentines breakfast with one's beloved, either bringing it in on a tray, or receiving it, feeding each other, cuddling up together under the duvet, making love in the morning, afternoon, evening.

The best Valentines gifts have been handmade ones. I have done my share: composing poetry for the object of my desire, handwriting it in calligraphy on parchment, tying it with a ribbon, reciting it for her from the heart. I have performed at weddings and led the occasional handfast. My friends commissioned me to write a poem for their wedding, held at Comlongon Castle in Scotland. That summer, I spent a week at a camp near Wheal Rose. It was the time of the total solar eclipse in 1999 (Cornwall was cited as one of the best places to witness this, and, if it hadn't been for the leaden lid of clouds, it would have been). It was also the time of the Grand Cross – I was at an 'astrology camp'. We worked with the planets – I picked Venus. Thinking about the poem I had to write, I visited the church at Zennor, famous for its mermaid. It is on the site of a temple to Aphrodite, apparently. I sat in the 'mermaid chair' and was overwhelmed with a feeling of love. I started to work upon my poem, which I called 'The Wheel of the Rose'. I learnt it by heart and recited it in the ceremony at the castle. An illustrated version of it was presented to the couple afterwards. The core emotion I felt in that mermaid chair I recreate every time I perform that poem, which I have done at several weddings since. This is my simple way of expressing something of love, and sanctifying a union, with the Goddess' blessings. It is intended to remind us that love is in all of us, for all of us. We simply have to share it. To do otherwise is against nature, like trying to block a mountain stream. Love is an opening up, a surrendering. To truly engage in it we should not follow the 'script of love', as given us by the media, by commerce, but express our own in-the-moment truth, with clear sightedness and complete transparency. To hold back is a self-deception and a waste of time. The true lover gives all of them self and puts the wishes of their lover before their own. If this is what St Valentine's Day provides the opportunity for, then it is a good and valid thing. But love does not run to a time-table.

Shrove Tuesday
16th February

All across Britain today you would have seen the strange sight of (mostly) women running along, flipping pancakes in the air – Britain's unique manifestation of the global calendrical custom of Shrove Tuesday. According to the BBC website, Shrove Tuesday is part of the Christian calendar, which commemorates the eve of Lent (forty days and nights of fasting and prayers before Easter). It is also known as Mardi Gras (literally, 'fat Tuesday' in French), Carnival (from the Latin for 'farewell to the flesh'), and Fasnacht (the Germanic 'night of the fast'). The word 'Shrove' comes from the Old English word, Shrive – to confess one's sins. Shrove Tuesday is a day where one confesses their sins and asks God for absolution. Shrove Tuesday is celebrated in many different ways around the world; the Brazilians samba in Rio and the people of New Orleans throw their most famous party of the year – the Mardi Gras. In England, the day is also called Pancake Tuesday. Eggs and butter were among food that used to be forbidden during Lent, so they were often used up in pancakes. Pancake races are also held where people must successfully toss and flip their pancakes into the air before crossing the finish line. Points are awarded for time, for number and height of flips, and number of times the pancake turns over. It is believed that the tradition of pancake races was born out of women rushing to church to confess their sins before the noon cut off time, clutching their half finished pancakes (a surreal image). Today, people tend to give up less vital dietary ingredients such as chocolate. But before the fasting, comes Fat Tuesday. The shops make the most to cash in on this, with prominent displays of egg, flour, sugar, treacle, plastic lemons and – for the supremely lazy or 'culinarily disadvantaged' – batter mix, or even readymade pancakes. It's interesting that Shrove Tuesday follows close on the heels of St Valentine's Day – this year, women had two days to consume the chocolate indulgences gifted them by their beau (perhaps for most not a problem), but an extreme shift from feasting to fasting. Many now forsake the brown stuff for 'forty days' until the displaced cocoa orgy of Easter, when the Lord rises on a sugar-high.

Some meaning can be restored to Shrove Tuesday, even if you are not a Christian, by considering what, in your life, you wish to give up. What do you *need* to give up? Instead of getting caught in the cycle of feast and fast, which gave fuel to today's binge culture, why not try and live a more balanced life? Some self-control and moderation would surely be a better method than our current obsession with 'magic bullet' diets and fitness fanaticism?

Today, I was too busy to watch the pancake race in Southgate, Bath, but had my own version, as I rushed from training event, to interview, to evening class, 'flipping my pancakes' as I went. Now I'm, well, battered.

Facebook has become a most up-to-the minute seasonal barometer. Regular users update their profile status with the minutiae of their daily lives. One 'friend' talked of 'eating her own body weight in pancakes'. Another shared a recipe for Welsh pancakes. Pancake Day is not quite as popular in the States, but an American friend who used to live in Bath and is a bit of an Anglophile, maintains the tradition; of the many enjoyable holiday observances of the odd variety, Pancake Day rates up near the top of the list. Any excuse to gorge on maple and other sundry syrups is a fine idea!

The gluttony aspect has persisted for centuries; in 1621, London satirist John Taylor wrote: *'They do ballast their bellies with meat for a voyage to Constantinople.'*

After the austerities of January and the bulk of February – lean months when nothing grows and little work is to be found – the 'putting away of fat' (on a day called literally 'Fat Tuesday' in the States) is an effective letting off of steam. Spring is on its way – and more fecund months lie ahead. It's the last blow out before Lent for Christians: a chance for a party to blast away the winter blues.

For me, pancakes will always remind me of my Mum, who used to make stacks, and so when I finally got round to making myself some this morning, the taste of the batter, sugar and lemon took me straight back to my childhood. My Dad loved them... and so did our dogs! We had them more than once a year. But for many, it is the 'last blow out' before Lent – no eggs for forty days, making Easter eggs especially welcome, like the return of fresh eggs after the powdered egg of war years and rationing. The round golden disc of the pancake, flipped into the air, like the sun itself, foreshadowing the return of the lighter, warmer months; also, the return of a more playful period after the hard months of winter – a harbinger of the 'silly season'.

The traditional tossing of pancakes could also be seen as a personal symbolic act – turning the wheel of fortune? An invocation to a personal sun; shine on me, bring me good luck for the coming year.

MARCH

St David's Day
1ˢᵗ March

There is always something satisfying about the start of the month, especially when it falls on a Monday. It feels like the clocks have been set back to zero – a fresh start. Larkin said: 'Afresh, afresh, afresh.' Seeing new daffodils unfurl their golden flags captures this feeling – brightness against the sombre palate of winter. Bright colours give you a buzz, just like they must the bees.

The national day of Wales' patron saint, St David's Day, hasn't caught the public imagination like St Patrick's Day (or rather it hasn't got a major brewery behind it). It is certainly celebrated in Wales with special concerts and services, but it seldom gets noticed or mentioned anywhere else, except in Welsh communities, or families. Only the token gesture of wearing a daffodil makes it discernible in the media. Nevertheless, I have celebrated it in my own way, not that I'm Welsh, but I am deeply inspired by its legends, literature and landscape, and I feel compelled to honour such a mighty but small nation that outpunches its weight in many ways. In previous years, I have gone to the Gower Peninsula in South Wales and honoured the 'dragon' of the Cymru, by running the gauntlet of Worms Head, a promontory only accessible at low tide; you have to be quick off the mark to reach the end and back before the tide turns, risking cutting you off. It's quite an adrenalin rush and has become one of my favourite ways of marking the turning of the wheel. Yet, if I cannot mark such an adventurous effort, I like to tell a Welsh tale or two at a local circle or my own gatherings. To take the time to learn the story of another culture is, I think, one of the best ways to show respect. It doesn't take away from that culture but points the way towards it, encouraging listeners to go and discover the land and its legend for themselves.

I made my own gesture, by putting on an event with the theme 'the green fuse', after Welsh bard Dylan Thomas' line: 'the force that through the green fuse drives the flower'. Here's to the awakening of Spring.

Severn Bore in the Sun
2nd March

The Severn Estuary has the second highest tidal range in the world (up to fifty feet), and at high tides – notably the Neap Tides of spring and autumn, around the equinoxes – this creates a natural phenomenon called the Severn Bore, a wave that increases in size as it is squeezed up the winding bottleneck of the estuary. This year the highest of these was due on 2nd March (8.55am at the Severn Bore Inn), and despite it being a 'school day', Tuesday, I decided to go up. Happily, Monday and Tuesday happened to be two days of spectacular spring sunshine.

I rode up in the late afternoon sun on my Triumph after class to stay at my friend Miranda's place, overlooking the Severn plain. This meant we could set off at a sensible time the following morning, as it was only ten miles from her lovely cottage. The frost was on the fields when I looked out first thing, but the sun had already flooded the plain and would soon burn it off. We quickly got ready and set off, dropping off Miranda's son first in Stroud, which meant we hit the rush hour traffic there, and then on the way into Gloucester. Realising we probably would miss it if we ran the gauntlet of that city, I persuaded my driver to try the back roads and find a viewing spot on this side of the river. We struck lucky, following a car that hared along the lanes, clearly on a mission to catch it as well. We ended up at a place called Stonebench, parking up on the roadside along with the many other cars and walked to the riverside, finding it hard not to get caught up in the excitement – some were running, desperate not to miss it. But we needn't have worried; it was a little 'late' (it can vary up to twenty minutes either side of the scheduled time, apparently). We had time to find a spot, by a large houseboat and tuck into our breakfast of coffee and chocolate croissants. The atmosphere was good-humoured. A group of guys next to us where sipping on cider. A lot of families were there. And men with serious cameras. It had the wonderful English air of something faintly ridiculous that we all find ourselves doing in public, fully aware of how daft it is.

A speedboat caused some excitement; we expected it to be preceding the bore, but it was just a group of surfers in wetsuits, maybe the ones featured on the BBC News that day, looking cool, surfing the bore in the early morning sun. I spotted a para-glider buzzing in the distance – a great way to see it. A couple more boats came up and this time, the wave was close behind. Everybody got excited as the level of the river suddenly surged – you could see the wave breaking against the shore opposite. It roared past us, spectacular and slightly unnerving. As it approaches there's a moment when you don't know if it's going to stop, or completely drown you; a feeling of the raw power of nature overwhelms you – humbling. A taste of what locals experience four centuries ago...

In 1607, what became known as the 'Great Flood', possibly caused by a tsunami, sent a massive wave up the Severn Estuary. It is estimated that 200 square miles (520 sq km) of land were covered by water. Eyewitness accounts of the disaster told of 'huge and mighty hills of water' advancing at a speed 'faster than a greyhound can run'. It caused massive destruction and the loss of two thousand lives. At its peak, it was travelling at thirty miles an hour and sending up waves over twenty-five feet, reaching fourteen miles inland to low-lying parts of Somerset.

Today was far gentler – a pleasant day out. We could all go home or to work having witnessed one of nature's wonders. Most of the crowds dispersed immediately afterwards, but we sat and watched the waters, changed 'from a river to a sea', as I observed, surging angrily like a stormy harbour. The levels were still rising; we were told that, in an hour, when the tide's at its peak, it breaches the river bank and floods the lane where several cars were parked. The bore carried a lot of flotsam with it. At one point I spotted what looked like a head. I joked that it was an unlucky surfer who had hit a low-lying bridge. With morbid curiosity we looked closer, laughing with relief when we realised it was an old football. In the gap between the boat and the quayside we noticed a large pike flapping about, clearly dying. The bore carries a lot of salmon upriver, who use its energy to return to their spawning grounds up in the Welsh hills. The owner of the houseboat seemed stoic about the whole thing. 'I just let it happen,' he said to us afterwards. Miranda had spotted some little paw-prints in the silt and we asked him about them. He hadn't a clue – possibly rats? As Ratty said in *The Wind in the Willows*: '*Believe me, my young friend, there is NOTHING – absolute nothing – half so much worth doing as simply messing about in boats.*' And Moley had an epiphany, watching the River for the first time:

He thought his happiness was complete when, as he meandered aimlessly along, suddenly he stood by the edge of a full-fed river. Never in his life had he seen a river before, this sleek, sinuous, full-bodied animal, chasing and chuckling, gripping things with a gurgle and leaving them with a laugh, to fling itself on fresh playmates that shook themselves free, and were caught and held again. All was a-shake and a-shiver – glints and gleams and sparkles, rustle and swirl, chatter and bubble. The Mole was bewitched, entranced, fascinated. By the side of the river he trotted as one trots when very small, by the side of a man who holds one spell-bound by exciting stories; and when tired at last, he sat on the bank, while the river still chattered on to him, a babbling procession of the best stories in the world, sent from the heart of the earth to be told at last to the insatiable sea.

An event like today's bore makes us see the river again as if for the first time. It suddenly becomes like TS Eliot's 'strong brown god' – a force to be respected. The BBC website reported the bore to be the highest in eight years – up to 5.4 metre (17.7 ft) high. An ancient legend connected to the river suggests a mythopoeiac explanation for its unpredictable character: amongst the older folk of lower Severnside it is told that Sabrina lives in the river Severn. She causes the flood tide to rise up and make the bore wave. Sabrina rides the bore in her chariot accompanied by dolphins and salmon, both of which were once common in the river. The bore reflects her mood: when calm it is small and unbroken, but when angry it is large, turbulent and foaming. Sabrina gave her name to the river, which eventually became known as the Severn.

The phenomenon of the tidal bore is a natural, and reliable, calendar. It is reassuring to see that there are still some certainties in a world where the climate has gone haywire. So many festivals are now out of sync with what they are meant to be celebrating, but this phenomenon remains as accurate as ever, something that man has not messed up, yet, although there are worrying plans for a tidal barrage across the mouth of the Severn, which would ruin the bore and the important effect it has on the ecology.

A river is not to be taken for granted or advantage of, as the people in 1607 discovered. Any development along such a powerful waterway – such as the proposed development of the Hinkley Point Nuclear Power Station – is doing so under a sword of Damocles.

St John the Baptist Church, Edge, 2nd March
(Field Notes): *Sitting surrounded by snowdrops in the graveyard of St John the Baptist, a tiny church in a triangle of land just up from Miranda's. I remember spotting the snowdrops here last year, when I met up with M at Nympsfield Barrow and she guided me back to hers.*

I vowed to come and see them in their glory and it's taken me a whole year to do so – a full turning of the wheel. Everything has its season. It wasn't right last time, but this year it is! The skies are filled with the cawing of the rooks, gathering twigs for their nests in the trees on the other side of the road, busy with traffic between Stroud and Gloucester. Stillness in the sun. Life is good. I'm glad to be here, alive, in this immanent moment.

We had visited the Rococo Gardens in Painswick earlier, famous for its snowdrops. It was busy, despite the chill. After such a hard winter it was heartening to see such a fine harbinger of spring – the equivalent of the Dove returning after the Flood with an olive branch in its mouth. A truce has been drawn between nature and humankind – Mother Nature's severity is meted by mercy. The prospect of warmer, brighter days keeps us going. The snowdrop is a sign of this annual covenant; by Gaia's grace we shall endure for another year.

St Piran's Day
5th March

Friday night, I had finally clocked off and I was looking for something relaxing to do, so I wandered down to The Star, an old real ale pub on the end of the Paragon, the longest stretch of Georgian terraced houses in the city of Bath, housed in a thin, apparently coffin-shaped building. It was their annual Cornish Beer Weekend and today happened to be St Piran's Day. Largely an invention of the Celtic Revivalist movement of the eighteenth and nineteenth centuries, patriotic Cornishmen felt there should be a day to celebrate the Cornish 'nation' in the manner of Ireland, Scotland, Wales and the Isle of Man. It seemed their powers of invention failed after the initial establishing of the date and name, for there is little description of specific traditions associated with this day. However, many observers note (presumably remaining sober themselves) the large consumption of alcohol and food during 'Perantide'.

The day following the St Piran's Day was known by many as 'Mazey Day', perhaps referring to the inevitable after effects of such patriotic bingeing: a term which has now been adopted by the revived Golowan festival in Penzance. The phrase 'drunk as a perraner' was used in nineteenth century Cornwall to describe people who had consumed large quantities of alcohol.

So, back to The Star. The landlord, Paul, is a Cornishman, and goes the whole hog, making the pub pretty unique in the area. St Patrick's Day has become pretty ubiquitous thanks to a marketing campaign by Guinness; Bombardier bitter has tried to single-handedly make St George's an English equivalent – do your patriotic duty and get pissed; St David's Day was on Monday and seemed to pass, at least in Bath, completed unheralded – I didn't see a single person wearing a daffodil. St Andrew's Day is even more of a non-event, replaced by Burns Night; it would seem you need a celebrity to front it. Is there a famous Cornishman who could front an annual celebration of all things Cornish? Kerno-phile Betjeman perhaps?

When I arrived, the pub was already pretty packed. I made my way passed 'death row', as it is referred to, where the older regulars congregate, making the odd laconic quip at any who run their gauntlet, and waited at the bar. Someone had just ordered a pasty and it was handed to him with a wink. 'Warmed under a barrel-maiden's armpit,' a punter smirked. I chose one of the Cornish Beers they had, An Gof, in a mug. It was dark, lovely and hazardous, like a Zennor mermaid.

The old oak-panelled pub was festooned with Cornish flags large and small. Saint Piran's Flag is regarded by many as the national flag of Cornwall, and an emblem of the Cornish people; and by others as the county flag. The banner of Saint Piran is a white cross on a black background. Saint Piran is supposed to have adopted these two colours from seeing the white tin in the black coals and ashes during his supposed discovery of tin. A curious fact is the Cornish flag is an exact reverse of the former

Breton national flag (black cross) and is known by the same name, 'Kroaz Du', which seems fitting for two countries that share similar landmarks (St Michael's Mount/Mon St Michel) and traditions (the identical legends of Ker-ys/Ys/Lyonesse).

Popping my head round the corner of the snug bar, I spotted my friend Marko sitting amidst the musicians, unusually silent (there's normally a session on a Friday). Three bodhran players had turned up and a piper, but no fiddler. With no one to lead the session (normally session stalwart Heather Brown) they just chatted quietly amongst themselves.

So, how do you celebrate St Piran's Day? Well, by getting 'peranned', it seems. St Piran reputedly lived until 250 but died of alcoholism!

Song sheets were passed around and we sang (badly) some Cornish songs like 'Lamorna' and 'Trewlawney'. Earlier, Cornish ice-cream had been handed around to the customers and, later, Yarg and crackers.

More beer was ordered – the barrels had been changed over already. I tried some 'Blue Hills' from the Driftwood brewery. My friends Kim and Phil turned up and revealed that it was the brewery of a Cornishwoman we know called Lou, who moved back to St Austell to take over a hotel and started up her own micro-brewery. Well, Lou's brew tasted good, better than the last one I tried, Kernow Gold, aka 'piskie piss'.

After another rousing version of 'Trelawney', we discussed the intricacies of Cornish history in a drunken, uncertain way.

Marko suddenly burst into a rendition of 'Between the Tweed' and expounded on the esoteric. At midnight we sang happy birthday to his friend Roger, who said he learned to enjoy the little things – and this has made him happy.

Rosie turned up, off to play an alien in a new film version of Edgar Rice Burroughs' *Carter, Warlord of Mars* in London for a month. We talked a bit about alien sex.

It was all getting a bit strange. Time to go home!

Sun and Steel – Vernal Equinox Ride-out
21st March

Cobwebs blown away, I have just returned from a 200 mile 'blat' to the coast and back with a bunch of bikers – a great way to see in the spring – on what the RAT group Swindon called the Mad March Hare run. This named proved to be prophetic. Though I set off in good time, with everything prepared after a (much-needed) quiet night in, I managed to miss the rendezvous at the Little Chef on the edge of Chippenham, finding it trickier to find than I'd anticipated (no luxury of Sat Nav for me, just a leisure map of 'Wessex'). I missed the group by about five minutes. Determined to catch up, I set off anyway, following the back road route south along the B3092.

It was a beautiful spring morning on the day of the Vernal Equinox and it felt good to be out and about, roaring along the country lanes. Although, at first, I was somewhat annoyed with myself and a little anxious to catch up, I decided to enjoy the journey; they'd be at Compton Abbas airfield (the destination), and I could connect with them there, and ride back with them. When I realised what was happening was entirely appropriate – half of the day riding alone/half with a group – I relaxed. This seemed to symbolise something uncannily equinoctial: the balance in my life, which seems to veer from industrious solitude to being in the public domain. The day was one of beautiful contrasts, from the land to the sea, from the flat to the rounded, the bare to the wooded, from going at my own pace to following the pack, from enjoying the scenery to concentrating on the road.

The route passed through beautiful towns and villages: Corsham, Bradford-on-Avon, Beckington, Frome, Maiden Bradley, Mere, Gillingham, culminating in Shaftesbury – the hill-top town like a giant Hovis loaf (I pulled up next to a model one, donated in honour of the restoration of Gold Hill, immortalised by before-he-was-famous film director Ridley Scott in the classic Hovis ad of the 70s – one could almost hear the brass band. At

least I didn't have to push my bike up the hill like the baker's lad!
Ee, by 'eck!)

Snaking down the steep serpentines lanes on the south flanks
of the town, I made it in good time to Compton Abbas, but could
not find the airfield (no signs). I tried calling the pack leader, Iain
on my mobile, to no avail. I returned to Shaftesbury to ask at
Tourist Info, but it was closed. Then I passed a bunch of bikers at
the garage and I pulled in. There was a guy on a Triumph, but he
was the only one. It turns out they were just off down to
Weymouth. Could I join them, I asked? Sure. The pack leader,
Steve, filled me in on their system (the riders are topped and
tailed by a blue bike (his) and an orange one (a KTM). If you are
behind the leader and he turns at a junction, you must stop until
the tail-man catches up – simple). I quickly filled up and grabbed
a Mars bar (no time for coffee) and off we went at a brisk pace! It
was like keeping up with the White Rabbit as Steve whizzed
down the back lanes. He had picked a cross-country route. What
had I let myself in for? But I loved the serendipity and
spontaneity of it – they were going to end up at... Compton Abbas
airfield. Since I hadn't met the other group yet, one lot of bikers
was as good as another. Once we all have our helmets on – some
with tinted visors – we become pretty anonymous. It was a thrill
to ride with a group of thirty bikers, all in a line behind you (I
spent a lot of time at the front with the leader). The ride was
pretty but hairy, with lots of gravel and tight bends, so I had to
focus. It wasn't as relaxing as riding at my own pace, and we
passed some places where I would have loved to have stopped
(e.g. Maiden Castle). But this was a butch biker blat – no time for
such 'feminine' distraction! Following on from Shaftesbury, we
passed 'masculine' places like King's Stag and Cerne Abbas –
appropriate it seemed for this petrol-head machismo, although
there was a mixture of riders, and they all were pretty sensible (it
turns out they were an Advanced Motorcycle club – WaBAM:
Wiltshire and Bath Advanced Motorcyclists!). In a line of

headlights, we roared on, passing the best of England; timeless, heavy-eaved thatched fastnesses; golden stone and wooded dells; the deep winding lanes of Dorset; bristled barrows on the rounded Downs, with rude giants gazing on.

The quality of light brightened as we neared the coast. The hills softened. And suddenly there was the sea! We made it to Weymouth, having lunch at the Cafe Oasis. I tucked into a veggie breakfast, sitting on the beach, gazing at the sea. I hadn't expected to see that today! It was a great feeling and made me feel anything was possible. The Triumph Legend has grunt and eats up the miles; feels like I could go anywhere on it.

Lunch over, we headed north to Compton Abbas airfield. A scenic cross-country route through Lawrence of Arabia country (images of Peter O'Toole roaring along...) took us there in an hour. Before we knew it we were sitting having a cuppa looking at the light aircraft take off. Stunning views over the Dorset countryside, towards golden topped Shaftesbury. The sun beamed down, warm on my skin.

I started chatting to a couple – a pilot and an older woman biker – but it was soon time to go. These guys don't stop! I bid adieu and deciding to head back the more direct route home. It was a relief to ride at my own pace again, but I was certainly going faster and feeling more confident. Some of those advanced biking skills have hopefully rubbed off on me! It was a lovely ride home in the late sun and I truly felt I had blown away the cobwebs of the week. After lots of mental work it was good to do something so 'in the body' and 'in the moment'. The wheel turned – and the brighter days have returned!

St Patrick's Day
17th March

St Patrick's Day has become a global phenomenon – Ireland's day of national celebration becoming a celebration of all things Irish. On one level, it seems nothing more than a promotional campaign by Guinness, 'turning the wheel' honoured by downing as many pints of the black stuff as possible: seldom has getting pissed been so patriotic. Yet fortunately, there's more to it than mass appeal alcoholism. There's the legendary elusive 'craic', as seen in the countless 'sessions' going on in pubs around the world, and of course the Cheltenham Races (on Monday at the Bath Storytelling Circle, in front of BBC cameras, I had told the story of Macha and the horse race). In Bath, I was running the Bath Writers' Workshop until nine. Afterwards, feeling very thirsty, I took a couple of mates to one of the two Irish pubs in town. The first one, Flann O'briens, was so packed out you couldn't physically get in the doors. Besides which, it looks rather bore-ish, with lots of yobs in silly hats, and so we went up the street to O'Neils, less trendy perhaps but more civilised. There was still a merry atmosphere, without it being like a rugby scrum. Nevertheless, it took about thirty minutes to get served, in which time I had got talking to a chipper lass from Galway. The ambience was pleasant. The Guinness was even pleasanter. But my mates left and I went home, wiped out from my class. I wasn't disappointed, because the next day I was going to another Paddy's Day celebration with my friend Marko, a man you don't meet every day, at the Weston, a far more authentic estab-lishment.

I was teaching another evening class, but blatted over there from Trowbridge afterwards. I got there at ten and luckily hadn't missed any of the entertainment. Not only was there an Irish band playing (Yon Canny), but a whole troupe of Irish dancers were up from Dorset – The Yetminster Irish Dancers. When I entered (still in my biker leathers) their lads team was dancing. Then the girls came on, all legs and straight arms. Then, finally, the mixed dance. I hailed my friend Marko across the bar and ordered him a jar of the dark stuff. A table became available and we ensconced ourselves, imbibing the lovely atmosphere. The Weston had been recently taken over by new management – no longer the dodgy dive it used to be – and it felt like a really nice family pub, a community pub. Whole generations were present for that special night. The staff wore plastic bowler hats. Green crepe bunting decked the ceilings. Shamrocks and cardboard leprechauns festooned the walls, but there was still something surprisingly authentic about it all – in the genuine feeling of community. When Yon Canny went into a rendition of *Black Velvet Hat*, Marko got up and jigged about. Always well turned out, he looked particularly splendid that night, in a smart black jacket with all his silver bling. He struck up the bones at another reel. Normally, he'd be playing along – as he was with them on New Years' Eve – but with a bass player in the band, he couldn't compete. But he acted like the unofficial 'fifth' member, in fine spirits. I didn't overdo it, since it was a school night, and I was riding, but still enjoyed myself. My friend Richard was over in Dublin, seeing The Waterboys perform Yeats' poems set to music at the Abbey Theatre. I tried not to be envious, but I'm sure that was magical. Instead, this was a fair substitute, on a school night in the middle of term. Elsewhere in town, there was an evening of poetry readings, The Harp and the Unicorn, at the BRLSI, and an evening of Romantic poetry at the Chapel Arts Centre, but tonight, having had my quota of words, it was nice just simply to listen to merry music and watch the dancing.

Dymock & Daffodils & Days of Song
27th – 28th March
Saturday, I set off 'in pursuit of spring', alluding to the classic book by First World War poet Edward Thomas, who, in 1913 (21 – 28 March), recorded his literary pilgrimage from Clapham to the Quantocks – the home of Coleridge. My destination was Dymock, where, during a brief time leading up to that fateful conflict, a coterie of poets, their spouses and offspring, gathered: Lascelles Abercrombie; Wilfrid Gibson; John Drinkwater;

Edward Thomas; Robert Frost; and Rupert Brooke – the Dymock Poets, as they became known afterwards. Their story, charged with poignancy in the shadow of war and the tragic death of two of their key members (Thomas and Brooke, who enlisted and never returned), inspires and moves me. Nearly a hundred years on, it seems more relevant than ever in the shadow of current conflict and the all-too-common reports of young men and women meeting their fate in a foreign theatre of war. Yet it was with joy I set off early on Saturday, having prepared the night before for a couple of days away. The forecast was good; the early reports were of heavy rain, but the nearer the time came, the more they improved, until I was fortunate to be blessed by a weekend of spring sun. It made the ride up to just south of the Malverns a real pleasure. It was great to leave the city, and my week of toil, behind. When the sun is shining it is important to seize the day! A sunny day is not to be squandered; they are 'golden', like the heartbreakingly brief days of bliss the Dymock poets shared together: the summer of 1914.

Twas in July
of nineteen-fourteen that we sat and talked:
Then August brought the war, and scattered us.
Wilfrid Gibson, The Golden Room

Following the precise directions to the wonderfully named village of Redmarley D'abitot, of Janice, whose writer's retreat I had booked for the night, I soon arrived at Mellow Farm – a charming cluster of red-bricked and beamed style farm buildings distinctive of the area – and was shown my room, in Courtyard Lodge, which had lovely views towards Dymock Woods and May Hill: two numinous poetic 'hotspots'. The charming garden vibrated with daffodils and birches, similarly associated with the Dymock Poets. Sitting in the window seat later, enjoying the late afternoon sun, I wrote:

The spring sunlight – the banks of daffodils – creates a 'golden' effect; dazzling after the gloom of winter. Now have the brighter days come!

Yet on my arrival, I didn't have time to linger. Shedding my biker gear, I headed off to the village hall, where the Friends of the Dymock Poets were gathering for their annual Spring Day. The first item on the programme was a walk to Cobhall Rough, the location of the famous altercation between Robert Frost and a gamekeeper.

I entered the hall, which was brimming with Senior Citizens in walking gear 'warming up' for the ramble, i.e. expelling hot air. Although it's nice to be the youngest one present, it did feel a little odd. Still, I was warmly welcomed and signed up to the Society there and then. And off we set! The walk wasn't very far – a couple of miles – but it took somewhat longer than it should have because the narrow track we took was 'boggy'. This proved a navigational hazard for some and so it was requested that the men present offered assistance. And so I found myself up to my ankles in mud, helping OAPs scrambled along the sides, offering encouragement and motivation, like some assault course for geriatric poets. This obstacle overcome with teamwork, we had 'bonded in peril' and carried on in an affable, ambling manner to the site of the gamekeeper's cottage in the corner of Cobhall Rough. Here, Frost and Thomas, while out on one of their customary perambulations, were accosted by a bullish keeper called Bott. Frost didn't take kindly to his manner and put his fists up in defiance. For a tense moment a kind of standoff took place between the Old and New World – feudal know-your-place politics vs the Land of the Free. Until, that is, Bott pulled down his hunting gun from the wall. After that, they 'moved off pretty sharpish', according to an eyewitness. Frost's blood was up, indignant and incredulous at such treatment. Thomas felt even worse, as though he had acted cowardly in some way. This, speculated our guide, might have influenced his decision to enlist soon after. The incident certainly ruffled feathers. Apparently, Gibson was entitled to walk the lands owned by the Lord of the Manor, Beauchamp, but not his guests; this put Frost out somewhat and spoiled their friendship. Still, it was an iconic moment, echoed in his poetry, e.g. 'Stopping by Woods on a Snowy Evening':

> *Whose woods these are I think I know.*
> *His house is in the village though;*
> *He will not see me stopping here*
> *To watch his woods fill up with snow.*

The whole incident was described memorably by our guide, Barbara Davis, who knew somebody who had witnessed the incident as a child (a ten year old boy, visiting a friend of his grandmother's) all those years ago – a living link with literary history. We had a stirring rendition of a 'Lincolnshire Poacher' by Roy, which some joined in with (it is customary for the FDP to pepper their walks with 'Guerrilla' poetry recitals). After inspecting the ruins of the keeper's cottage, we finished with a stirring reading of a poem by Wilfrid Gibson, *To John Drinkwater*, which was interrupted by a man on a quad bike, rattling along like a Gatling gun. The spell broken, we continued on our way. The temperature had dropped and so, woolly hat on, we walked up through Ryton Firs, the setting for another classic from the Dymock Poet cannon, this time by Drinkwater.

At the edge of the woods, before we turned back to the village, our guide speculated on the repercussions of the incident and Wynne read *The Road Not Taken*, which had extra resonance and meaning now. As I lingered, gazing at the track. The secretary, Cate Luck, said this could have been the very track that Frost referred to. Certainly, his phrase 'the yellow woods', could certainly describe the wood that day, brightened by daffodils and spring sun. It was a tantalising thought.

I shall be telling this with a sigh
Somewhere ages and ages hence:
Two roads diverged in a wood, and I –
I took the one less travelled by,
And that has made all the difference.
Robert Frost, The Road Not Taken

We returned to the village hall, where people dispersed for lunch. I ate my sandwiches in the sun, then wandered to the local churchyard, found a grassy gravestone, and promptly had a nap in the warm spring sunshine, a local cat curling around my legs. The early start – and my cold – had taken its toll. I was wiped out!

Yet my cat-nap got me through the rest of the spring day. The afternoon consisted of two talks, one about 'Dymock Poets: Wives and Muses' by Sue Houseago; and then 'Swords and Ploughshares: rivals and reputations in pre-war poetry' by Dr Lynn Parker. Both were interesting, but I started to flag towards the end, despite being shored up by tea and cake.

I left the hall and returned to my lodgings, running the gauntlet of some lively young bullocks, who insisted on seeing me off their muddy field, despite their scaring easily whenever I turned and waved my arms. The two little grey goats in the horse paddock were cuter, as were the two dogs belonging to the family who lived in the main house. I made some tea and sat in the sunny window seat, reading up on the Dymock Poets in Linda Hart's book, *Once They Lived in Gloucestershire*. I was about to go to Ledbury to buy a copy when I found one on the shelf in my bedroom, inscribed by the author to the hosts. Gratefully, I curled up with it, recharging batteries for the evening jaunt.

'Colour and Savour of Spring' was an evening of 'Dymock poets and friends in music and words' at St Mary's, Dymock. I set off in good time but hadn't reckoned on the labyrinthine back roads and lack of signs for Dymock; there were signs for Ledbury, Gloucester, and Newent but not my destination. Taking May Hill as fix, I struck out along the most likely lane on my Triumph Legend. It was dusk and the trees silhouetted in the deepening sky. Bats flitted past my helmet – some looked huge! DH Lawrence's poem came to mind – a visitor to the Dymock Poets:

Dark air-life looping
Yet missing the pure loop...
A twitch, a twitter, an elastic shudder in flight
And serrated wings against the sky,
Like a glove, a black glove thrown up at the light,
And falling back.
from Bats by DH Lawrence

I eventually found Dymock – lost in its own becloaked time warp – and pulled up opposite the church, from which a promising glow exuded. I jogged over to the doorway – it was 7.30pm – and burst in to a packed congregation and a concert in progress. The 'stage' was right by the door, so everyone looked at me. There was no way around it. I had to walk past the performers and down the middle of the aisle to find somewhere to sit. Rather than waiting for a suitable gap, which would have been the sensible and polite thing to do, I strode to the back, hoping to look like I knew what I was doing. A man accosted me halfway – Bob May, the organiser. I gave him a tenner and he handed me the change later. He found me a seat, bless him – a row of ladies had to shuffle up – and finally I ensconced my Bardic behind on the hard church pew. The children of what sounded like 'Am Dram School' were in full song (turned out to be Ann Cam School), but I'd only missed a couple of tunes (four seasonal songs by Eleanor Farjeon). There was a maypole, of all things, set up in the middle of the church and I surmised that the evening must have started with a dance. There followed some cute poems by the pupils. Next up, a little skit on the Friendship of Eleanor Farjeon and the Dymock Poets; then something on a poorly-tuned cello (that's how it sounded to me) by a lovely young lass; Heroes & Heroines by the St Mary Singers – again, lyrics by Farjeon – this time accompanied by a 'fancy dress' parade of each of the respective historical figures: Devonshire Drake; Grace Darling; Wellington; Florence Nightingale. After an interval, when refreshments were served and I picked up copies of the Poets Walk maps, there was a presentation of prints then a reading by a local poet about daffodils – daffodil doggerel – and an extra contribution from another 'local poet' of similar quality. Fortunately, the standard picked up again with a masterful recital of Brooke's immortal poem, *The Soldier*, by actor Peter Thorpe. More tuneless cello followed then the reading of *The Golden Room*, once more by Thorpe, but this time he didn't stand so close to the mic and the power wasn't carried so well. When I had read this earlier that day I was deeply moved by the vision it presented, of a brief, fragile flowering of fellowship:

Was it all for nothing that the little room,
all golden in the lamplight, thrilled with golden
laughter from hearts of friends that summer night.
Wilfrid Gibson, The Golden Room

The penultimate act was a pleasant surprise – a whole bevvy of young lovelies got up (Sixth Form pupils of St Mary's School, Worcester) and sang Brooke's trio of sonnets, entitled *The Dead*, in haunting falsetto voices. Thorpe returned to the mic for his version of Edward Thomas' *The Sun Also Shines*; and the evening ended with a sing-along to *A Song for Gloucestershire*, by Johnny Coppin. There followed lots of thank-yous and the handing out of bouquets – the contributors getting well-deserved applause for their efforts: a fine community event.

Afterwards, I browsed the display at the back of the church about the Dymock Poets, deciding to return the following day to read it when I was more awake.

It had been a lovely evening of poetry, song and music. It was wonderful to see the Dymock Poets honoured in such a way. They have clearly been taken to the heart of the locals and their words have become also liturgical in the way they mythologize and sanctify the local landscape. And quite rightly so – that is the true poet's role.

I walked out into the night, taking in the sky full of stars, the moon shining merrily. The interior of the remarkable Norman church of St Mary's reminded me of the abbey on Iona, and so too did this experience, from sacred space to Sacred Space: the cathedral of the Stella Maris. The change of scale, and and shift from interiority to exteriority, brings about an oceanic feeling of amplification. Looking up, it feels like you could fall forever and be drowned in the night.

Before I floated off into infinity, I popped to the Beauchamp Arms next door for an ale, needing to ground myself and enjoy the atmosphere of human company before I struck out alone once more into the dark, Frost's line 'Yes, I have been acquainted with the night,' ringing in my ears.

But first I supped my pint and made some field notes.

And then off I went, fortunately finding it easier to get back – a needle in a haystack – to my dwellings. I gratefully fixed myself a hot drink and retired to bed with a book – not the liveliest of Saturday nights, but certainly fulfilling and wholesome. I felt like I had drunk from a purer font, took a road not travelled (by many), and that, I hope, makes all the difference.

The next day, I visited the various dwellings of the Dymock Poets, which was particularly moving – from such humble, unassuming places came words of lasting power. No blue plaques adorned their walls; all were private residences; no tourist signs pointed snap-happy hordes to their doorsteps. At Oldfields Farm, Thomas's residence, a woman came over to see what I 'wanted': 'To pay my respects to Mr Thomas,' I said. She was friendly enough after that. I said they must get fed up of all the people traipsing by (it is easy to think the footpath runs through their garden, which it apparently doesn't), but she replied that 'surprisingly few' walk in the area.

I made it to Dymock in time for the afternoon 'Daffodil Walk', a permanent marked trail that has become an annual tradition – a way of seeing in the spring. First, I had stow my togs. In a rush, I found a place to stash them in the church – my helmet, trousers and jacket – in the pulpit! I joined the group of two dozen tourists just as they set off from the lych-gate of St Mary's. We went on a relaxing hour's amble to simply go and look at daffodils, as though we don't see them anywhere else (they're coming out in my garden, but these were smaller wild ones). Folk took photos – and yes, I did too, caught up in the herd instinct and photo-frenzy.

We bimbled in a long, lazy line back to the church. I went to get a cuppa at the village hall, where the Spring Fair was taking place. Realizing my change was back in my bike trouser pockets I went back to the church and found, to my surprise, a young waif curled up asleep on top of my gear. He drowsily awoke. 'Sorry to disturb you,' I said. 'What's your name?' 'Ryan.' I gave him my hand and introduced myself. I asked him where his folks were. His mum was in the Spring Fair next door – good, he wasn't homeless then! Perhaps still rumpled from his nap, he did look a bit of a ragamuffin: like Master Robin Goodfellow – the spirit of spring himself – awakening from his winter's sleep! I said I didn't mind him using my things as bedding; the pilot jacket, with its thick fleece lining, would make comfortable for a temporary nest, as I know. I apologised for disrupting his siesta – his afternoon nap, I explained – and went on my way, charmed by this lovely encounter. How special!

I got myself a drink from the pub – the thirsty walkers had all arrived and there was quite a queue – and sat in the sun, preparing for my journey home. It had been a very pleasant weekend and I felt very relaxed. Peaceful. Dymock had worked its magic on me. I had something of an epiphany of the hill overlooking Thomas' place: I had a glimpse of an 'English heaven'. As Brooke put it, paraphrasing his classic poem: here was a little corner of England that will be forever sanctified by the lives and words of the remarkable Dymock Poets.

APRIL

April Fools & Easter Tricks

The lead up to Easter has been a busy time, with the completion of projects – teaching, publishing – and the tying up of loose ends. Good Friday serves as a severe deadline; the hiatus of Easter is imposed on us, whether we like it or not, as everything shuts down for at least the Easter weekend, although the holiday can stretch over one or two weeks. As with Christmas, it has become a national time to 'down tools' and, after the hectic spring term, it comes as a blessed relief – thank God (or maybe we should thank the Romans, that 'advanced civilisation', for nailing a thirty-three year old from Bethlehem to a cross).

The morning of April Fool's Day has become a time to take everything with a pinch of salt, for it is the customary time for pranks, practical jokes, hoaxes and general foolery. The media run their usual brace of dubious 'news' items: the Circle Line is to be used as a substitute for the Large Hadron Collider; ferrets are to be used to deliver broadband cables; AA men will use jetpacks to beat the traffic jams; Shakespeare was French; England didn't win the World Cup in 1966. My favourite was in Denmark: recently the famous Little Mermaid statue had been removed to be displayed in the World Expo in Shanghai, leaving her rock bare – someone had replaced it with a mermaid skeleton.

We joined in the spirit of this by announcing the launch of *The Art of Self-publicity* in the Bath Chronicle ('Hungry for Self-publicity? Then this is the book for you'). In the Editor's column, ('Spotted our April Fool yet?') Sam Holliday asked: '...perhaps you are convinced that our April Fool joke this year is that we have given publicity to a man who has written a book about how to get publicity'. Actually, the book is genuine (the latest title from my small press, under the imprint Writers' Workshop: the

first in a series of practical guides) and we decided to use April
Fools to gain some publicity – it worked! It was due to be
launched on Easter Sunday and we wanted to let people know
about the event in advance – part of my Garden of Awen.
Typically, we were on tenterhooks about the books arriving on
time (no matter how well-planned our new books are this always
seems to happen). Yet, by Thursday, I had the first batch arrive
from Stroud Print – phew! Publishing can be an act of folly and
you can easily end up with egg on your face (e.g. a book launch
with no book).

We weren't the only ones launching a book that day; contro-
versially, Philip Pullman was in town talking about his new book
at Topping & Company: *The Good Man Jesus and the Scoundrel
Christ*.

This is territory I am familiar with. While studying my Fine
Art degree I got obsessed about the Fool archetype and made a
film called 'My Life as a God', which had a main character who
was part-fool/avatar/insane/even an ODed drug addict having a
near-death experience. A lot of it was filmed in guerrilla style
around the mean streets of Northampton. I remember one scene
where my fool character dragged a ladder up the street as though
he was carrying the cross up Golgotha. A black woman
harangued me, probably justifiably. It wasn't a very subtle satire
on religion – a low budget *Life of Brian*. Yet behind it were ideas
influenced by my research into mythology and Jungian
psychology. Cecil Collins' luminous book *The Vision of the Fool*
was particularly inspiring. This project culminated in a free May
Day festival I launched called the Fools' Fete in Abington Park,
Northampton. This I saw as the completion of the Fool's Journey,
from setting out like Chaucer's pilgrims at the start of April, to
becoming feted as king-for-a-day, Lord of Misrule, at May.
Thousands of people attended the first Fools' Fete, which ran for
three years every May, with the help of the Umbrella Fayre
people, who have since gone on to run the Green Fair, which

happens in late summer, replacing the official town show. Yet, an act of 'folly' started the ball rolling. I recall walking by the bandstand one day and thinking: 'this would be a great venue for a festival'. I came up with the name and format, booking the bands and devising the programme. All creativity starts like this, with an act of awareness and an adventurous spirit. Blake said: *'If the doors of perception are cleansed, man will see things as they truly are – infinite.'* Being a big fan of the LA psychedelic rock band, The Doors, at the time (who took their name from Huxley's book, *The Doors of Perception*, inspired by Blake), I identified with this, perhaps too closely at times!

Good Friday came along and I found myself munching on a hot cross bun, like a lot of the population, wondering why eating sugary dough is a way of celebrating the death of an avatar. Clearly, the Cross has become the Christian symbol, but it seems a strange custom to remember a crucifixion! I absent-mindedly pondered on when this tradition began, but rather than trace its origins (which has been done in other books) I want to share a lesser known tradition. On Easter Monday, in the beer tent of Mells Daffodil Fayre, my friend, Kevin Williams, RNR officer, shared with me a wonderfully quirky custom that takes place on this day, in East London: The Bun Day at The Widow's Son. This is the story behind it: A young sailor went to fight in the Napoleonic Wars; when he finally had time, he wrote to his mother asking her to save him a hot cross bun for Easter, when he planned to be home. Alas, he failed to return – he became one of the numerous fatalities of that conflict – but the mother dutifully saved a bun for her son that year and every year since, until her death. The pub in the neighbourhood of the mother became associated with the story and has gone through various incarnations over the years; it has been pulled down and rebuilt, burnt down and rebuilt, again and again, mirroring, in its own way, the resurrection connected with that time of year. Its name has changed with owners and with the times, from The Bun

House to The Widow's Son, named in honour of the woman. Every year, Navy personnel gather to honour the tradition with a lot of drinking and singing (including the modern 'tradition' of karaoke) and the 'hanging of the bun', when a bun is ritually placed by the youngest sailor present in the net above the bar. The bar is in the east end of London, in the Stratford area, with rough-and-ready locals and Navy guys mixing together in a good humoured way. It is perhaps one of the Navy's most unusual traditions – and that is saying something, since they have more than their fair share!

The following day, Easter Saturday, I loaded up the Triumph Legend and set off over the Cotswolds up to Northampton to visit my Mum and sister, whom I haven't seen since last summer (winter isn't the time for long bike rides). It was great to catch up with them and my friend Justin, that night down the Malt Shovel; we opted for a relatively quiet pub because we too had a lot of catching up to do. Earlier that evening, I had sat down with a meal cooked by my Mum and watched the new *Doctor Who*, starring Northampton-born Matt Smith – it felt like being a child again! Watching *Doctor Who* at Saturday teatime was a childhood ritual. Who would have thought it would become popular again?

The next day, after visiting the memorial tree planted in memory of our Dad in Delapre Abbey with my sister (and enjoying a mighty Sunday lunch cooked by my dear Ma), I bid farewell and set off, roaring back over the Cotswolds. I decided to break the journey about halfway at a place of literary significance: Adlestrop, one of the soul-springs of England.

Here, in June 1914, renowned critic Edward Thomas, on a train (on his way to Dymock, where a coterie of poets were gathering), paused and made some notes. Later, when he started to write poetry, encouraged by his friend Robert Frost, then living in the Dymock area, he wrote *Adlestrop*, which has become a classic of English verse, much anthologised and imitated. It was very poignant to pull up there, kill the engine and hear the same quality of birdsong he wrote about (*'And for that minute a blackbird sang/Close by, and round him, mistier,/Farther and farther, all the birds/Of Oxfordshire and Gloucestershire.'*) . I sat in the bus stop, which has the old station sign and Thomas' poem engraved on a brass plaque, and soaked up the peaceful ambience of this quintessentially English hamlet, a corner of England which motivated men like Thomas to go and fight – to live and die for.

I returned home in time to listen to a Radio 4 feature on the Blakean poet, Michael Horovitz, who has recently turned seventy-five. Hearing his antics inspired me to make the Garden of Awen a lively 'happening' later that evening.

The tricksters were making their presence felt when I arrived to find the place locked up. We were told somebody would be there from 6pm – it was 6.30pm. David and Terry arrived and we sat over the road in the Lamb and Lion and waited anxiously. I had tried to ring the director, but he was away on holiday in Cornwall. He had left his team in charge. Fortunately, the bar manager turned up at 7.15pm and let us in. We hastily set up – doors opened at 7.30pm – and the evening kicked off. We had a good crowd; the place was packed, almost standing room only, until they got some more chairs. I had arranged some champagne (well, Prosecco) to toast David's new book, and there was free chocolate on the tables. The atmosphere was great; there was a colourful crowd of creative types present, including a group of girls from Glastonbury all dressed up as Victorian harlots!

I kicked the evening off with my poem, *Phone Tree*, then David gave a talk about his book, regaling us with adventures in media. There followed an open mic section, with some excellent contributions from the floor: poems and songs. The second half started with a fabulous set from Crysse Morrison, poet from Frome. Then there was more open mic, including an improvised shambles from 'Ben and friends'; Ben was going around Britain recording songs, a kind of British song-line. It was a brave attempt at something experimental, which is what I love to see. Afterwards, I said: 'Creativity is an act of folly – a leap of faith. You step off the cliff and hope for the best.' We finished the evening with a sublime set from singer/songwriter/guitarist Ali George. It was a great night – my folly had paid off for once!

One of those attending (and contributing a poem), Lizzie, said afterwards: '*Congratulations on creating a lovely, fun evening at the Garden of Awen event last night. I am so glad to see this happening in the heart of the city at a community space... It is what our city needs!*'

The following day, I went to the Mells Daffodil Fayre with a couple of friends. My friend Kevin drove us over in his 1985 Mercedes SL 'panzer' with Creem blasting out – very Withnail-like but not doing much good for my hangover. Still, it was a merry way to travel. Pulling into the car park we were let in for a quid as a 'classic car'. I got us all a hot drink and we took in the atmosphere. Everyone and their dog were out, gorging on chips and beer, listening to the bands in the marquee, or elbowing their way down the packed narrow streets lined with stalls. I showed Kevin the grave of Siegfried Sassoon, First World War poet and personal hero. Then I took them into the church to show them the Burne-Jones designed tapestry.

Mells is such a charming, unspoilt village, preserved in a kind of time-warp: a perfect setting for a *Hammer House of Horror* episode (a couple lose their way in the fog...). Today, it couldn't have been merrier, or more picturesque – the grassy banks glowing with daffodils. In previous years, the daffs have often passed their prime by the time of the fayre, but with the late spring this year, they were in their glory. We supped beer, browsed the stalls, missed the Morris Dancing and checked out the lovely Manor House Gardens. As the afternoon progressed, we become 'daffed' out. I offered 'tea and buns' back at mine, so off we set, finishing off the last of the hot cross buns. Agreeably bulging, I found it hard not to nod off on the sofa. The week/end had taken its toll; it had been a memorable Easter, but thank Christ we don't have to do it for another year!

MAY

Padstow May Day
1st May

There is no better place to be in England on May Day then Padstow in North Cornwall, where every May 1st for many years (no one knows exactly how long it has been celebrated here, but it is probably a couple of centuries at the least) visitors are greeted with a spectacle both exotic and quintessentially English – locals dressed all in white, and either red or blue neckerchiefs and sashes, proceed through the streets following what is called either the Old Oss (red) or the Peace Oss (blue): an alarming dancer wearing a round black skirt of waterproof material (like an alien sou' wester, or a cake on legs). This is topped by a black pointed head-dress decorated in an African style, and the dancers wheel and jig through the packed crowds, lured on by a 'teaser', usually a nubile local girl wielding a phallic 'bladder-stick', accompanied by a hypnotic drum-beat, accordions, whistles and singing. The atmosphere is at the very least merry; although, at times, it becomes wildly un-British, something you might see in a Mediterranean religious street festival or in say India. Such unrestrained exuberance is uncommon in a small English village, and that makes it all the more special. The narrow streets of the small fishing village are festooned with foliage and flags. There's a fun fair and the pubs do a roaring trade. Thousands of visitors descend, causing the tiny village to gridlock. Yet, the ambience remains pleasant. After the winter, especially a hard one like we've had this year, there's a palpable sense of 'easing off' as we celebrate the start of the summer. The silly season starts here!

The last and only other time I had made it to Padstow was in 1997, on the eve of a Labour landslide. I had visited it with my new friend from Bath, Stephen, and I have a shot of him mischievously running off down the road with a Tory placard. A number of these kept us warm at night as we camped on the beach. Thirteen years later and it feels like full circle – we're on the eve of another general election and it looks like Labour is on its way out, the euphoria of their victory, when Tony Blair seemed like the Britain's new hope, long gone in the squalid aftermath of a second Gulf War. Then, Padstow seemed to capture the 'feel good' factor that was sweeping the country – New Labour's election anthem (now deeply ironic), *Things Can Only Get Better*, in the air. This time – who knows? A sense that, if the country is going down the tubes, let's party while we can?

This time, I was picked up from my flat on Bathwick Hill, (where I had been living for ten years to the day I moved in on the first of May 2000) by my friend Kevin in his 'Panzer'. I helped him take the hard roof off the day before and we rode down 'topless' – hair blowing in the wind. As we left Bath early Saturday morning, the Skipper played Maddy Prior's Padstow Song on his ancient car stereo – the song, he told me, that had started it all for him (piquing his curiosity to go and check out the source of such a lusty tune). It blasted out across Combe Down (where the last Tommy, Harry Patch, grew up) and we sang along to the (until then) quiet, empty streets, probably waking up half the neighbourhood. We were in good spirits; it was great to be setting off on an early May morning, the energy not only of the day, but the whole of summer, the whole of awakening nature, behind us.

Kevin took the scenic route, over the Mendips via Shepton Mallet and Glastonbury, where they were many celebrations going on over the weekend. No doubt, folk were up the Tor or in Chalice Well. We saw some likely suspects dressed in robes, obviously on their way home for breakfast after greeting the dawn. A couple of years ago, I had leapt the Bel-fire in the field above Chalice Well and helped raise the maypole. It's a great place to celebrate it, but I was glad to be going to Cornwall today.

We cruised across the Somerset Levels, crossing the M5,

running the gauntlet of Taunton and out the other side. Kevin decided on a whim to go 'cross-country' and we ended up on some obscure back roads. We managed to find a pretty route along a B-road via Wiveliscombe, Bampton and other lovely places. We stopped off at Clovelly, much in need after a cuppa, after the weather turned damp and chilly, and found ourselves in a surreal complex. It turned out that you had to *pay* to get into the honey-pot village – all we wanted was a cuppa! There was a bizarre deal at the cafe where it cost more to have a straight black coffee, than a latte. The girl at the counter was unable to explain the logic of this – she was 'only following orders'.

A little recuperated, on we went, eager not to miss the celebrations. We arrived around midday and parked up in the campsite a 'couple of miles' from the village, as Kevin somewhat euphemistically put it. Five miles later, dying for a pint, we made it into Padstow; it seemed like all the celebrants were leaving, but it was just the 'morning shift' breaking for lunch. The next dance was at 2pm – time for a much-needed pint and pasty. We sat on the quayside, amongst the crowds and boats draped in bunting, and tucked in. We had made it!

We went to see the Peace Oss at 2pm, although it was impossible to get near the institute where it 'lived'. My heart sank, thinking I was not going to be able to see it properly. I didn't remember it being that busy thirteen years ago, but Padstow is a changed place. Rick Stein has set up shop and the yuppies have moved in. It has become somewhat gentrified as of late, going by the shops and some of the crowd. But there was still an excellent atmosphere.

We tagged along with the Peace Oss procession as it wended its way up the 'high street' towards St Petroc's church; it became easier to see it the further it went as the hills thinned out the crowds. Finally, some decent photo-opportunities! We followed it into the church and I was told by a bullish Blue Oss follower not to bring my pint into the hallowed place, but a frolicking pagan fertility icon was obviously okay! The drums sounded extraordinary in the church, as though inside a long barrow. It was great to see the church come alive with the drumming, dancing and merry crowds. Out the other side it went and back down into town for a while. We left it as it seemed to 'die' halfway up a little side street then walked back towards the Ship, where we met up with Kevin's old university buddy, Steve and his family. More pints were procured and downed, quaffable local ale – Doom Bar was a popular choice. Not much of that to be had in Egypt (where I was off to in a couple of days for the remainder of May) so I made the most of it. Kevin's biker buddies, John and Aaron, rocked up, a little tender from a lock-in at the Tintagel Arms the night before. They had ridden across from Sussex on their Harleys – an impressive ride. We took a stroll to the quayside and enjoyed the sites, including a fine wooden figurehead on a ship with impressive curves.

I needed a cup of tea desperately. It was all catching up with me (a fortnight of storytelling workshops in Italy, followed by five days trying to get home thanks to the travel chaos caused by the Icelandic volcano ash cloud; a weekend workshop in North Wales directly after; a week's marking; an early start and long car drive). I found a cafe and gratefully took a seat. I ended up chatting with a local lady and asking her about her colours: 'How do you become a follower of the red or blue Oss?' I wanted to know. 'You are born into it,' she explained. Her grandfather, then father had been Old Oss stock and, thus, so was she, and her children and grandchildren. It seems an accident of birth then, which creates this friendly schism. The Peace, or Temperance Oss was started after the Second World War, so perhaps belonging to that indicates 'incomers', as opposed to old Padstownians. The woman enthused about it, saying how 'It's a kind of freedom,' until that is the politically-correct brigade (anathema of *Daily Mail* readers) come along and 'spoilt it', which they've already done, she complained, with the banning of the dubiously named 'Darkie Day', when Padstow's temporary black population used to be celebrated, on their annual day off. She became increasingly racist in her opinions after that – what Gordon Brown would call 'a bigoted woman' (but not to her face). 'Are you one of those Liberalites?' she asked, sensing my disquiet with her loathsome opinions about asylum seekers and so forth. This somewhat tainted my impression of events, which now looked, in the light of this conversation, to be a thinly-disguised white power demonstration, (a kind of 'Klu Klux Kernow') but the Oss transcends that. Really, it's just a bit of good old fashioned silliness. People like to 'justify' it by saying it's an ancient fertility custom, practised since time immemorial, but it probably is only a couple of centuries old (Kevin thinks there are Napoleonic references in the songs, but the lyrics he quoted could easily be read in all sorts of ways). Ironically, the tradition of the Oss – the trappings of white costumes and black masks – might have been imported by Moorish mariners, but I didn't feel like pointing this out to the Tory racist. Her theory about its origins sounded just as feasible – during the Napoleonic Wars, a French ship was seen approaching. All the men were away and so the women dressed in white, as sailors, to make the French think the place was 'manned'. It seemed to work. When the men returned from war they were so taken by this, they started to do it themselves and, ironically, women were not allowed to take part.

Leaving *Daily Mail* woman, I rejoined my friends. We walked around the harbour then up to the war memorial, which afforded fine views over the estuary mouth. The sun was just setting behind the headland and, after a rainy afternoon, the clouds broke. It felt like a *Last of the Summer Wine* moment, I observed. I shouldn't have invited in such 'thought-forms', as later on someone called me Compo, since I was wearing my woolly hat in an attempt to retain my rapidly vanishing body heat!

Our small but merry band made its way back into the village

to get another one before the six o'clock dance of the Old Oss. This time I was determined to get a good view, and so I waited outside the Golden Lion inn, the 'stables' of the original Oss. At 6pm the Ossers emerged, sporting different coloured rain macs, as though part of their ritual regalia. The slick black Oss squeezed out of the narrow front entrance – a painful birth – and started to jig about furiously, falling into the crowds and being pushed back into the middle, (like some kind of punch-drunk fighter) as it zig-zagged down the lane. Touching its black skirt is meant to bring luck – get taken under it and it's meant to make you pregnant!

My friends found me in the crowds and we followed the Oss to the 'village square' where it converged with the rival Oss, jigging around the enormous maypole. The crowds packed in, but we were right up the front. The atmosphere was fantastic; the Oss was really going for it. The rain didn't dampen our spirits. It really felt like we were tapping into something powerful and primal here – rightly or wrongly. It felt real. You could feel the sap stirring and the carefree spirit of summer coming in after the sombre days of winter.

Buzzing, but in need of some hot food, we went to get some from the quayside. More beer followed and I was beginning to flag; it had been a long day and it wasn't over yet! The final dance was at 10pm. A siesta would've been good, but seating space was at a premium. We went to the Golden Lion, with its incredibly low ceiling, as though at any moment it's going to collapse in like a soggy takeaway. Finally, a seat appeared and with relief I slumped down into it, trying to save some energy for the final stint.

The drumming started again – the pounding rhythm would stay with me for days – and we made our way outside, girding our loins with, you've guessed it, a final drink. I had a shot of Jagermeister, which seemed to do the trick, that is, reviving me temporarily, in Oss-like manner. The frisky Oss appeared – the dancers and drummers in a kind of shamanic trance (induced by a day of drumming, dancing and beer). They were wilder than ever; the atmosphere was positively Bacchanalian and I felt we had all become lost in a kind of collective folk consciousness. We followed, we sang, we cheered – with the slightest of encouragement.

With one final loud cheer the drumming stopped – the dancing stopped – the day's celebrations were officially over. Folk stood around chatting, bubbling with the good vibes. I was ready for bed though. It took a while to extricate the lads from their respective chinwags. We made our way up out of the village, passing a couple of police. 'You must be relieved it's over', I suggested. 'Same again tomorrow,' one responded, to my surprise. Apparently, it's repeated the day after, which was news to me – a 'second May Day' being not widely advertised. Maybe it was a recent addition, to cope with numbers and the uncertainties of the weather?

We made our way back along the dark country roads, feasting on a sky full of stars. We had a couple of torches between us to help us avoid being run over walking along the main road in the pitch black. I led the way like a Signalman, sending a warning flash to approaching drivers.

Despite the slog back to the campsite we were in good spirits, but not completely sozzled. The walk soon sobered us up, which made it easier putting up the tent in the dark. Finally, I slipped into my sleeping bag and closed my eyes, satisfied at experiencing such a magical, unique celebration of British culture. Oss, oss, wee oss!

Raising the May

After Christmas and Easter, May Day is probably celebrated more than any other seasonal festival in Britain. It has become 'secularised' as Internal Workers' Day, or Labour Day, but it has always been a festival of the people (so much so that the Tories wanted to ban it at one point in the nineties).

The first Monday in May is a 'bank holiday', which we seem to have instead of Holy Days (showing where society places its values) and the May Day bank holiday weekend is often the first decent one of the year, when legions make a break for the coast. There's a general sense of joyousness and relief – summer is a-come! (in principle at least). Over the years, I have experienced several different May Day celebrations, include the Hastings Jack-in-the-Green Festival, when a veritable army of Morris sides jig through a foliage-festooned town after a walking bush, the Jack-in-the-Green, ending up on the heights of Hastings Castle, where he meets his fate, to be torn apart by the revellers, who grab a bit of him for the 'luck in the leaf'. Bristol have their own Jack-in-the -Green, which proceeds from the Harbourside, via St Nicholas', the indoor market (where it blesses the stalls with a dance), onto Broadmead shopping centre, before leaving the centre to pass through several estates; it's quite a surreal experience, following a green dalek through some of the city's back streets, stopping occasionally to quaff an ale at some dodgy-looking local. The procession culminates on a green, Horfield Common, where the Jack meets his inevitable fate. In Shropshire, I attended the Clun Green Man Festival one year, where there is a colourful procession of the Summer and Winter courts, headed by the Green Man and the Ice Queen respectively, leading to a 'standoff' on the bridge, involving a bit of ritual banter and a 'battle'. If the Queen wins, winter will prevail, but fortunately the Green Man and his followers gain victory every year, to much cheering. This is all charming but genteel in comparison to what occurs in Edinburgh, which has a massive spectacle organised by Beltane Fire Society event, which my friend Helen Moore used to be involved in. The Seelie and Unseelie Courts – in either red or blue body paint and little else – proceed with much drumming and dancing up to the volcanic heights of Arthur's Seat, where the fire festival culminates in much wildness. Yet, in most cities towns and villages across Britain on and around May Day you are likely to catch sight of at least some Morris Dancing, and perhaps a flash of green, as I did one year – arriving in Oxford early one morning after a night at the Rollright Stones – catching a glimpse of the Oxford Jack scurrying along backstreets, accompanied by the tell-tale jingle and clatter of Morris. Here, there has been a long custom of students leaping from Magdalene Bridge, a practice which has been banned after several broken limbs – not the kind of behaviour you'd expect from Britain's brightest and best. But the lunacy of May is infectious, a verdant virus sweeping the land.

Just up the road from the dreaming spires of Oxford, in my old home town of Northampton, at the end of May, there's the Oak Apple Day event, when the statue of Charles the Second, above the portico of All Saints Church, is crowned with an oak garland to commemorate the time he hid in an oak tree to escape his Parliamentarian pursuers (although there is an element of symbolic power statement about this show of Royalist sympathy in what was a Cromwellian town, as well as a deeper echo of the time when the king was associated with the sacred oak, blessed by the druids in the ancient grove). The monarch became popular for reinstating the May Day revelries, practices which the Puritan Roundheads had outlawed; maypoles were once more raised in village squares and the people were allowed to party, at least for a day.

Cheese Rolling, Cooper's Hill, Gloucestershire
31st May
Every year in late May a group of (mostly) strangers throw themselves down a steep hill in pursuit of a round of cheese. The now famous cheese rolling that takes place at Cooper's Hill on the edge of the Cotswolds overlooking the Severn vale – now on Whitsun bank holiday Monday – started in 1884 and has continued, even through the War Years and rationing (when a

symbolic cheese was used, stuffed with paper and a symbolic piece of Double Gloucester) with only three official cancellations (1998, due to concerns over casualties the previous year; 2001, due to Foot-and-Mouth; and 2003, when the Mountain Rescue Team weren't available, having been called to the Algerian earthquake). It has to be one of the most eccentric and loved events in the British seasonal calendar.

I was unable to go this year, being out of the country, but it had been officially cancelled in March anyway, due to Health & Safety concerns (not, as you would think, over the lunatics who throw themselves down the steep slope, often breaking limbs, but due to the large crowds who gather there). Richard Jefferies, of the event's organising committee (interviewed 12th March in *The Daily Mail*) said: 'We have had to cancel on the advice of the police and local authorities. Last year 15,000 spectators tried to come to the event, by far the most we have ever seen, and we just could not cope. As well as concerns about the safety of the crowd and the competitors, landowners were worried by the amount of damage done by people climbing over fences and that sort of thing.' And so the event was cancelled. In such circumstances a cheese is rolled by the committee, 'to maintain the tradition'.

But this year the unprecedented happened – enthusiasts ran an unofficial event. The Cooper's Hill website showed photographs of this guerrila cheese-rolling. The organiser, Chris Anderson, many times a competitor and multiple winner, said in an interview, that he was compulsively drawn to the hill and would run down, even if there was no event nor even a cheese, 'just for the joy of it'. Media gathered there in anticipation of an unofficial event, and were not disappointed. The website describes what happened:

There were four downhill races as normal, starting exactly at the Official starting time of midday. The 'Organisers' of this unofficial event had arranged their own Master of

Ceremonies and a fine line of catchers at the foot of the hill. A Double Gloucester Cheese, as is the tradition, had been obtained and dressed in white with the customary blue & red ribbons. The cheese was somewhat smaller than usual, this to reduce the danger of injury if the cheese went astray! The event played out to an estimated audience of 400 – 500, not only locals, but also to visitors, both regular and new, from as far away as Sheffield, some commitment there for an event which was officially cancelled two months ago!

The website congratulated the 'unofficial' organiser: '*The event really is in your blood Chris, you are the true spirit of the Cheese Rolling.*' And so the tradition was maintained for another year, heralding perhaps a new spirit to the event, the secret of its success – a real grassroots imperative. This is the heart of any authentic folk custom – the participants do it for themselves. It is an almost unconscious urge. To feel valued and accepted – however hilarious the reason – is also why these traditions perpetuate. To be part of such a custom fosters a sense of belonging, of community, of continuity. You are 'making (local) history' and helping the wheel to turn. You are no longer just a consumer – passively experiencing festive time – but a partic- ipant. Even the spectators are all part of it and can indeed get caught up in the action. The website reports:

Spectators too have sustained injuries whilst attending past events; some have slipped and tripped on the precipitous hill, sustaining injuries in their falls. Occasionally a wayward cheese has rolled into the spectators. One year a spectator was caught by the cheese which sent him tumbling down the hill where he received treatment from the paramedics.

The committee clearly state the hazards, including a sobering toll of injuries, concluding that 'Running down a 1 in 2, in places, 1 in

1 hill, could never be considered a safe pastime!' When I went to see the Cheese Rolling in 2004 I got to see some of the fromage carnage myself. After an early morning drive along the Cotswold Edge, we parked the car as close as we could along the narrow leafy lane and made our way to the hill, which loomed impressively before us. We looked around for the best spot still available, which involved half standing in a tree. It was quite surreal, seeing hundreds of people peep out from the undergrowth, the bushes buzzing with anticipation, a load of Ents, waiting to be entertained. We probably shared some snacks, maybe even a flask. Some people had brought picnics – with plenty of cheese, of course. There was the usual slightly amused atmosphere – a self-conscious whiff of the absurd: 'God, look at us, aren't we mad!' The paramedics got into position. There were some attempts at announcements on the Tannoy, reduced to crackle and feedback. Then it reached noon and the races started. The first race was the men's; over the top they went like a load of lemmings and the first man down broke his ankle in spectacular fashion – it stuck out at an unpleasant angle. A mountain rescue team came and carried him off. The winner of the men's race was a Ghurkha, who rolled like a Tonka toy to victory. The women's winner was a Kiwi – not surprising from a nation of extreme sports nutters – Dionne Carter (who went on to win it three years running, or slipping, sliding, bouncing...). There were more casualties in the wake of the cheese, which bounced down the hill like a Barnes Wallis invention. The battered winner would hold the cheese triumphantly aloft – not much to break a limb over! Clearly it meant far more, but what? I'm madder than everyone else? I'm faster? There's other, less dangerous, ways to prove that. I am sure some would like to see it as a continuation of some kind of ancient sun cult – the pale round of cheese symbolising the wheel of the sun – but I doubt many competitors or spectators see it that way. It certainly celebrates local distinctiveness, the rounds of cheese usually Double Gloucester, even if

made by guest farms from far and wide. The 'reason' has to be a lot simpler. Such an event is a joyous defiance of sane, sober rationality and the mundane, a chance indeed to step off the wheel and do something completely purposeless. The fact that it is usually free (unless you park in the official field) and a little crazy makes it all the more appealing – one can't imagine it getting corporate sponsorship. Other similarly hazardous events have continued in a similar vein, such as the International Bognor Birdman, held in early September.

Long may the cheeses keep rolling down Cooper's Hill. I can't see them stopping now.

June

Making Hay
11th – 13th June
Just back from three days in Avalon – Scythe Fair today, book launch yesterday and storytelling show on Friday (which was actually in Taunton, but it was called 'Otherworlds', so I'm including it!).

Friday afternoon, Richard and I made our way down in the sun to Taunton, where we had a gig at the Brewhouse Theatre. We compiled an anthology show called 'Otherworlds'. I did a couple of stories from hotter climes (Al-Andalus; Yemen) and an Irish myth. Richard did stories from Scotland, Ireland and 'the fifth quarter', as he fondly calls his homeland, Romney Marsh. The set seemed to complement and flow well, but we could have done with a few more listeners. We were competing with a squaddie dance company in the main auditorium – clearly more to Tauntonian taste (or perhaps it was the footie and the sun). Still the venue was impressive and we felt well-received by our small but appreciative audience ('absolutely brilliant!') and had an enjoyable jolly. We sank a couple of well-earned beers ('Wayland Smithy' from the White Horse Brewery) when we got back. It was good to be doing some pro-storytelling again (last time was in Italy in April).

The next day, I prepared for my big book launch at the Cat & Cauldron in Glastonbury that afternoon. I enjoyed riding down to Avalon on my Triumph Legend with a box of books on the back. It promised to be a special night and it didn't disappoint.

We had a decent turn-out at Trevor and Liz's shop; the launch had been timed to coincide with the OBOD (Order of Bards, Ovates and Druids) summer gathering in Town Hall. When I launched the companion volume, *The Bardic Handbook*, four years ago at Gothic Image we had a great turn-out, with the late John Michell, Philip Carr-Gom, Ronald Hutton and Michael Dames turning up (it turned out they were in town for the OBOD bash, which I didn't know was on. Afterwards, I was invited along, so I organised this one to synchronise). Making it feel like full circle was having the first Bard of Glastonbury, Tim Hall, there, who kindly played a mini-set, as he had done at my launch in 2006. It created a lovely atmosphere. I introduced the book and read out a small selection of poems, which were well received. There were some good questions and the vibe was pleasant. I left with only a couple of copies of the book remaining, which soon got snaffled up at the OBOD gathering. It was great to go there afterwards, as a guest. Thanks to Philip, I also got my friends, Nigel and Ola, in as well. We got ourselves a plate of food and enjoyed the Bardic entertainment. I ended up having a dance with my old Dutch friend Eva, who I met on Glastonbury Tor one summer solstice twenty years ago! We bid farewell to my friend Nigel and staggered back to Amanda's yurt, which she had kindly offered me for the night. My friend had the short straw – sharing with me – and having to put up with wine-induced snoring, but we're good friends and she didn't kick me once!

The next morning, after a much needed Full Monty (breakfast) and walk up the Tor, I went to the Green Scythe Fair in deepest Zummerzet, riding passed scores of bikers on classic bikes out for a blat heading in the other direction. I passed hamlets with names like Little Gurning and finally found the site – a campsite called Thorney Lakes near a village called Mulcheney Ham. It was only a fiver to get in and you got free tea and cake if you came on a bike – that is, a bicycle – I tried my luck but didn't convince the lady in the tea tent (who had come down on a Bonnie). I bumped into folk and bimbled about, enjoying the ambience. You felt like you were breathing in carbon credits just walking about. It's a very positive event with lots of green solutions – alternative fuel, food, housing, clothing, education – as well as being relaxed, picturesque (and picaresque) and just the right size. If it had a theme tune it'd be *Heavy Horses* by Jethro Tull. It was very Hardy-esque and felt like something you'd expect to see Gabriel Oak at. There were scything championships – all very serious stuff (involving plenty of liquid preparation). Competitors carefully whetted their blades and assessed the quality of the grass, scratching their chins, shaking heads, and drawing in breath. There were lots of wonderful craft stalls, info tents and music, including my friends Tim Hall and the Archetypes, who performed on Sangers fabulous horse-drawn solar-powered stage. There were bands with names like 'Bag o' Rats', who played 'psychedelic folk' to a good-natured crowd mellow on cider. There were plenty of fresh grass cuttings for kids to play with, which kept them amused for hours (a Battle Royale grass fight lasted all afternoon and several grass burials took place).

The sky had been darkly ominous all afternoon (a bit Bergman-esque with the reapers hanging around, as though waiting for a game of chess with Max Von Sydow). At one point the heavens opened and I found myself standing under a gazebo in a sandpit to stay dry. A rainbow came out soon after. After a suitably drunken delay (a missing trophy), the scything champion was announced (a local, winning it for the fourth year in a row) and the MC said the standard was so high he was confident we were now 'ready for Europe'; though the World Cup and Olympics might have to wait, he wagged. I made my way back soon after, glad to get back after a fine weekend away.

I thought the magic would be over with a stack of OU marking facing me Monday morning, but then a call from my friend Helen at midday meant I ended up going on a lovely trip down the river Avon to celebrate her birthday ('life's too short,' she said, and she's right – *carpe deum!*).

We found a sunny spot to stop for a fabulous picnic. I read out some of my poetry, including 'Let Love Be Our River', and on the way back recited some Elizabeth Barratt Browning and Thomas the Rhymer as the ladies rowed (they insisted, after us guys had rowed on the way out). It was all very Wind in the Willows. Most relaxing! We can step off the wheel at any time and make any day, any moment, sacred time. Quality time with friends is probably the best of all.

Mad Dogs and Englishman
20th – 21st June

The summer solstice is one of those deadlines of the year – it is for me anyway. Everything seems to build up to it and there's a millions things to get done before it; as though time will stop after. Of course, it will carry on just as before, like the millennium or 2012. Significant dates – lines in the egg-timer sands – turn normally sensible people into headless chickens, and the 'doom' that we expect becomes a self-fulfilling prophecy (our mounting panic causing accidents, hysteria, conflict, suicide, down-sizing to a remote Scottish islands, etc). On a microcosmic scale, summer is the 'silly season', when lazy journalists, recovering from long liquid lunches, dig deep into the odd box. But it's not hard to find stuff – druids at Stonehenge being a favourite 'isn't life a bit weird sometimes/don't worry about the economy' piece. Images of ragged revellers at the World Heritage Site – usually with some wally raving on a trilithon – mark the turning of wheel in the same iconic fashion as a groundhog in the States or bluebells over here. Here's a typical report of the event, from the Beeb:

Revellers at Stonehenge to celebrate Summer Solstice

About 20,000 revellers were at Stonehenge to mark the Summer Solstice, each hoping to see the sun as it rose above the ancient stone circle at dawn.

Police described the event on Salisbury Plain in Wiltshire as one of the safest in years, although 34 people were arrested for minor drug offences.

Sunrise, marking the longest day of the year north of the equator, occurred over the circle at 0452 BST.

Peter Carson from English Heritage said:'It has been quieter this year but it's been a great solstice.

It's an improvement on the last few years – the last time I remember seeing the sun rise was in 2003 – so it's great to see the sun has put in an appearance.

This year there are about 20,000 people and last year it was about 35,000, so that is quite a bit down which has meant the operation is a lot easier.'

He said two years ago the solstice happened early on a Saturday and about 30,000 people attended.

He added:'I think the days of the week do make a considerable difference to the number of people who come along – this year it's a Monday morning.

The people who are streaming out now – a lot of them are going to work.'

Victoria Campbell, 29, was among those marking the solstice.

She said:'It means a lot to us... being British and following our pagan roots.'

The Londoner, who works in the finance industry, added 'getting away from the city was a major draw.'

On Sunday police chiefs said they had planned for 'all eventualities' ahead of the event.

Last year a record 36,500 revellers attended, causing traffic chaos and road closures.

[BBC website, accessed 22.06.10]

I have attended the Stonehenge celebration at the summer solstice (when they first re-opened it to the public after ten years), but found it complete chaos and as far from sacred as you can imagine, with many people off their heads and so much conflicting energy/attitudes it defeated the point. It seemed to me the 'mob' where desecrating the very thing which had drawn them to a jumble of stones on Salisbury Plain very early on a June morning – a sacred site at a sacred time. Any attempt at ceremony became a circus show spectacle, tolerated in the libertarian atmosphere, or laughed at. Priests were mocked. Anarchy ruled. It might as well have been a dodgy football crowd, chanting: 'Innggerrrlunnddd'. Couples got hand fasted in the hurly burly. Others snogged, skinned up, threw up, danced naked, chanted, shouted or blew horns. A young lad tossed somebody's ashes into the crowd and it blew into our faces. A group of Maoris looked on aghast – was *this* how we treated the dead? I felt ashamed for my country. Stonehenge *is* amazing and at other times of the year (winter solstice can be more civilised and atmospheric) or via private access, you can feel the awe and majesty of the place and connect with something sacred. But avoid the summer solstice, unless you can gain private access outside of the popular 'slot', which several groups choose to do instead.

But what of my own revelries?

After an intense couple of weeks meeting all my (mainly marking) deadlines, I was looking forward to a couple of days of downing tools and just enjoying the sun – and he certainly had his hat on for us, which makes the world of difference. Nature smiled, filling everything with a benign quality.

I went to a picnic on Solsbury Hill, organised by my friends Peter Please and Kirsten Bolwig. Taking my friend Sally on the back, we rocked up there on the Triumph, finding them to one side, underneath a rocky ledge. There ended up being about twenty of us – a splendid picnic with splendid people. Poems and songs were shared. We 'broke bread' together and relaxed in the sun.

Alas, we had to shoot off early, as I had a previous

commitment to run the Independent Creatives Forum at the Gaynor Flynn's Being Human weekend, Frome.

The venue – a warehouse tucked away in the obscure outskirts of the old wool town – was difficult to find. A couple of small easy-to-miss arrows pointed in vague directions. Finally, I found it, after a few dead ends, and it felt like a lazy Sunday afternoon chill-out with a small group of friends (in publicity it looked like it was going to be some amazing ground-breaking happening, not a house-party). My forum was meant to take place in a yurt, which had been taken over by children, but I managed to claim the space and set up; the event was announced and... I had one person come in. I can't blame folk for wanting to sit in the sun and drink beer (I wouldn't have minded doing that myself). Sunday 2-5pm is the wrong time to have an intellectual forum. Nevertheless, we had a nice chat about creativity (there were four of us in the end). One woman who had come all the way from East Grinstead for the event said she was so glad I had come along; all weekend she had been hearing discussions about technology and I was the first speaker to talk about *people*, about being human. If you connect with one person, or make one person's day – sowing the seed of something, an idea, a thought, inspired in some way – then it's all been worthwhile.

It was nice to bump into my fellow Bard of Bath, Helen Moore and her partner, Niall from London. There's a healthy creative scene in Frome, and Gaynor's outfit is one aspect of it, showing that provincial life doesn't have to be parochial. Later, Banco de Gaia played and a little backstreet of a sleepy Wiltshire town became plugged into the global groove.

I returned at speed to finish setting up for my annual solstice 'Bard-B-Q', with the help of my friends Sally and Ola. It was a lovely gathering, blessed by a perfect summer's evening, with friends sharing poems, songs and stories. I got my mead-horn out – as I am wont to do as such occasions – and we offered heart-felt toasts as it was passed around. This jump-started an excellent discussion on the BP oil disaster, and I found myself having successfully facilitated a creative forum after all, albeit in my own home.

After a lazy breakfast (getting up at sunrise would've been a bridge too far; I have learnt to be gentle with myself lately. The solstice doesn't have to be a triathlon, although it can feel like that, racing from event to event), I headed over to Avebury for midday with my friend Sally once again on the back. It was a lovely run in the sun and we got there just in time to catch the noon ceremonies (solstice was 12:28pm). A wonderfully raggle taggle mixture of sun worshippers hung out between the stones and the atmosphere was relaxed. No doubt the all-night/or early morning revelries had worn out most. Avebury is big enough to accommodate for everyone's 'thing'; the energy is far more feminine and less antagonistic than Stonehenge, which I feel has been tainted over the years by all the conflict that has focused around them: stones of contention. One group was having a dual gong shower. Another sat in worship around a giant stone egg. Druids in full regalia chanted hand in hand. People meditated, picnicked, slept – it was hard to tell. Everyone was in a kind of placid state, like a load of cows in a field, contentedly chewing cud – stoned bovines. If anyone was on grass, they were keeping it discreet as the token bobby strolled around. There was no crowd control trouble here; many had come from Stonehenge that dawn, but something about Avebury chills people out. We did a ceremonial ambulation, with frequents stops in the scorching heat, before culminating in the ritual pint at the Red Lion, where the party continued on the benches outside. We sat in the leafy shade of the 'fertile triangle' nearby and ate our sandwiches. I bumped into an old Bardic acquaintance, Jim, who updated me on all the ins and outs of the druid scene. He'd played four gigs that morning and was involved in getting the ancestral sculpture to Stonehenge. He was excited about the media coverage they had gained – druids can be complete media tarts, preening and pontificating in front of the cameras. Certainly, it can be used as a platform to discuss real issues, but often the media treat such people like a novelty news item ('And finally...'). Jim's band, Druidicca, feature in a new movie partly filmed at Avebury called *The Stone*. He talked at length about his big scheme to bring all druids together and I wished him good luck. We stopped off at Silbury Hill to hail the 'Mighty Mother' then hit the road back home.

Rounding off the solstice revelries nicely was the Bath Storytelling Circle, which happened to be on at the Raven that night. I went along and contributed a story and a poem, and enjoyed the ambience, helped by a couple of ales.

Satisfied, I returned home. Finally, I was able to be still, which after all is what the solstice signifies. The sun puts its feet up for three days and has a well-earned rest!

Midsummer Magic
24th – 27th June

We have been blessed with magnificent weather the last few days; the sun has well and truly had his hat on. When the sun does shine, the English summer is a glorious thing and I would not want to be anywhere else on Earth.

Shaman-poet of *The Doors*, Jim Morrison, once said, 'No eternal reward shall forgive us now for wasting the dawn,' and having missed the solstice sunrise I thought I'd better make an effort to see it while it was at the same place (over the solstice, the sunrise stays at the same time for 3-4 days, 4.44am), so on Midsummer morning I awoke before dawn and, after listening to the exquisite pre-dawn chorus over a cuppa in my back garden, I headed up the hill to Bathampton Down (home of an Iron Age tribe who sculpted it into earthworks and field systems; an effigy of the triple-aspect goddess was discovered dating from that period in the road above mine). I made a beeline for Sham Castle, a local folly, which I thought would be the perfect place to greet the midsummer sun. While I waited in the brightening light I made some notes and had a flash of inspiration for a story, which I wrote up later that day. Although the sun decided not to make a dramatic debut that morning you could still feel the quickening of nature – the surge of energy rippling across the land like a tidal bore. On this wave of solar power – the sun at the 'high tide' of the year – I launched my latest book the next day. The 25th of June was the official launch date of *The Way of Awen: Journey of a Bard*, and I planned to do something to 'wet the baby's head' in Bath. When I discovered that penbeirdd Robin Williamson was playing at Chapel Arts Centre on the same night (an event I did not want to miss) I decided to find a way of bringing the events together, so I booked the Live Arts Cafe downstairs for 6-8pm, leaving time to see Robin's show after – and it all worked beautifully. Robin had generously contributed to *The Bardic Handbook*, which came out four years ago, and so it seemed apt to combine the events. He was most accommodating about it, and popped down at the start, after I had given him a hand bringing in his instruments. To have him there was such an honour, as he's been such an inspiration – so to Greywolf, aka Philip Shallcrass (founder of the British Druid Order), who was one of the key people to introduce me to the concept of Awen in the mid-nineties. I was delighted when he turned up with his friend Eva and his son Joe. I thanked both these awesome Bard-druids at the start of my talk – presenting them each with a copy – before reading extracts from the book. There was a good crowd (including Franklin, the Bard of Basswood all the way from Buffalo, USA) who seemed to respond well to what I shared. The mead flowed and the atmosphere was pleasant. It felt like a very successful launch.

Afterwards, we decamped upstairs to enjoy a fabulous concert from Robin Williamson, probably the best I've seen him do. He did some amazing Celtic tunes on his harp, weaving stories, jokes, anecdotes and songs seamlessly together. He did a fantastic cover of Dylan's *No Direction Home*; some of The Beatles *Within,*

Without You; The Irish Rover; and even a blues number – on the harp! It was a pleasure to hear a couple of his new songs, and some from his back catalogue (e.g. the ever poignant, *Political Lies*); a deeply touching one about his son, Gavin; as well as one from his time in California in the sixties. He did a couple of classic British ballads, *The Death of Robin Hood* and *Lord Barnard* – overall, an impressive set showing his incredible range. One could really appreciate the fact this was a man who has been performing as long as I've been alive; his technical virtuosity and repertoire is awesome. He truly is Britain's greatest living Bard. To enjoy such a concert after my book launch really was the icing on the cake; when one works on such a big project like my book (really twenty years in the making, as it draws upon journals and notebooks from that period), organise the launch, entertain everyone, play the host, give a reading, etc, one can feel depleted, but a concert like Robin's really replenishes the well.

The next day, I had to get up early and get my act together for a creative writing day school in the lovely Wiltshire town of Devizes, followed by a camping trip with friends. The plan was to rendezvous at the Barge, Honeystreet, but when I rolled up there on the Triumph Legend I found it to be completely jammed with revellers, there for the bicentenary bash – a mini music festival. You couldn't swing a cat, let along pitch three tents and park three vehicles. I looked around for my friends amid the merry but mellow crowds, to no avail. I procured a pint of Croppie – brewed by the Barge – in my pewter tankard and supped it on the canal bank, cooling off after a hot day's work and riding. After trying to contact my friends I discovered a text explaining the change of plans; they had found a campsite in Bishop Cannings and so I togged up again, into my sweaty leathers, and set off down the back lanes. To my relief, I found my friends pitched up in a quiet campsite and I was offered a cold beer – things were looking up. I finally managed to erect my tent, somewhat hampered by the ale.

The campsite – little more than a lawn – could hardly have been more different than the chaos at the Barge. Yet later, after a meal, my poet friend Jay arrived and drove us over to soak up some of the Bacchanalian vibes. A band called The Hub was on – young, loud and belting out various covers with the same three chords and hoarse vocals – but the crowd was dancing and Jay and I joined in. There was a certain hick chic to the whole thing. You really feel you're in the Wild West Country at the Barge, with its eccentric demographic of boaties, croppies, bikers, yokels, druids, Bards, boozers and glampers (glamorous campers – the word of the weekend). We didn't stay long enough to incur brain damage, from the cider or the music, shooting off into the tranquil night with a little relief (and great relief at not camping there).

Jay insisted we visited Avebury in the light of the full moon, which was truly enchanting and worth the effort. We three poets – Jay, Dawn and I – wandered around in the silvery light, savouring the spell-binding beauty of the place. There wasn't a soul in sight and the place regained its ancient glory in the glow of the moon, the enchantment not challenged by the traffic and crowds of the daytime. We processed along the chalky ridge, as hard and bright as compacted snow, our shadows proud on the opposite bank like an ogham. At the beech grove, contained within its matrix of roots, we lent against the smooth grey trunks and nearly descended into Rip Van Winkle-like slumber, from which it was hard to extricate ourselves. With the honey moon lambent through the leaves, sheep huddled quietly nearby, a deep peace over the land, and a benign golden warmth pervading everything; it was like falling asleep in a Samuel Palmer painting. We left, inspired. Independently, each of us penned a poem about this experience, which we published later in the summer in a small pamphlet: *Avebury Moon*. It presents an interesting 'holographic' rendering of a magical night. The next day, after resurrecting ourselves, we struck camp and headed up to the

Wansdyke, parking up in the droveway by Milk Hill and heading up to Adam's Grave to enjoy the 360 degree view. The cool breeze was a relief – it was scorching – and the light and space helped to clear my head. You can really get a perspective on things at such a place.

Starting to feel weak – having only had a handful of strawberries for breakfast – we wended our way over to Avebury, where we grabbed some lunch at the Red Lion. I bumped into my biker buddy Nigel, who had been up for the whole week. He had played the Oak King in the ceremony at Stonehenge the day before, duelling with, and ultimately being defeated by, his rival/brother the Holly King, who takes his place as consort to the Goddess for the second half of the year.

This was my third visit to Avebury in a week (it's the hub of things at this time of year, as it probably was thousands of years ago), but I wished to be there for my friend Michael Dames' launch – who was celebrating the publication of his new (and apparently last) title, *Silbury: resolving the enigma*, by The History Press. He was standing outside the National Trust shop with a kind of 'art altar' illustrating his theory of the hill – the largest manmade mound in Europe, aligned with the phases of the moon at certain times of the year. He gave a colourful demonstration, placing his model of Silbury on his head at one point. He seemed prepared to act the clown, but like many clowns, he was prone to fits of grumpy despondency. Yet, he would 'revive', like John Barleycorn, regaining his sunny persona and merry twinkle and pass round glasses of wine. I chatted with the publisher of my book *Lost Islands*, Bob Trubshaw (Heart of Albion Press), who videoed the whole thing for posterity. I was wilting by this point – after a lot of sun, beer and little sleep – and so I headed home for a much needed 'quiet night in' (watching Christopher Eccleston on superb form in *Lennon Naked*). I felt I had truly made the most of this exceptional weekend – apparently a time of great cosmic events (full moon;

lunar eclipse; Grand Cross; the sun and moon in alignment with the centre of the galaxy!). It was exhilarating, exhausting and utterly memorable.

JULY

My Week

It's been a busy week, Bardically, with lots of talks and travelling.

Tuesday, I performed with my friend, fellow poet Crysse Morrison of Frome, in the Arts House Cafe, Melksham, as part of their food and drink festival. We were billed as a 'Poetry Fest' and were given the theme 'Feast and Famine', which we both responded to in typically atypical ways. I read out poems from my recent Egyptian residency. Our hostess was Sue, who looked after us extremely well and made things flow beautifully.

Wednesday, I travelled to London to give a talk to the Moot with No Name in the Devereux Arms – a charming olde worlde pub usually frequented by City types (its opposite the Royal Court of Justice on the corner of Fleet Street and the Strand, tucked away in its own 'Dagon Alley'). My friends Geraldine and Bali from Atlantis Bookshop were there to greet me and sell books on my behalf (*The Way of Awen* was stacked up – the focus on the night's talk). Steve Wilson was hosting and introduced me. I raised the Awen and this seemed to break down barriers. I ended the talk with a story, as requested by G&B – one of my desert ones. I managed to catch the last train home (just) and got back late.

The next morning, I was on the train again – to Bristol – to give a poetry reading to Can Openers, at the Bristol Central Library, a monthly open mic event hosted by Claire Williamson. I declaimed through the mic in the middle of the library – I don't normally like using mikes but with building work going off in the background it was essential. I joked that it was like some kind of industrial art happening: Beatniks meet Bob the Builder. 'Howl, we can!'

Saturday, I performed at the Camerton Batch Green Fair – my second gig on its slagheap, albeit a very pretty one now it's been reclaimed by nature and made accessible with a lovely nature trail. Various fluffy crafty folk did their thing – bodging; making stuff from felt; willow; clay; dream-catchers. A resplendent old steam engine powered a scary-looking saw mill. A mighty shire horse helped extract timber. The ladies of Polka Dot Pantry tempted passersby with their cakes. I performed a couple of thirty minutes sets of stories in a bell tent that was furnished comfortably with fleeces. My audience ended up being very young – something to do with it being incorrectly billed as 'children's storytelling!' (despite my briefing them not to) – but it seemed to go down okay, although, by the end, the adults were laughing more than the kids. Saravian provided moral support. The sun shone and it was a pleasant affair.

Sunday, I needed a day off and so I went for a spin on the bike, up to the Banbury Hobby Horse Fair and back, over the Cotswolds on my own 'cock horse'.

Banbury Hobby Horse Fair
4th July

This charming event has been running since 1999 and I made it along to its eleventh anniversary after being told about it the week before in Avebury by Bob Trubshaw. I imagine one could travel the country this way, on a chain of serendipitous causality (the 'word of mouth' tour). I was planning to go to the Beyond the Border International Storytelling Festival in St Donat's, South Wales, but after my gig at Camerton Batch Green Fair, I was rather wiped out, and decided to cut myself some slack – taking the night off and heading up to Banbury the next day. Nevertheless, a 'quiet pint' with my old friend Marko outside the Coeur de Lion (the smallest pub in Bath) turned into a bit of a Bardic experience – a tune from his whistle greeted me as I turned the corner into the picturesque passage. Marko was in fine voice and did a few songs, as did another fella, AJ. Despite the jar or two of dark stuff, I managed to do my poem 'Heartwood' on request, before I slipped away to avoid too much brain damage – or a hangover; I had a long ride the next day.

In the morning, I blatted up over the Cotswolds on one of my favourite runs – along the free roller coaster ride of the old Fosseway, a fast straight road with some hills and thrills.

Here are the field notes from the event:

The sounds of a bell, an accordion, and a booming bass drum, echoes along the High Street. I am standing by Banbury Cross, decorated with its foliate horse heads, about to watch the procession from the Town Hall to the People's Park of the Hobby Horses that gather here this time of the year. Suddenly, the street is full of hobby horses, clacking and jigging along. The Mayor and other VIPs join the procession. Rotary Club volunteers steward the route, temporarily halting traffic as the colourful cavalcade wends its way around the Cross, paying their respects to the statue of the 'fine lady upon a white horse', the magnificent bronze statue erected in 2005 and inaugurated by the Princess Royal. There are schoolchildren upon their own cute steeds; 'grown ups' riding fabulous beasts. It is calm and civilised, like a Girl Guide parade, not a parade of frolicking pagan beasties. The crowds are naturally drawn into the procession, Pied Piper style, following it along Horse Fair, to the bottleneck of The Leys, a narrow alley they slowly squeeze down to the People's Park, where a fête awaited amid the trees – all part of the Town Mayor's Sunday and Hobby Horse Festival. The hobby horses politely queue up by the village green to await their turn in the Parade of Beasts. Punters line the central 'green', where the Beasts enter – announced by the MC, a lady dressed in medieval style jester gear from Radio Horton: the 'fine lady' (a guy in drag with false legs and a blonde wig); a cluster of endearing schoolchildren's efforts; a Fair-trade horse; the Four Horsemen of the Apocalypse; the Sailors' Horse from Minestead, which jigged about vigorously to its own band – then proceeded to 'mount' the MC, with ten ceremonial 'bangs' – virtually covering her with its skirts. At one point the MC, announced: 'And here are some school-children on their cock horses' – a sentence you could probably only get away with at the Banbury Hobby Horse Fair. I grabbed a pint of 'Old Hooky' from the Hook Norton Brewery van (for a splendid £2.50) and sat under the shade of a tree to write this – glad I had made the effort.

There's a relaxed atmosphere in the warm sun. The quaint festive ambience is enhanced by old-fashioned funfair amusements: try your strength; the pop of a cap gun; the burnt sugar scent of candy-floss; the sizzle and reek of burger vans; raffle stalls; charities; lost children tent; village stocks (an officious girl in red insisted I make a donation for taking a photo of it); a merry-go-round; lots of families. People bimble about amid the leafy glade, trees swaying gently in the breeze, heavy with foliage. I succumb to an ice-cream, sit on a chair and take it all in. Ah, the glory of an English summer. Just then, a woman in a full burqa walks by with her husband, looking strangely like a sibling of one of the hobby horses. Smiling to myself, I imagine taking a photo of them side-by-side – a symbol of multi-cultural Britain – but think better of it.

Such events help synchronise a community with the seasons, with the place and with its own. They foster a sense of civic pride, and make citizens feel peaceful, knowing that something distinctive is happening in their neighbourhood. It makes you feel that it is not elsewhere – it is *here*. I have made the right choice/s. I'm with the right person, in the right place. All is well.

The main arena continued its programme of various events: Morris Dancers in white; Martial Arts pupils in black; Dogs for the Disabled demonstrators in orange sashes. The hobby horses lay dormant while their riders enjoyed some fodder. Other provincial delights awaited: Line Dancing (the ladies in pink were limbering up and posing for team photos); hobby horse races (adult and children) and no doubt some prize-giving – but

I departed, keen to be back on the road, heading home.

Rollright Stones (later)
I stopped off at the Rollright Stones on the way back, to catch my breath and reflect on things. Because I make it to such places infrequently (maybe once a year at the Rollrights, often as a pit-stop on the way back home from Northampton, my former home town), when I do it feels like the wheel has turned significantly in the meantime. Where am I at? Where have come from? Where am I going? What have I done? Am I happy in my life? Such monuments of endurance act as positive touchstones – reminding us about the bigger cycle.

The Rollrights were the first stones that I consciously inter-acted with. I had visited Stonehenge in 1987 as an A Level Geography student – sketching them (I had seen them on *Arthur C Clarke's Mysterious World*; and *Quatermass: the final sequel,* so knew they were something special!) and had passed through Avebury on the way to my first Glastonbury Festival in 1989. But it wasn't until 1991 that I really engaged with these places, going there with my friends Keith Lord (medicine pipe carrier) and Bernard King (rune-master) to dowse and meditate. Since then, I have been back several times, liking their slightly understated quality; they are impressive, but not in the way the larger stone circles are. It is the ritual landscape and how it all connects that contributes to the overall effect: the King's Men (a late Neolithic ceremonial Stone Circle dating from 2500 to 2000 BCE) are only part of it; there's the King Stone on the other side of the road, in a separate county – Warwickshire; the Whispering Knights further down the field (the 5000 year old burial chamber, believed to be part of a Neolithic long barrow); and a small circle by itself, possibly the remains of a Bronze Age barrow. I've slept there and been there for dawn; it's often cold, being exposed and relatively high up. Many pagans use it, but it doesn't feel drained or tainted like some sites do. Its isolation helps, and perhaps its

own genius loci help to protect it. Inevitably, with such a place
there is a clustering of folkloric accretion, 'explaining' the origins
of the stones, and adding to their continuing mythic ambience. It
is tradition that the stones are impossible to count accurately
(indeed, as I was leaving a couple asked me how many I had
counted). I hadn't bothered this time, but had tried before.
Because some of the stones are split or part buried, it depends on
what is classed as a 'stone', hence the frequent disparity – that is
my prosaic explanation, anyway – and yet such places can also
make you feel dizzy, as happened to a friend when we visited in
the early nineties. We were told to stand in the middle by a
curious old man there with twinkly eyes and you could certainly
feel a swirling vortex of energy. Paul Devereux with the Dragon
Project in the 1970s carefully measured the energy field of such
places. But it seems to me that people find what they want to –
earth energies, sacred geometry, alien technology; they act as
conduits for the subconscious. For me, they inspire me to write
poetry and stories. There are some good ones about these stones.
One of the most interesting relates the consequences of moving
or damaging the stones, which goes like this:

*a man from Banbury took a chipping from one of the stones – on
returning to his cart he found that the wheels were solidly locked. A
young soldier took a chip with him to India where he promptly died
of typhus. Another relates how a farmer from Little Rollright is said
to have removed the capstone of the Whispering Knights to build a
bridge across the stream. It took a score of horses (and the death of
two men) to drag the stone down the hill. Strange and eerie noises
gave the farmer no peace – every morning the stone had turned over
and lay on the bank. The farmer finally decided that enough was
enough and that he had to take the stone back. With the greatest of
ease, one horse pulled the stone back up the hill.*

What does such a story tell us? I interpret it in a metaphorical way – that one shouldn't go against the tides of nature. By living in disharmony with the Earth, exploiting its resources in a disrespectful way, you will suffer the consequences – of ecological justice. It also suggests turning the wheel is about working *with* the flow. In this case, pulling the stone up hill was easier than dragging it down, for it was contrary to the geomantic integrity of the site. When the Dragon Lines of the land are synchronised, things move 'effortlessly' – and that's how it feels whenever I ride the Fosse Way across the Cotswolds back to Bath. It feels as though I'm swimming *with* the current, rather than against it; maybe it's just the prospect of getting home, but it feels so much faster. The wheels turn as I ride the lines of the land.

Stone Temple Biker
(Written at the Rollrights)

I listen
to the wind
sifting through the trees
sitting in these ancient stones
embraced by old strong arms –
mottled, gnarled, lichen-dappled
liver-spotted with age. A congregation of crones
silently they share their knowledge.
Centuries of counsel.
From the nought of the desert
to the zero of stones.
Full circle.
My two wheels carry me,
and I carry on down the road.

Tynwald Day
5th July

In 2004, I fulfilled a long-held ambition of mine and travelled to the Isle of Man – that quirky island at the centre of the British

Isles (a circle, extending from the island in the middle of the Irish Sea, encompasses the whole of the UK and Ireland – from John O'Groats to Lands End, with Snaefell Peak at its exact centre) to witness the biggest day in their calendar, Tynwald Day, the Manx National Day (equivalent to St George's Day for England; St David's Day for Wales; St Andrew's Day for Scotland; St Piran's Day for Cornwall; and St Patrick's Day for Ireland). At the heart of this is a ceremony, which has reputedly continued unchanged, except in detail, for more than 1,000 years. The annual outdoor sittings of Tynwald, the Manx Parliament, date back to the Viking settlements, which began in the eighth century of the first millennium CE. No other parliament in the world has such a long unbroken record. This venerable ceremony is celebrated at St John's, on Tynwald Hill, the four-tiered sacred mound repre-senting the symbolic heart of the Isle of Man – very similar to the Brythonic *gorsedd* mound, with the ceremony echoing those of the National Welsh Eisteddfod – where laws are decreed in English and Manx with much pomp and ceremony and Manx citizens can make petition directly to their government. Policemen in the distinctive white helmets stand soberly on guard. VIPs parade solemnly along the processional route linking the church of St John the Baptist to its pagan past. There's a wonderful feeling of local pride. Here, for centuries, the ancient laws of Man have been enshrined in what is the oldest unbroken parliament in Europe. It is one of the key ceremonies in the Celtic calendar, where a Celtic country declares its autonomy in dual-language. The Isle of Man is not part of the United Kingdom, but a Crown Dependency. Strangely, Her Majesty the Queen is acknowledged as Lord of Mann, presiding over the ceremony in 1979 when the Millennium of Tynwald was celebrated.

It has strong connections with the All Thing in Iceland, from the roots of which it draws its name (Tynwald stems from *thing-vollr*: field of the parliament). Not surprising, when Tynwald is a legacy of Nordic colonists who first came to the island around

800 CE and ruled for four and a half centuries. By the time it was ceded to the King of Scotland in 1266, the Norse settlers had indelibly stamped their own administrative system on the island, and the Tynwald was preserved from then on.

Witnessing the Tynwald Day ceremony feels like you are watching something very special. Victorian novelist Sir Thomas Henry Hall Caine, when visiting it in 5th July 1893, said: 'You may go to the ends of Europe and see nothing of the kind that is half so interesting.' His description of it is colourful, vivid, sometimes fanciful and biased with the pomposity of its period:

The day was bright, brilliant, even dazzling, and at an early hour the streets of Douglas were thronged with vehicles. Brakes, wagonettes, omnibuses, private carriages and cadgers' carts, all loaded to their utmost capacity, were climbing out of the town by way of the road going towards Peel.

Visitors, boarding-house keepers, shop-keepers, boatmen, members of the Legislature and officials of every class, were driving in thousands to Tynwald Hill. They looked as cheerful as the weather was beautiful. The town seemed to shout; the old island rock itself seemed to laugh.

It was a drive of eight miles, and we were driving in a line of some hundreds of carriages. By the time we got to the breast of the steep hill going up to Crosby the road ahead was like a funnel of dust, and the road behind was like the tail of a comet. Out of the dense cloud, in front and at the back, came sounds of singing and laughter. At one moment there came wild whooping behind, and presently the line of carriages swirled like a long serpent half a yard nearer to the left-hand hedge. Then through the grey dust a carriage shot past at a rapid pace. It was the carriage of the Governor.

When we came within a mile of Tynwald, we could see the flags, the tents and the crowd as of a vast encampment, and hear the deep hum of a multitude like the murmur of a distant sea.

Tynwald Hill is an open green in the very midst of the island, with hills on three of its sides, and on the fourth a broad plain dipping down to the sea. The shape of the green is that of the frame of a guitar. Down the middle of the guitar there is a walled enclosure, which may be said to be of the shape of a banjo. At the key end, the east end, stands a church. The round drum is the mount, which is built in four circles, the topmost being some six paces across.

The open part of the green was covered with booths, barrows, stands and show tents. There were cheap-jacks selling shoddy watches, phrenologists with two chairs, fat women, dwarfs, wandering minstrels and itinerant hawkers of tin hat-boxes containing sticks of toffee – these and other shiny, slimy creatures, with the air and grease of the towns. At one corner there were a few oxen and horses, tethered and lanketed, and kicking up the dust under the dry sod.

The crowd was dense already and increasing at every moment. As the brakes arrived they drove up with a whoop and a swing that sent the people surging on either side. Some brought well-behaved visitors, others brought an eruption of ruffians blowing tin whistles and Jews' harps, and yet others brought farmers and fishermen disguised, out of all recognition, as lodging-house keepers, and pretending not to understand the salutations of old comrades when addressed by them in the Manx.

Down the neck of the enclosure, and round the circular end of it, a regiment of soldiers was ranged with rifles and bayonets. Inside their lines there was a company of marines with drawn swords. The steps to the mount were covered with rushes from the Curragh. Two arm-chairs were on the top under a canopy hung from a flagstaff that stood in the centre. These chairs were still empty; the mount and its approaches were being kept clear.

The sun was hot, the heat was great, the odour was sometimes oppressive. Now and again, sounds of singing within the church mingled with the crack of the toy rifle-ranges and the jabber of the cheap-jacks. It is usual to begin the proceedings of Tynwald Day with Divine Service, and the Governor and Legislature were at prayers.

Presently the crowd gathered thick down the neck of the enclosure and dense round the mount. Then to the strains of the National Anthem played by the band of the regiment, the Governor, his Council, his Clergy, and his Keys, came out of the church. His Excellency wore cocked hat and Court dress, and the Sword of State was carried upright before him. He walked through the lines of soldiers and marines and stepped to the hill top. There he took one of the two chairs under the canopy; the other was taken by the Bishop, who was wearing his lawn. Their followers came behind, and broke up on the mount (I am bound to confess it) in an irregular and indiscriminate mass. A number of ladies were admitted to the space on the topmost round. They stood behind the two chairs of the Governor and the Bishop, with parasols still open. From the Governor's seat the scene was a splendid and even magnificent one. Fifteen thousand people in holiday dress, with brakes and wagonettes, a company of soldiers and a company of marines, stood closely packed in the brilliant sunshine on the green below. To the east was the church spire against the green background of Greeba Mountain, to the south the strong outline of Slieau Whallian, to the west the broad plain going down to the sea. Not, perhaps, a spectacle such as Thingvallir must have been, with its craggy hill of laws, surrounded by its natural moat and encircled by the snow-clad Jokuls. But a beautiful and wonderful scene, nevertheless, revitalised and ennobled, too, by a real national sentiment.

And this custom seems in no danger of diminishing. The BBC reported that at the 2010 Tynwald Day: 'Thousands mark Isle of Man's Tynwald Day event'. The article reported that 'The day was also a chance for people to air their grievances to politicians.' In the light of the recent election debacle on the mainland (a hung parliament), and scandals over MP expenses, banks and the like, such a democratic custom seems not so archaic – but more valid than ever. A tradition endures if it serves the needs of the people; beneath its eccentric Pythonesque trappings the Tynwald ceremony preserves the heart of democracy upon its 'craggy hill of laws'.

When I was there, there was the week-long Peel Viking Festival. Viking re-enactors from all over the world (not only Scandinavian countries, but also Russia; there were even some from Alaska) camped out in the 'Viking village' on the beach. Every day there was an impressive Viking raid, with mock long ships pulling up on the shore and surly warriors leaping out, recreating the devastating raids that the Isle of Man endured, sitting as it was in such a strategic position. On the final day, there was due to be a 'spectacular Viking funeral' with the burning of a longship, but unfortunately heavy rain put a dampener on things. The final battle had to be cancelled – rain doesn't agree with chain mail, nor does it make lying 'dead' on damp sand very pleasant. The audience bravely faced the lashing rain, wrapped in emergency bin bags, until finally the plug was pulled. It was meant to be the mist of Manannan's cloak that protected the island from unwanted visitors (as in the Royal visit in 2000) but here it was the mere rain that held off another Nordic invasion. Afterwards, on the way back to the bus stop, we briefly met two rain bedraggled Slavic Vikings, wandering the bleak streets of Peel, with a desperate look in their eyes. They stopped us and cried: 'We need wod-ka!'

The Viking culture, although surviving in re-enactment, has a modern incarnation in the biking culture which converges on

Man for the TT races and can be seen in evidence all year round. Manx man John McGuiness has won the TT races several years running. To see gangs of bikers roaring around the winding country lanes of the island, or hanging out outside bars and cafes, you get a glimmer of that former warrior culture – although most are pretty harmless: middle-aged men on a jolly with mates away from the wife and kids (or sometimes in tow). The fact is, even the 'wild ones' want to settle down eventually and that also went for the Viking invaders, who married local women, who gave them bright-haired children; children they raised and taught the local tongue – so in the end the 'victory' was theirs. This cross-fertilisation can be seen in the distinctive place names of Manx – a mixture of Nordic and Gaelic.

Apart from the infamous 'tail-less cat', the Isle of Man is renowned for its wheels. One of the key landmarks in the Isle of Man is the Laxey Wheel. Set upon the hills near the village Laxey rests a giant. The 'Lady Isabella' is named after former Lieutenant Governor Hope's wife, and is also known as the Laxey Wheel. Built in 1854 by Robert Casement, a Laxey native and talented engineer, the Laxey Wheel remains the largest working waterwheel in the world. The wheel has a diameter of 72 feet and a circumference of 227 feet. It was used to pump 250 gallons of water a minute from the Laxey mines some 200 yards away and 1500 feet below ground. The mines employed over 600 miners at its peak – producing lead, copper, silver and zinc until the mines closed in 1929. In 1965, the government bought the wheel and site. Restoration occurred and in 1989 it was put under the control of Manx National Heritage. Tourists had long come to see the wheel, even when the mines were still in use, and they continue to come to this day. The landmark sports an unfortunate livery of red, black and white, making it resemble a Nazi monument. Flags bearing the Legs of Man (red background, white circle with black symbol) also resemble, in passing, the Swastika – unfortunate, since both originated from the ancient symbol of the sun (the sun wheel is a symbol in Sanskrit). Critically, the Legs of Man rotate clockwise, radiating, rather than absorbing energy as Hitler's flag did. Perhaps a colour change would help – how about pink?

The Isle of Man is an enclave of charming, and harmless, eccentricity. It seems stuck in a 1950s time-warp, with its old-fashioned buses, quaint coppers and slow pace. Luckily, it has been preserved from the worst ravages of the late twentieth century/early twenty-first century, as though protected by Manannan's cloak itself. Manx fishermen to this day say a prayer to the Celtic sea god:

> *Manannan beg Mac y Lir*
> *Little Manannan, son of the sea,*
> *bless our boat and all those in it*
> *going out strong*
> *coming back*
> *with both living and dead aboard.*

On a boat trip around the Calf of Man, the skipper admonished me for whistling – bad luck on a boat, apparently. The island's economy survives from tourism, as a tax haven, and from investment from the film industry – it has provided locations for several films in recent years (e.g. *I Capture the Castle; Waking Ned; Me and Orson Welles*).

The wheels keep on turning on the Isle of Man – and, as a biker myself, I like to wear one of my favourite T-shirts, bought on Man back in 2004, bearing the Legs of Man and the national motto: 'Whichever way your throw me I shall stand.'

Long may Ellen Vannin endure.

Tewkesbury Medieval Festival
11ᵗʰ July

Early on Sunday, I made my weary way (after getting only two hours' sleep the night before) northwards along the Cotswold Edge to the Tewkesbury Medieval Festival, now in its 27th year. I had been meaning to go for a number of years, hearing good things about it – what, I couldn't quite say, but there was a general consensus it was 'a good one'. It had started, in the words of the introduction to this year's programme, as 'an idea thought up over a pint by some of the Companions of the Black Bear' (the local pub).

I raced through the sunshine to be there in time for the opening ceremony performed by druid friends, Elaine and Greywolf. Apparently, they had a countdown for me to arrive. I might have made it if not for the army maidens demanding a parking fee at the entrance, and clumsily dropping my gloves several times in my exhausted haste. I parked up by a mobile home and raced in, across the tilting field and over the little wooden bridge that provides a threshold into the festival's medieval time-warp. They said to meet by the beer tent – typical druids! I saw a suspicious looking circle in the distance and headed towards them. Sure enough, the druids were in a circle outside the Drunken Monk Inn. I arrived and joined them just as they chanted 'And may peace prevail throughout the whole world!' They finished casting the circle with air in the form of Greywolf's flute; fire – with incense; and spring water – scattered before us. In a brief lull, I pulled on my Bardic cloak. Phew – made it! Elaine, clad in a beaded 'Pocahontas' dress, asked people to speak on behalf of whomever they wished to. Immediately, the PA kicked in with a screech, which made everyone laugh. The ceremony was good-humoured, especially with Greywolf's light touch, and such disturbances didn't derail things (indeed the success of any good ceremony is about being fully present in the moment and opening to all). Heartfelt words were said about those fallen at the Battle of Tewkesbury – one of the decisive battles of the War of the Roses – that took place on the site, on 4th May, 1471. Around two thousand five hundred souls met their end that day, on what became known as the Bloody Meadow, aka the 'Main Arena', where the battle would be re-enacted later. Fortunately, the festival was a far more peaceful affair, even though many of the stalls sold armour and weaponry. Strange how so much creativity and culture has thrived off the back of a slaughter. Warfare seems a peculiar thing to celebrate, but for many I imagine it is just a chance to escape from the mundane activity of their daily lives with a bit of dressing up and role-playing. Yet, some take it very seriously – the cost of the costumes and equipment isn't cheap. I wonder what draws people to certain periods. Why do people re-enact? Is it a past life thing? A way of connecting with and honouring ancestors? or a form of OCD (as my friend Jay suggested later when we discussed it over a pint in the Woolpack in Slad, Laurie Lee's local in the Five Valleys near Stroud)? It is easy to mock the likes of the 'Sealed Knutters' (members of the Sealed Knot Civil War re-enactment society, The Sealed Knot). I used to know one in Northampton who was a bona fide eccentric clearly born in the wrong century – a complete obsessive, with leather tankards, Roundhead armour, and bits of metal to hit Royalists with cluttering up his bedsit in a tower block. His great-great (...) grandfather had fought in the battle of Naseby and he still took it personally. But I can see how it gives those who participate a sense of tribe, of community. A reassuring idyll where everyone has a clearly defined role and life is simplified to a village green arcadia, with all your needs met by individuals like the black-smith, the baker, the brewer, etc. It is healthily low-tech yet highly skilled – craftsmanship is highly prized. Things aren't mass-produced but handmade, often bespoke. When I had a chance to wander around the market – rows of stalls offering a wonderful assortment of medieval wares and archaic skills such as alchemy and leech-craft; beautiful things in leather, velvet, clay, ring mail, wood; and more wimples and snoods than you could shake a bladderstick at – I was impressed by the sheer creativity and craft. It also occurred to me that a lot of this is Peak Oil proof and might be a glimpse of how society could be in the future (as imagined by Richard Jefferies in his visionary post-apocalyptic novel, *After London*, published 1885). However, I can imagine such a scenario not being so picturesque and bucolic. Folk lolled about in the sweltering sun (one of the hottest days of the year), enjoying a flagon of cider while watching 'knight combat' or listening to a band of prancing loons in the beer tent. There were a couple of guys with 'pet dragons' on their arms – but these were trumped by a man with a *real* python wrapped around his neck, the ultimate in festival bling, all scales and muscle, which he was letting small children stroke as it devilishly darted out its forked tongue. I had to have a go as well, running my hand lightly over its sinuous length. 'Some pythons can be mean, but he likes people,' the owner reassured. There were lots of panting dogs around, tongues lolling (imagine sweating through your tongue), including several large, shaggy wolf-like varieties. One husky pulled a small boy along in a cart – 'it'll all end in tears,' I said, seeing the strange sight hurtling along. Next thing, the cart jack-knifed on a tussock, throwing the boy out. Fortunately, he wasn't hurt; indeed, seemed to enjoy the experience. Health and Safety appeared marvellously absent from the whole affair, although St John's paramedics were there in force, especially for the final battle, where there services were required after one particularly rough skirmish resulted in an ambulance arriving.

I watched an archery demonstration – just for a chance to lie back on a grassy bank in the sun. Far more impressive was the archery-on-horseback demo later, where Korean-style horsemanship/archery was shown in dramatic fashion by three folk dressed up like Mongols, giving examples of Parthian shots. The grand finale was spectacular – two thousands re-enactors marching onto the field of battle in all their armour and colours, waving their banners, shouting insults at the opposition. The crowds were encouraged to join in with this good-humoured ribbing. I ended up on the Yorkist side – by chance, not choice – so I suddenly found myself a Royalist for the first time in my life. When the King and the Young Pretender finally met for parlez in the middle of the field, there was a certain frisson about the whole thing – enhanced by the commentary from the PA tower. It reminded me, visually, of Arthur and Mordred at the Battle of Camlann – it seems this 'script' has been played out through time. The young will always try to overthrow the old and perhaps that's healthy, as one generation must make way for the next. Yet there is something Darwinian and brutal about how the upstart, eager to prove himself, will try his luck against the established pro with his reputation (like an old stag – the alpha male – with his hinds, having to defend himself against a young rival). The battle slowly got under way – large armies don't move fast: an unwieldy behemoth, once it gets lumbering in one direction, it's almost impossible to stop. The chain of consequences led to the inevitable endgame, the slaughter of Bloody Meadow – men bashing the tin crap out of each other, rather than talking it out (a display of relentless stupidity – all violence is an insult to evolution, to the sacredness of life – as I witnessed in microcosm with my friend later, as we sat on a bench in the churchyard where Laurie Lee is buried, opposite his favourite local, The Woolpack in Slad. A booze-fuelled altercation broke out, complete with screaming girlfriends, shattering the peace of a quiet Cotswold village on a Sunday afternoon). After watching about an hour of the 'carnage', albeit with the Tewkesbury miracle of battlefield resurrection – swathes of arrows darkening the skies, the report of cannon and rifle fire, the shouts of men – I grew weary of it all and decided it was time to leave. It's sad that so much energy and talent is put into recreating death and destruction rather than the arts of peace. I'd had enough; it had been a full-on weekend and I needed to rest, but there was still the ride home, via Stroud, where I met up with my dear friend

Jay, for a heart-to-heart over a pint. We do not need to use our fists. We can be better than that. Jay shouted over to the brawling boozers of Slad: 'Stupid! Stupid!' – there is something Neanderthal about such behaviour. Yet, despite such reflections, it had been a worthwhile endeavour. The medieval festival in Tewkesbury is worth seeing. It makes for a colourful and interesting day out. It certainly brings history alive, which has got to be a good thing (for if we learn from the past there's a chance we don't make the same mistakes). We can take the best of it – the value of craftsmanship, of 'human scale' social structure, of etiquette, of community – and leave the rest.

Dog Days

For the first time in a long while we've been having a decent summer – May and June have been glorious and so were the first two weeks of July. It's hard to do any work when it's like this, as any schoolboy or girl could tell you. The ancient Romans had their own theory about what caused the hot, sultry weather – the 'dog star' Sirius rising just before sunrise, giving its name to the 'Dog Days', which began in July and were believed to be an evil, stagnant time 'when the seas boiled, wine turned sour, dogs grew mad, and all creatures became languid, causing to man burning fevers, hysterics, and phrensies (sic)' (*Brady's Clavis Calendarium*, 1913). Due to the Earth's precession of the equinoxes, Sirius has changed the time of his rising, so we no longer need to appease his rage, as the Romans did, by sacrificing a brown dog to him. Instead, we lounge around in our gardens, on balconies, in parks, taking it easy, as the classic Billie Holliday song declares: 'Summertime and the livin' is easy.' Great Britons mark this time of year with the ritual burning of meat (B-B-Qs); libations (drinking lots of beer, wine, Pimms, etc); songs (e.g. World Cup chants), as well as campfire classics; dancing (at festivals and summer night spots); ceremonial garb (Kiss Me Quick hats; Bermuda shorts; bikinis; 'I've visited such-

and-such and all I got was the lousy T-shirts); tribal paint (again popular in the World Cup); pilgrimages (to the beach or beauty spots); penitent suffering (sun burn; traffic jams; family arguments; dodgy stomachs); and the paying of indulgences (toll bridges; car park fees; entrance fees; overpriced cream teas, etc). The British summer is summed up best of all by that most genteel of events, the summer fête – stalls of kindly donated but unwanted/unsellable rubbish; mediocre events, such as dog shows; inexplicably starting at 2pm; lost children; the inevitable argument, or village drunk. These seem to be destined to be annual offerings to the rain gods – to end with rain lashing down onto soggy, half-finished sandwiches, abandoned deck-chairs, and broken gazebos. They are among the dullest forms of activity known to humankind. Why we persist in doing them remains a mystery unless it is as some kind of ritual appeasement of the calendrical gods. And yet when they come these days, the Dog Days are always welcome. I went to the Paw Pals Picnic just up the hill from my house, at the Claverton Cats and Dogs Home. My friend was playing in support of this worthy animal shelter. The small stage was set up next to one of the several kennels. I got myself a ploughman's and settled down on a plastic garden chair to watch. It was overcast and not exactly heaving with people. The edge of the field was lined with lonely looking stall-holders. Dogs howled and barked in the background – the continual soundtrack of Claverton. Nearby was the steep lane known as Brassknocker Hill, where in the seventies an infamous 'beast' was spotted – alarming walkers. It was described as a hairy ape-like creature. A group of men with what looked like blunderbusses – pictured in the local rag – went on a 'beast hunt'. It turned out to be an escaped llama – not quite Bigfoot, but certainly not what you would expect on a Somerset hillside either. Nothing quite so exciting was going to happen today at the Pawpals Picnic. The only hairy beasts were rather endearing ones, whose eyes I tried not to catch. They all were asking to be taken home with big pleading puppy eyes. It is said that every dog has its day, but it seemed unlikely that some of the mutts would ever get re-housed. Yet, who knows. Some people root for the underdog.

Tolpuddle Martyrs Festival
16th – 18th July

I went to this in the early nineties, when hitching along south coast, sketching portraits to earn a few bob. I met some folks and was offered a lift there, in the spirit of the festival. So what is it about? Every July thousands of people come to Tolpuddle to celebrate trade unionism and to remember the sacrifice made by the six farm workers of the village. The tiny Dorset village has been a place of pilgrimage for trade unionists and socialists ever since the Martyrs came home in triumph. The festival is a popular mix of political discussion and speeches, great music to suit all tastes, entertainment for all the family and the traditional procession of banners, wreath laying and Methodist service. I remember a picnic on a hot summer's day, but little else – I was more interested in the girl I got a lift with, who had very nice legs. There were lots of worthwhile things being discussed and promoted, but it became blurred after a few visits to the Workers Beer Co. marquee. I don't recall much after that. The revolution would have to wait for another year.

Carnival!
Newport Carnival, Isle of Wight
24th July

I am sitting on the war memorial brimming with pansies, over which a small wrought iron spitfire soars, on Newport High Street, waiting for the annual carnival – one of the many that proceed through the towns on the Isle of Wight throughout July and August. It was just after seven in the evening and the temperature was pleasant after a hot day. I had decided, on a whim, to visit the Isle of Wight, which had managed to elude me thus far, although it is probably the easiest of islands that cluster around the British coast to get to for someone from the Midlands (a couple of hours from Bath). I had rung up my biker buddy Nigel from Plymouth in the week and he seemed up for it, so we had rendezvoused at the car ferry terminal in Portsmouth on our respective steeds and off we set for the weekend. He'd gone to get us some chips and a group of lads to my right were occupying themselves while waiting by throwing coins and then stones into the drain opposite, directly in front of Fields Menswear. It looked like it would end in tears, until a big guy to my right growled at them to stop. We'd been told that the carnival was due to come by at 7.30pm. It actually didn't arrive until about 8.30pm being a slow beast. We had seen it go by the end of the street, near where we had parked, but it took an age to get round to us. It felt like an hour burnt from my life – what was I doing here, in this rather prosaic town, on a Saturday night? Surely there was somewhere better to be? In fact, we'd had a great day, waking up to a stunning vista on St Catherine's Point, having wild-camped at Blackgang Chine, which made us feel like a couple of smugglers. After a fry up, we had taken a bimble up the hill to the impressive St Catherine's Oratory, known locally as the Pepperpot (nearby is the Salt-cellar, an unfinished church now housing a telecommunications mast). Built in 1328, the Oratory, which resembled a stone rocket (like the ones once tested on the Downs by the MOD), was built by a repentant lord. It served as a beacon and a chapel for souls lost at sea. We huddled into the narrow tower and did an impromptu Awen, which felt like a psychic shower – both for us and the place. Afterwards, we had mosied into Shanklin where we ensconced on the beach, enjoying the sun while licking ice-creams. I had taken a walk up into the old village to connect with the spirit of Keats, who had stayed there in 1819. Carrying along the coast, we had a pint of refreshing outside the King Lud on Ryde Esplanade before heading to Newport. While waiting for the carnival, we visited Carisbrooke

Castle, which we were both impressed by, as was Keats: 'I have not seen many specimens of Ruins – I don't think however I shall see one to surpass Carisbrooke Castle.' Opposite here, on Bowcombe Downs overlooking the ruins, the poet had written the lines 'a thing of beauty is a joy forever', which I pondered on. After such a picturesque day, it was quite a comedown to be sitting on the High Street of this blue collar town, waiting for a small carnival – but hey, when in Rome...

Nigel returned with sustenance (well, stodge) and we tucked in. Then folk started to move to the end of the road – it turned out that the route had been changed at the last minute and we were sitting in the wrong place! Everyone seemed to take this with good humour and the atmosphere was convivial. The longer we waited, the more people took to entertaining themselves. But it wasn't drunken; the crowd consisted of mainly families. We stood on the steps of the impressive Queen Victoria monument, with its muscular lions and formidable goddesses. The crowds lined the street. A couple of pushbike PCs kept an eye on everything. A guy rode down on his bike and got everyone's attention. Finally, I could see blue flashing lights reflected in a shop window; the fire engine appeared, which was heading the parade. The marching bands could be heard, booming along. The Salvation Army stopped and did a couple of numbers, marching in formation. I puzzled over why anyone would want to join such an outfit – I suppose it's all about belonging. A carnival is a great leveller. Everyone has a chance to participate. Each town has a carnival queen, with her respective 'handmaidens' – each on their particular float. Some are surreal and some slightly sinister; some simply kitsch. More marching bands followed, then some fabulous dancing nuns – a phalanx of them, doing a 'Sister Act' routine. Things livened up. This was more like it. The costumes got more exotic – real carnival confections – strange animal-human hybrids, angels. This was grassroots creativity. Democratic. Everyone can shine. It was so simple

– the cavalcade of life – but it works. Despite the wait, it was a pleasant way to pass an hour or two. It was all very mild-mannered – not the Bacchanalia of other carnivals around the world. It was hardly Rio! I suppose it was emblematic of our English reserve. Slightly embarrassed exhibitionism – as though the participants had suddenly found themselves in costume by mistake, like as in one of those classic anxiety dreams. They shuffled about half-heartedly (apart from the Terpsichorean nuns). Still, it was pleasant fun. But as soon as the parade had past, that was it. The crowds dispersed. There was no atmosphere. I thought back to other carnivals I had been to. St Pauls, in Bristol, which was an exuberant sensory bombardment – the booming sound systems, the crush of people, a pungent aroma in the air, the smells of stalls selling jerk chicken, curried goat, fried banana, ginger beer, cans of Red Stripe, whistles, women dancing friskily in colourful costumes, men in pristine singlets, shell suits, bling – a heady sexual energy. And Notting Hill was like this but on an even larger scale – vast, virtually impossible to move – one sluggish mass of people. Making it there one year by myself I ended up dancing with a lovely local. 'You're beautiful,' she said. I smiled a little shyly and replied: 'So are you!' It is the cross-cultural fusion that can occur at carnivals which makes them so colourful. White working class culture is perhaps too anaemic to create something heady enough. I remember the Northampton Carnival when growing up, which was always a bit under-whelming, although more exciting when you're young, throwing pennies at the floats. The Bridgwater Carnival is well known, touring Somerset in, for some inexplicable reason, the depths of winter. I saw it one year in Glastonbury on a cold November night. It was hard work, standing around, trying to keep warm, although the floats were dazzling, with their numerous light bulbs and gaudy costumes. Some were very impressive, like a load of vampires on the 'Goth' float. I guess it brings some light and cheer into the dark nights – like the Blackpool illuminations

- a very Anglo-Saxon diwali. The Carnival groups work on their floats all year round; it provides a community focus and raises money for good causes. The carnival culture is one of the most inclusive and popular in the country. A local carnival – with all the various community groups parading along – provides a narrative for that place, in a visual linear fashion, like a moving Bayeaux Tapestry. It is the pageant of the life of which we are all a part, with our role to play. It lets everyone shine – the local distinctiveness to be praised, its genetic stock (in the Carnival Queen; its generational regiments) appraised, and grassroots creativity celebrated.

First Fruits Full Moon Party
26th July
Every year on Twelfth Night I hold a small wassail in my back garden to bless my fruit trees and to sow the seed of dreams for the coming year; I ask people to visualise what they wish to manifest as ripening fruit, working with the tide of growth. So it seems only right to give thanks when those actual fruit are ready. The apples still have a month to go but my plums were ripe and so I decided to hold a First Fruits Full Moon Party. I knew it was going to be low-key affair – as fitting the gentle start of a new cycle (the beginning of harvest, in a similar way to how Imbolc marks the first inklings of spring) – but it turned out to be even smaller than anticipated. With many friends away, we only had four in the end – two men, two women – but this was just enough to make it seem worth doing. My house guest, Karola Mueller, and I prepared food. I got the fire going. We ate and then gathered around it to share poems, songs and stories. Ola (as Karola likes to be called) fashioned for us garlands of ivy, which made us look like the fairies from *A Midsummer Night's Dream*. We made merry and whiled away a pleasant evening. It wasn't especially 'sacred' – it didn't feel appropriate to do some full-blown ceremony – but it was enough to mark the start of the

harvest and share some of its fruits. Louder, livelier harvest celebrations will follow – it seems wiser to go wilder after the harvest is home, not before. There is much work to be done to 'gather it in' – I think of the projects I need to complete, deadlines to meet, the preparations I need to make before the new season and term starts. I have to 'put my house in order'. Yet, at the same time, there feels a languid easing off at this time of year. You can feel the Earth starting to breathe a sigh of relief. On the ebb tide of summer we can coast. Savouring the golden days and lengthening shadows, the heavy fecundity and sense of fulfilment I begin to feel the need to retreat and rekindle – burnt out from my year's teaching and life's wildfires.

Smooring the Hearth
An important part of turning the wheel is knowing when to stop, when to turn inward, to nourish and nurture oneself. At times, life demands everything from us; we have no time or energy to call our own; our days are crammed with too many things to do; a thousand things clamour for our attention; the world insists we pay attention to it, like some noisy infant. At such times we can step up to the mark and truly shine. But we need to balance this outward spiral – essential, healthy – with the inward, with what I call 'smooring the hearth', when we bank down our fire to ensure it doesn't blow out, as we take some much needed rest. Winter for me is the natural time to do this, although my longed for hibernation is rarely possibly until the din of Christmas and New Year have died down. However, at certain times in the year, it is also essential to smoor the hearth, to avoid burn-out. After the academic year finishes I definitely need time to recuperate; mountains of papers have been marked and my head feels like it is finally my own again. I try to make the most of the summer, capitalising on the (hopefully) good weather and abundance of creativity on offer – the plethora of events, festivals, gatherings and so forth. However, towards the end of the summer I feel the

need to turn inward, to go on retreat. This normally happens in early September – a final, precious hiatus before the wheel of the academic year grinds into life once again. I have organised week-long 'Bardic retreats' on Bardsey Island, off the Llyn Peninsula; last September, I went to Iona with my friend, Anthony. But before then I undertook a mini-retreat by myself to a 'place of truth', as my fellow poet, Jay Ramsay, called it, down in the westerly most corner of Somerset. Hidden away in a wooded fold of the Somerset coast-line, just along from Porlock Weir, Culbone is the smallest complete parish church in England. There is a small cabin one can stay in, by private arrangement, and this is where I headed last June/July, in need of some seclusion.

Here are my field notes:
Arrived at Culbone – raw and ragged after a precipitous descent down the track – a test of nerve! – but more from the life which has worn me out. I am in sore need of this retreat, away from the madding crowd. At last! Three days at the Exmoor Camp and three days here by myself – a good balance. The inner and outer spiral.

Culbone is famously inaccessible (the coastal path is your best bet), nestled four hundred feet up in a wooded coombe above the wild north coast of Exmoor. Hidden in the deep folds of a plunging valley, it feels removed from the world; yet it has been, at times, a leper colony, an open prison, a religious community, and now a popular place for passing ramblers. There is evidence of human activity over six thousand years: its ancient name was Kitnor (from Anglo-Saxon for cave 'cyta' and 'ore', sea shore, suggesting what might have been the nodal point that originally drew people here – the summer rising sun floods into the vale, as if for it alone). The church is a mixture of styles from different centuries and cultures – Saxon being the earliest. Its name derives from a Welsh saint, St Beuno, (pronounced 'Buy-no'), born in the late sixth century, died 642; Kil Beun, the chapel of Beuno, became eventually Culbone. Beuno, said to be the most important Welsh saint after St David, follows in a long line of Celtic saints who graced the West of England, leaving their names as relics. The church is still used, with fortnightly services, and an atmosphere of deep peace pervades the place.

Drinking my first cuppa, I read some of *The Book of Peace* (a favourite poetry anthology I had brought with me) and instantly related to the poem, *To Mr Izaak Walton*:

How calm and quiet a delight
it is alone
to read, meditate and write,
By none offended, nor offending none.
To walk, ride, sit or sleep at one's own ease,
And pleasing a man's self, none other to displease.

A three hour jaunt to get food – on the hottest day of the year; nothing here you can take for granted: gas lights, a compost loo, a narrow bed and a simple stove – the basics. All you need really. I guessed staying here for long would become a bit grim – hand baths and hand washing. After a while, one would murder for a hot bath and a washing machine, the odd movie, a cold beer. Yet for now, I have all I need and I am content. Complete unto myself. Not quite Thoreau, but it'll do.

Porlock always waits – the world always waits. I think about the infamous 'man from Porlock', who so inconveniently inter-rupted ST Coleridge while he was working on his poem 'Kubla Khan' (at Ash Farm, close by); he is a symbol for the world itself; the jealous world of man and matter, always wanting its pound of flesh, banging on your door, never leaving you alone, always clawing for more, clambering for attention, creating patterns of interference to stop the flow — the signal from the Otherworld; the way out; to a transcendent reality far richer, far real, than this one.

I was inspired to write about the infamous visitor. I settled outside on the little porch, surrounded by silence and seclusion. As I put pen to paper, I suddenly had callers: Barrie (the owner and steward here) and a neighbour had to brush right by humble yard, where I sat in the sun, to gain access to the little foot-bridge by my cabin, making measurements, talking – this was the only time over the three days I had 'visitors'! Back and forth they went, threatening to break my reverie, but I couldn't help but smile – I had my own men from Porlock!

In the churchyard there's a seat in the top corner dedicated to the Earl of Lovelace. It is known as the Lovelace Seat and has been noted for its powerful energy and inspiring properties. The inscription runs thus:

Let all who rest here give glory to God and have in remembrance one who loved this place – Ralph, 11th Earl of Lovelace and XIIIth Lord Wentworth, Born July 2nd 1839 , died August 1906.

The trickling ribbons of the stream, the gentle cooing of a wood pigeon. No other noise. Secluded silence. Not a soul in sight. Here at St Beuno's Cell an underground river from Wales feeds the spring (the only water source) confirming Coleridge's vision: '...where Alph, the sacred river ran through caverns measureless to man, down to a sunless sea.' Pure clear source – Celtic under-currents, bubbling up in unlikely places... secret outposts of Awen.

On the Lovelace Seat, I ponder on the infinitesimal interlace-ments of love; I think of my friends, close friends, dear friends and how they enrich me. How I feel connected to them here – Jay (who introduced me to this place); Anthony (who is a fellow literary pilgrim); and our mutual friend Mary (whose tragic death earlier in the summer has left us reeling). Humans are so delicate, so complex, so astounding – each one is a small miracle and should be honoured as such, yet we seldom do ourselves credit. We seldom live up to the grace given us.

As I sat in the Lovelace Seat I felt elevated, not just from the marvellous prospect over Culbone and its small churchyard, but within. My soul seemed to rise up like the yew tree I face – crown level – from deep roots, roots it is said grow through the mouths of the dead, and I imagine I shall speak to the ancestors if I stay here long enough...

Washing out my clothes in the stream (flowing with water from a Welsh source), I have never been happier. I had a blissfully peaceful night, writing and reading Joan Cooper's wise words; my Book of Peace; Richard Jefferies. Daisy, Barrie's black-and-white tabby, came a-visiting late last night. About 11pm, deep in my solitude, I saw something pushing against my door – I called out. No reply. So, nervously, I opened it and there she was! She sidled in and had a sniff around then came and sat on my lap, fussed about a lot then finally settled down – falling asleep between my legs. It was pleasant having such an agreeable easy-to-please companion. Cats have a knack of picking up energies, of finding comfort zones, of bringing healing. It was a shame I had to chuck her out when I went to bed, but I couldn't have her waking me up in the middle of the night wanting to go out. No cat-flaps here. This morning, I awoke to the sound of birdsong and the stream after a profound night's sleep. Very peaceful. Made myself some breakfast, listening to some classical music on my little radio. Serenity.

I feel I would be happy living somewhere like here – at least for the summer months. It's nearly perfect – all that's missing is a place for a real fire and a place to watch the sunset (although I discovered one up the hill later). Other luxuries would be electricity for a laptop, a broadband connection – although it's nice to be off the grid – and a hot shower. The latter could be rigged up easily enough – solar-powered, fed by the stream. A nearer shop for provisions would be handy, but it's the isolation which makes this place so special.

Being here, in this pared down place, made me consider the essentials of my life:

- Creativity – *to write, perform, publish.*
- Nature – *woods, water, sun, stars. The elements. Landscape and wildlife.*
- Freedom – *ride-outs, camping, visiting new places, diverse experiences.*
- Friends – *kindred spirits, a cultural scene, gatherings, community.*
- Spirit – *sacred places/sacred time, connection with the Awen, festivals.*

I was asleep in the churchyard on the Lovelace Seat, until disturbed by a trio of lady walkers, congratulating each other on reaching the church. 'Well done! Well done!' I read some of *The Messages of Sacred Places* then realised I hadn't brought my glasses or any water along (feeling rather spaced out after my siesta). I get up to leave. Passing the two sitting on the stone cross, I bid them a good afternoon. Another seems to be trying to cut off my escape route. 'Are you local?' she calls after me. 'Well,' I hesitantly reply, 'for a while.'

Hildegard of Bingen coined a term: *viriditas*, greening power, which seems to sum up the 'Culbone Effect'. She embodies its voice: '*I am that supreme and fiery force that sends forth all sparks of life.*' This *viriditas* seems akin to Dylan Thomas' green fuse: '*the force that through the green fuse drives the flower.*'

One can feel this power, this viriditas, so lucidly here. It is incredibly comforting – it is like being in the arms of a parent. I feel so languid, overcome with weariness, on the verge of tears or exhortations of joy; a raw place; a vulnerable place – or rather a place in which to be vulnerable. It provides the shell so we can come out of ours. DH Lawrence wrote in an essay on the spirit of place: '[E]very great locality has its own pure daimon, and is conveyed at last into perfected life.' Here the genius loci feels hidden, feminine – rivulets of water, deep valleys dripping with lush foliage, silent, soothing, safe. A green womb. The embrace of the goddess. Mother Culbone.

I walked up to the top of the track – to check if I could make it out! The way down was most precipitous and the uncertainty of whether my bike, laden with me and my kit, could get back up the hill has been hanging over me a little since I've been here. This is one of those places that – once you're in, you're in! It's an escape from the world – returning takes concerted effort, a conscious act of will. It's easy to stay – comforted, cocooned. Why would one want to return to the madness? Yet one must – until it is time to retreat for good. But I must take my 'vision' back to the tribe, my renewed enthusiasm and clarity. My rekindled strength and sense of purpose. Though, looking over the ageless landscape, the mighty coast of Exmoor, all else seems vain ambition. Efforts to achieve recognition, critical acclaim, success – so many dandelions scattered on the breeze. Yet, I believe in my stories, my ideas, my Awen and want to share it, share the beauty. This dramatic Exmoor coast, plummeting in deep green folds down to the sea, dotted with content sheep, so Arcadian – one can see how it inspired Coleridge with lofty, noble thoughts, visions of grandeur, immortal words. It's the stuff of a Caspar David Friedrich painting. Cue Romantic pose!

I nearly went into Lynmouth, but was glad I didn't – it would have broken the spell. Walking up onto the hill did the trick. It's good to get a perspective – to see a horizon. I'd been in the valley for three days and was starting to develop early symptoms of cabin fever. I hate feeling trapped, cooped up.

On the way back, I noticed a lamb caught on the wrong side of the fence. I opened up the five bar gate and let it through. It was reunited with its mother, and I felt a shepherd-like satisfaction!

Time to Leave

And yet his very silence proved
How much he valued what he loved.
There peered from his hazed, hazel eyes
A self in solitude made wise;
As if within the heart may be
All the soul needs for company:
And, having that in safety there,
finds its reflection everywhere.
A Recluse, Walter de la Mare

May I be a 'self in solitude made wise' and may I carry this peace with me – take it back into the world, and not lose my centre. May I always carry myself with grace and act with wisdom – look with the heart, not with the head. Respond with love, not ego. May Culbone's blessing stay with me.

I woke up at dawn to see the sunrise – watched its virgin light flood the vale – and realised its benediction may have been the original prompt for early man to linger here, to consider it a sacred place. Standing there, a man in a forest, beholding the new sun, I felt ... primal. I felt connected to its earliest inhabitants, and probably looked not dissimilar in my shaggy state, all stubble and grubby clothes!

I locked the cabin, loaded up the bike and paid a final visit to the church then sat one last time in the Lovelace Seat – paying my respects to the man on his birthday. I wrote my impressions in the church visitor's book and left, negotiated the steep hill out of the woods, taking it real slow on the gravel and ruts. I startled a deer, who bolted across the track in front of me, startling me, and for a brief moment, still half asleep, I thought it was some kind of dryad, one of Jefferies' 'fern maidens'. I kept going, revved it up the really steep bit and was clear – relief! I stopped to close the gate and enjoyed the view at dawn over the wooded dell that had been my home for the last three days, before hitting the road back home, ready to rekindle my fire.

August

Lammas – Avebury Champion
1st August

For the last ten years, a group of friends have gathered at Avebury at the time of Lammas, the Saxon festival celebrating the start of the harvest, also known as Lughnasadh – the funeral games of the Celtic sun god Lugh. Keeping to the spirit of the festival, they have held their own games to find the Avebury Champion. Although serious in intent, they are run with light-hearted good humour. Having myself been involved in the Lammas Games – a small festival set up by The Druid Network, which culminated in the Bardic contest for the Spear of Lugh, over which I presided – I was intrigued to see how these were run, and so I headed down there on Saturday morning from Worcestershire. I had paid a flying visit to the Resurgence Readers' Summer Camp, where I helped my friend and fellow poet Jay Ramsay run a poetry workshop and performance the day before. The event was held at the fabulous eco-resource, Green and Away, 'Europe's only tented conference centre'. The demographic there – nice middle class greens – couldn't have been more different from the raggle taggle crowd that converged on the stones that day, to participate in the midday ceremony, run by the Gorsedd of Bards of Caer Abiri: a large public ceremony with perhaps an over-emphasis on showbiz, media relations and point scoring than true magic. Nevertheless, the god and goddess were duly honoured and the start of the harvest marked; the inevitable hand-fasting took place. From the henge, I watched another wedding party dressed in Scottish Highland attire cross the road that runs through the stones and make their way, laden with bouquets, swords and the like, to the 'altar stone' used by pagan groups. Although they looked like a typical 'catalogue' wedding, albeit of the tartan variety, they were clearly using the circle as a sacred space, and not just a backdrop for wedding photos. The beauty of Avebury is that it can accommodate all. I was glad to sit on the hill in the sunshine with my Dutch friend Eva and eat some lunch while we waited for the games to begin (I had rushed to the contest ground, the 'Avebury end of the Avenue', for 2.30pm – the start time on the poster – only to find no one there). Typically, it was running on 'Druid time', which seems merely an excuse for poor time-keeping – the opposite of what a Druid should be capable of, if observant of the cycles of the sun, moon and stars. However, I wasn't expecting anything else from previous experience. But, to be fair, it was hard to rush around on such a muggy summer's day; just because I had been rushing about like the white rabbit on my bike, I shouldn't expect anyone else to be!

We went over to the Avenue, where a small crowd had gathered and slowly, liked a stoned sloth, things got under way. In anticipation of the event, I read some of the information about the Games on a display board, which explained things as follows:

The competition to decide the Avebury Lammas Champion is meant to be tough and will test candidates strength, stamina and skill so that the prize is one that is hard one [sic] and worthy of honour. The winner will have proven themselves to be a true warrior in the manner of the old way.

The prizors had to commit to four events – a 2.5 mile run along the Avenue; wrestling; stick fighting; hammer throwing; test of agility and endurance ('prizors will balance on one leg whilst 'the tribe' throw things at them. Points awarded for the three remain standing longest'). They were entitled to play the 'John Barleycorn' card should they wish to drop one event. Not surprisingly, all dropped out of the run, which came at the end, to avoid prizors being too out of breath for the other tests! The games were presided over by Steve the Stag – so-called because he has a penchant for wearing a set of antlers on his head. The rules state: 'the Avebury Stag has the final word and judgement on all matters', with the caveat comically underlined. 'These rules may change subject to the whim of the stag'. Despite the Pythoneseque rules, the games were well-managed, with health and safety in mind. Children's games were run side-by-side, as well as other activities for the kids. The audience consisted mainly of families with young children – the group of friends who had been meeting for the last decade, informally. There was much ribbing, but it was all good natured.

The contestants consisted of: Steve Stag; Leon Archmage of the Multiverse; Drac the Invincible; Chuck the Mighty; Oiley the Very Lazy (who dropped all events); Dennis the Menace; and Gary the Undefeated. Things finally got under way around 4ish – an hour and half late. I reclined amid the stubble of the Avenue, chatting to my friend Eva over an ice-cream, when we could get a word in between the boasts of Jim the druid 'rock star', who, if there was an Olympic sport in bragging, would win the gold medal. Occasionally, we got caught in the friendly fire of water-bombs or straw fights.

The first heat was the hammer-throwing. Prizors had to knock a bucket off of a pole with a mallet. Watching this below Waden Hill (apparently named after Woden/Odin) was quite something, even if the men didn't quite match up to Thor. There was the occasional cheer or jeer – all in good fun – as things progressed and the points were notched up, with plenty of stops for refreshments. The adrenalin got going for the wrestling and the stick-fighting, after which wounds were tended to. The 'test of agility and endurance' quickly degenerated into a water/straw/anything you could lay your hands on fight. A bucket was slam-dunked onto Steve the Stag's head when he refused to accept defeat (thanks to a sneaky push from an opponent). Everyone lunched out from the run, as the winner (a foregone conclusion) and the champion, Leon, was announced, and crowned by a 'maiden'. He held the Mallet of Victory aloft and tried to look manly. 'May the enemies of Avebury be smote down and destroyed!' he challenged, with an almost macho tone. Steve the Stag declared the games over for another year and we repaired to the Red Lion, where an informal Lammas celebration was happening – a colourful collection of hippies, druids, warlocks, corn-maidens, bikers, minstrels, bemused tourists and locals communing with John Barleycorn. Beneath floppy fringes and hats guitars were strummed. A kid banged a drum by my ear – I turned round to say something (after fifteen minutes it was getting wearying) only to discover it was a bloke with a very basic sense of rhythm. Bumping into biker buddy Nigel, we ordered chips, cheesy garlic bread and ale and 'grounded ourselves'. Later, Nigel joined us as we camped by Silbury Hill. We shared some mead and nibbles, as we huddled around our symbolic hearth – an instant barbecue raised off the ground by my frying pan.

For hundreds of years, feasts were held by Silbury Hill around the time of Lammas. We continued the tradition in our own low key way. We held a small ceremony, holding hands in the dark and expressing what Lammas meant to us. After, I did a dodgy rendition of the British ballad, Sir *John Barleycorn*, and Eva sang a beautiful song in Spanish by an Argentine woman. When the waning moon rose by Silbury, we stood in silence to greet it. I was overwhelmed with fatigue after a tiring couple of days... weeks... months... years... but it felt like I had marked Lammas appropriately. Even with my borrowed airbed half-deflating – mine had died on me the night before – I slept like a log (and probably snored like a dog).

In the morning, we woke to the magnificent sight of Silbury at Lammas; alas, there were not the right conditions to witness the Silbury Glory, visible around Beltane and Lammas, when the rising sun casts an aurora around the hill's shadow as it stretches across the dew-soaked fields. Nevertheless, it was very special to see such an awesome harvest hill at such a time. After breakfast, we started to pack up the tents when an interesting looking couple walked up to the viewpoint. They looked suspiciously pagan and so I greeted them with 'Happy Lammas!' This failed to illicit a response, and so I tried 'Happy Lughnasadh!' This didn't work either, so I tried a simple good morning. They responded with Germanic accents. It turned out they were from Austria, and were visiting British and Irish sacred sites. Eva spoke some German and was able to engage them in a more fluent conversation. It was heartening to meet some fellow pilgrims – and ones that had come a long way, from the cauldron of Celtic culture in fact. We ended up swapping details, suggestions of places to visit, and being invited over to their homeland. And so the wheel turns.

Awen in the Abbey
Bardic Picnic, Northampton, 2nd August 2009
In June 2007, I took part in a small event organised by John Morrissey to declare the Bardic Chair of Northampton. Moving back to the town with his wife from Portland, Oregon, he managed to secure a little bit of funding and planned a cluster of community arts events under the banner of the WOW! Festival. It began in a modest way, as his initial outlined thus:

A community mandala will be laid in the outer gardens (to centre the picnic and declaration) from midday, the abbey courtyard and FODA cafe will close at 6.00, there will be gongs and drums till 6.30. Then your storytelling followed by the declaration till about 8.30.

It was a very small event. I recall about a dozen of us gathering by a tree I called the 'heart tree' as a child, because of a shape of one of its cut-off limbs. It was very 'gentle'. A couple of friends were there, Rob and Carrie, although when I went to do my set, they upped and left (they had young children and it had been 'a long day' they said). We joined hands, formed a circle and I got people to raise the Awen, inviting it into Northampton, to inspire budding Bards, to bless the Bardic Chair. We let off some balloons. As we looked up, a hot air balloon passed right over head. We took this as a good omen.

From this humble beginning, the following year, the event took place in a nearby field (as the council didn't turn up to let them into the grounds of Delapre Abbey). I was invited up to be the judge but nobody came forward to enter (shoe town got cold feet). The attendance was low and it seemed a bit desperate. The highlight was when a Lancaster bomber rumbled overhead – on a flyby to a nearby History Festival. The event ended in a painful fashion, with feral children allowed to bawl into the stage mics any pop song they could half-remember. It felt like the Bardic Picnic was dead in the water. But in 2009 things finally came together...

This was the third year I was invited up for the Bardic Picnic at Delapre Abbey (a very special place for me, since going there pretty much every day as a child with my dog) and the first year it was a real success. After the groundwork of previous years, my old home town finally 'got' the notion of the Bardic Picnic and it was a great day, thanks to the hard work of the Three Jays, as I call them: Justin, Jimtom and John – and all the crew behind the scenes. I was asked to judge the contest again. This year half a dozen had put their names forward. I rode up on the Saturday afternoon, waiting for the rain to pass, but it stayed with me most of the way there, so the usual run over the Cotswolds wasn't as much fun. I was told that the crew were gathering there around 4pm – I got there about 7pm and things were still very 'in utero'. I ended up helping putting the marquee up with a good crew of about twenty volunteers. It was great seeing people working together in Northampton. Justin and Jimtom had been running a monthly event called Raising the Awen, and this had built up a groundswell of support and performers. Finally, the marquee up, the promised BBQ got going (when the forgotten grill had been collected), beers were bought and we could start to relax. It was nice to hang out with my old friends and new there on the eve of the event, and to be able to stay over at the 'Green Abbey', as I called it in a poem of mine, which was a real highlight.

The next morning, after waking up in a sunny glade to the strains of a harp (Justin in Alan a Dale mode), I popped over to my Mum's to freshen up and have some breakfast (hooray for mums!), before returning to rehearse in the glade. I was ready to start at midday (I had arranged an early slot) but unfortunately the festival wasn't. The scene before was looking pretty desperate. Stages and stalls were half-up. A broken white gazebo (the backstage) blew across the site, rolling towards my friend's car until I stopped it, and it was all looking like it was going to be disaster – but finally it came together and people started to arrive. Two hours later than announced, the Bardic Picnic commenced, and I went on after the Jays announced the start.

I started my set with my old green man poem, *One with the Land*, connecting it to the theme of the festival: 'Northampton, my home in the heart of England.' Then, warmed up, I recited my epic praise-song to Albion, *Dragon Dance*. I finished with my version of the Taliesin story, which seemed apt for a Bardic contest. After this, I was able to relax; I grabbed my complimentary veggie burger and beer from the bar tent and hooked up with my fellow judges, Caroline Saunders and Jimtom, both old friends. The contest was in three parts: a general performance; statement of intent; Northampton piece. Between these were some great bands and other performers including the psychedelic prophet, the 'Shaman of the North'. On the open mic stage, hosted by Ripping Pages (a Northamptonshire writers group who run a monthly spoken word event), other spoken word performers got a chance to do their thing. The day was blessed with glorious sunshine and there was a lovely atmosphere as family and friends picnicked and enjoyed the Bardic enter-tainment – this is what Bardism is, for my money: the arts acces-sible for all. Everybody there could see the Bardic Tradition in action – celebrating the cultural biodiversity of the community in an engaging way.

We had to go and deliberate, then make the announcement. I was asked to speak on behalf of the judges and comment on each participant's performance, before finally declaring the winner: a 'blow in' from Wolverhampton, Donna, who won the final heat with her great praise song to Northampton, *Finding my feet in Shoe-town*.

Afterwards, there was a great band, which got everyone dancing. Then… it was over, officially. People helped tidy up the site. The core crew stayed on site, looking after the marquee and PA. Folk stayed around chatting, glowing in the buzz of a good event. Finally, some veggie chilli was warmed up and we chilled out, enjoying the dusk at Delapre with a glass of wine. An Asian doctor called Azam strayed upon the event by accident and stayed behind, sharing our supper. It turned out he was a singer and I encouraged him to sing for us, and so we ended up having a comic version of X Factor, with folk impersonating the different judges. I ended up being Piers Morgan! Azam said he had been waiting for this for twenty years and had a truly great day. This sums up the Bardic way – it's for everyone. We all should be able to express ourselves and be heard. Three cheers to the Three Jays, the new Bard and to next year's Bardic Picnic.

Bardic Picnic
1st August 2010
After riding up from Avebury, I arrived at the Abbey – the spiritual heartland of my childhood – at midday and could see things were being set up, so I roared onto the site and passed, unwittingly, in front of the main stage, only to discover somebody was on! Amazingly, they had started on time, despite

the setting up still taking place. I guiltily parked up by my friends' van and hugged my old friend Justin, one of the three main organisers. I was down for a slot at 3.30pm, although I wasn't holding out much hope for it to be on time. In the meanwhile, I chilled out – a cup of tea was the priority after a longish ride up from Avebury that morning. I put up my tent, dumped my stuff, got a coffee and collapsed on the lawn, listening to the nice music coming from the main stage (Greg Cave and the Village Hall Band). I felt the sun on my face and felt glad to be still. It had been a tiring couple of days and my back was aching from unreliable airbeds.

I got changed into my Bardic costume – loose, light clothing a relief after wearing my biker leathers – and put out a few of my books on a cloth next to the mandala and tarot reading. More picnickers were starting to arrive and the place was filling up. The organisers were clearly stressed – and not really present when you tried to engage them in conversation (heads clearly full of a million and one things) – but it was looking promising. The relaxed ambience was a result of a lot of hard work though – months of planning, fundraising, community liaising, calling in favours, negotiating egos and old grudges, etc.

My sister turned up with her baby daughter, Kerry, in a buggy, and a picnic, which was most welcome. I needed something inside of me before I went on. The former Bard, Donna Scott, did a poem. There was a round of contestants – five had stepped up to the mark. And then I was on. The theme of this year's contest was 'Global Tree with Local Roots', and so I did one international story, and one from the town – *The Garden of Irem*, from Yemen; and *The Legend of Ragener* from Hamtun, Saxon Northampton. I spoke of how special it was to be there, in the place I went every day as a boy, with my Welsh Border Collie, Ben – the place it all started for me. It was strange to see so many people gathered in my sacred soul place. A private dream had become a public one. Suddenly, I was no longer alone – a lonely boy daydreaming in a garden...

After my set, I cracked open a beer – finally able to chill out. I caught up with my sister and old friends. This is the main attraction of such an event. It has become something of an annual reunion, our own 'Cropredy' – Fairport Convention's long-running get together, which takes place a week or so later just down the road. There was some fine music – by the likes of The Morrows, who played fey tunes on harp and guitar; the rock-twins, Enki; and the popular Celtic Rasta, who ended the evening with their dancable reggae. Capel Spence ran his inclusive and supportive Ripping Pages open mic stage in the beer marquee. Children ran amok. Adults got merry. After the final band, there was a lovely informal session by the Bardic Banqueting tent – some of the performers played covers of The Doors, Jefferson Airplane, The Beatles, The Stones... even one of my old ones, 'Gypsy Nation', courtesy of Jimtom, howling into the night. It felt like a good tribal spirit – a vibe as good as you'd get at any decent festival. Gratefully, I went to crash in my tent – falling asleep to the sounds of the singing drifting over.

In the morning, I packed up my tent and said my farewells, hitting the road once again. I left with a warm glow in my heart, kindled by my old friends and family, and the success of the event. Alas, the future of the Bardic Picnic looks uncertain, with John going off to Oxford to study and Jimtom planning to buy some land in Eastern Europe to set up a collective, but I hope it continues – now it seems to have become established. A new Bard was awarded the Chair – a young man who was a popular choice with the crowd – and so a tradition is born. Others might have read out a poem for the first time in the Ripping Pages tent and felt inspired to enter next time. A beautiful framework was provided for people's creativity to shine. Northampton has talent!

Shire Horses at Poulshot

6th August

My friend and fellow poet, Dawn Gorman, mentioned a charming little event that takes place in the small Wiltshire village of Poulshot, just down Caen Hill (with its famous flight of sixteen locks) from Devizes, home of Wadworth Brewery, who use a team of four Shire horses to pull drays of beer and other drinks, delivering them to customers within a two mile radius (admirably carbon-friendly and 'cheaper than diesel', according to the Wadworth rep on hand). Every year, in early August, the horses are taken to Poulshot, given a mug of Wadworth 6X, led along to a field and let off the harness to enjoy a two week holiday. This small event has grown in popularity through mainly word of mouth, because it is not widely publicised, except via the Wadworth website.

I rolled up there on my Legend and was ushered onto the parking field, alongside the burgeoning ranks of vehicles, which would eventually stretch right along the long village green. I could see why Dawn recommended getting there early. We rendezvoused outside the Raven, where a marquee had been erected for a mini-beer festival, including a hog roast. We caught up as the crowds gathered. Soon after, the massive Wadworth show dray team trailer pulled up and the crowds buzzed with anticipation as the horses were unloaded and led to the pub forecourt. Here, they were lined up in a row – the four of them – and each given a mug of 6X. The one nearest clearly didn't like it and wouldn't drink ('you can lead a horse to water...'), but the others slurped it down happily. A lot of photos were taken. The sheer scale of the horses became apparent up close, with children close by, looking on with delight. Up to eighteen hands high, the horses even dwarfed their respective grooms. Their names and ages were Prince (7), Percy (3), Monty (6) and Max (7). All four come from Jim Yates of Duffield, Derbyshire. Their working life lasts as long as they are fit, and they live up to twenty years.

Originating from England, a descendant of the medieval war horse (bred to bear knights in heavy armour), they were later developed to work on farms as draught horses. Friesians and Flanders horses were taken to England by the Dutch and were bred with local specimens. The result was a resistant horse able to work in the land and carry heavy weights. They work in pairs, pulling a dray – the cart carrying up to two tons. Wadworth have used Shire horses to deliver their wares for over a hundred years in the area. Before the arrival of the internal combustion engine, they had more than forty Shires working. With the reality of Peak Oil on the imminent horizon, we might see an increasing number of working horses back on the road. They are a Janus-like symbol, pointing backwards and forwards.

Their thirst 'slaked' (one would imagine that it would take more than a mere pint to do that) the horses were led along the street, getting increasingly frisky (at one point, the rear one kicked backed – fortunately no one was in the way). The crowds followed in Pied Piper fashion. They were lead into a field, stationed in a line as their grooms took off their harnesses. The remarkable thing was, when the first one was free, it didn't bolt straight away – it waited until its comrades were also emancipated, and then they bolted as one, galloping wildly around the field, 'like a boy on a beach', observed one of the elderly spectators. It was a magical moment, which brought a tear to the eye of some of the onlookers. It was hypnotising, watching the horses gallop around the field – pure freedom.

Witnessing sentient beings released from servitude is touching. It makes one consider personal 'prisons' and the small freedoms we enjoy. The whole spectacle is a poignant metaphor for retirement, when we slip the harness of our duties for good. For some, work defines them and they feel at a loose end afterwards. It is common for men to die soon after retirement; so much of their identity and self-worth is wrapped up in their work.

I remember my neighbourhood grocer, Ken. I used his shop on Bathwick Hill for ten years, favouring it over the supermarkets in the area. He offered a valued personal service, always making you feel welcome in his shop. He would ask, in his West Country twang, 'What's for tea today then, hey?' When you brought your items to the till he would comment on them and say, 'You go home and cook that up! That'll do yer!' If you didn't have the right money he would 'put it on tick', and would always get in what you asked for, catering for the idiosyncratic needs of his customers. He was a lifeline for the old peoples' home across the road, always having time for a natter – a real community asset. A certain major supermarket wanted to take over the old car showrooms next door, and he managed to fight them off three years' running, with local petitions and press coverage, but finally they got in – probably with a few backhanders along the line. Ken defiantly remained open, even though it was inevitable he would be forced out of business. It was heartbreaking to see the cruel law of economics deprive him of his customers and, though I still got some items from his store, it was hard not to succumb to the cheaper prices and greater range next door. The last time I went in there, there was just Ken and an old customer propping up the counter. Then the shop closed. Locals held a special farewell BBQ for him. Clocking off from twenty years' service, Ken went to Thailand to visit his brother-in-law. He came back early. The last time I saw him, a few weeks later, he was just leaning against the wall outside his shop, looking at people go into the 'express' supermarket next door (many probably his old customers). I greeted him, asked how he was doing. He was clearly unwell, but I didn't realise how ill he actually was. I shook his hand and said thank you for all he'd done for the community. His son arrived and helped him into the car and drove off. He died of cancer a couple of weeks later, within two months of his shop being forced to close. He had served the community for two decades and had worked into retirement (he was seventy). I am certain that his work kept him going and if he had been able to continue running his shop, he would still be alive. It was his life. Without it, he passed away.

It is good to feel one has a role within society, or at least within one's social group; that one's skills and experience matter; to feel valued, respected; that one can make a contribution, even a difference. Ken made a difference in his community. Now, you can go into the supermarket, use the self-service and not even speak to anyone. The manager is unfriendly and unhelpful; the staff little more than bored automatons. The place is soulless. It has forced two businesses to close (the off license also went bust) so that the little row of shops now looks desolate, with empty units in a row. So much for progress.

I watched the Shires galloping around the field, savouring their freedom. It was a beautiful sight.

We all have our own drays to pull.

And we all need time out.

Satisfied, we returned to the Raven for a pint and a bite to eat. I joked to Dawn that I felt a bit like the Shires – ready to step off the wheel and have a well-earned break.

Rivers Deep, Mountains High
North Wales
9th – 15th August

As my fortieth year drew to an end I journeyed to North Wales for my most intense experience of sacred time yet and, in many ways, it was the culmination of my journey, exploring the way we make and mark the turning of the wheel.

And it was completely out of the blue.

At the beginning of the month, I went to the Resurgence Readers' Summer Camp in Worcestershire, to co-run a poetry workshop/performance with fellow poet, Jay Ramsay. I was on my way to Avebury (via a roundabout route reminiscent of Britain's famous 'drunken roadmakers') and wasn't expecting to stop for long, let alone have an encounter that would radically change my life.

I had zero expectations – not of the event, the venue, or people there (all lovely) but of my participation in it, due to recent devastating disappointments. Yet, to my surprise, I made a connection with a lovely woman called Jenni, who runs eco-psychology workshops on The Work That Reconnects (a system devised by deep ecologist, Joanna Macy). Over dinner, we talked around the communal campfire, and later we danced in The Rising Sunflower canvas tavern to Dragonsfly. This raised the temperature a lot! Afterwards, at my spontaneous suggestion, we went for a midnight skinny dip in the river Teme to cool off. As we stripped off, somebody appeared with a torch, sweeping it down to us and calling out. We felt like we had been caught red-handed by the fun police, but it was just someone looking for their teenage son. And so we plunged in, the dark liquid coolness taking my breath away. We whooped with delight, laughed and splashed about. It felt wonderful – a magical moment. The warm summer night cast its spell. Naked, we held each other in the water. Suddenly, we found ourselves kissing. We made our way to the shore and dried off, returning to huddle up by the fire, joining a group of teenagers. We felt a little adolescent ourselves, heady with the night and the wildness of our swim. We had connected! We wished each other good night, returning to our respective dwellings.

Over breakfast, we were all grins. Before I left, our plans for the next week or two were discussed. Jenni was due to have her annual two week leave, before the new term started. She fancied seeing some mountains and Cae Mabon, Eric Maddern's place by Llanberis, was mentioned; suddenly, we were swept away by the idea of going there together! I had initially planned to go to Ireland for the Puck Fair in Killorglin, but when I realised this was a 'bridge too far' at the time, I considered alternatives, and Snowdonia sounded like an excellent one. And so, swept along by the Awen, we decided to go.

I made my goodbyes – after our all-too-brief time together – and hit the road, heading to Wiltshire. On the way, I tried to make sense of what had happened, and failed! It was the last thing I was expecting, or even wanting, but deep down it was what I *needed* – a chance to heal my heart.

Afterwards, I discovered that it was an auspicious time; we had met initially on Solsbury Hill at the summer solstice, and now we had finally connected on the eve and morning of Lammas (31 July/1 August): Lammas comes from *hlafmaesse* – the Anglo-Saxon word meaning loaf-mass, one of the earliest celebrations of the first harvest of the year. Lammas day used to be a day for foretelling marriages and trying out new partners. Two people would agree to a trial marriage lasting the period of the Lammas fair (usually eleven days) to see if they were really suited for wedlock. At the end of the fair, if they didn't get on, they could part. This seemed uncanny considering what we proposed – a week in deepest Wales with a relative stranger. It would be make or break. By the end of the week we should have a pretty good idea if there was something there, or whether it was just a 'festival fling', something that would vanish in the cold light of mundane life. And so we met in Bristol to confirm things, going on our first 'date' (a meal at the pleasant Thali Cafe in Clifton; a test ride over the suspension bridge; a drink in the Avon Gorge Hotel, with its terrace overlooking Brunel's masterpiece – all lit up and glowing with promise, a bridge into the future) and booked three days in a gorgeous looking 1940s renovated Showman's Caravan at Pistyll Rhaeadr, one of the highest waterfall in England and Wales. Travelling up on my Triumph, we were restricted to one pannier and one small pack each, but somehow we managed to take everything we needed for a week.

I set off on Monday morning, negotiating the maze of Bristol's inner city to find my beautiful companion, who shares a house in St Werburgh's. We loaded up and off we set, into the wild...

Pistyll Rhaeadr
9th August

This majestic waterfall is reached along a narrow, winding lane lined by mighty trees that catch the late afternoon light like the tree of leaf and flame described in that collection of Welsh legends, *The Mabinogion*. I made perhaps an unlikely Peredur on my motorbike, but savoured the Otherworldly vista I beheld nevertheless. It was as though, at any minute, meaning would break through – a message from beyond. Suddenly, you are granted a glimpse of the silvery horse tails of water cascading over the sheer cliff. The nineteenth century author George Borrow, in his book *Wild Wales*, remarked of the waterfall:

What shall I liken it to? I scarcely know, unless it is to an immense skein of silk agitated and disturbed by tempestuous blasts, or to the long tail of a grey courser at furious speed. I never saw water falling so gracefully, so much like thin, beautiful threads as here.

Its name, Pistyll Rhaeadr, means 'spring of the waterfall', and it is formed by the Afon Disgynfa's falling, in three stages, over a seventy-three metre cliff-face, after which the river is known as the Afon Rhaeadr. Whether it is the tallest in England and Wales, as is commonly claimed, is disputed, but its sheer beauty and enchanting effect cannot be denied. It is as though a little section of the Greater Realm has broken off and appeared in this world. A cascade of white water, shimmering unicorn tails of urgent energy, fall from a precipice two hundred and forty feet into the depths of the gorge below – into a great bowl gouged out by the ceaseless action of the water, the whole thing a powerful metaphor (I felt) for the irresistible force of woman meeting the immovable object of man, the water shaping (and shaped by) the rock it wears down! By its incessant force, the descending water has gouged out a natural arch, like a larger version of St Nectan's Glen. From one angle, the rock-cut arch looks like a heart, through which the water pours. The sheer rock face is festooned with dripping foliage, ferns and mosses. Trees cling tenaciously to the side; older brothers look on, stately – Scots pine, oak, hawthorn, ash, sycamore – gathering around it as if to drink an Ent-draught, to commune with this sacred source. A dragonfly flits dramatically about, alighting on the timbered uprights in front of the lodge, which commands a dramatic vantage point. On the terrace of the charming lodge (its name *Tan-y-Pistyll* means 'little house under the waterfall'), visitors sit and enjoy the view while sipping beverages. Chaffinches boldly dart by, flashing their bright liveries.

There is a sense of witnessing something remarkable, as though stumbling upon an ancient sacred mystery being enacted – by and for nature. It is not merely a backdrop for some human drama; it is a drama *in itself* – nature having sacred dialogue with itself. The continual flow of the water – millennia's worth – has deepened this place, and its effect deepens us. Such places gently crack us open; widen us; awaken us. We become more fully ourselves. We step into our true being – and our shining self is revealed in its glory.

As soon as we arrived, Jenni and I found ourselves slowing down. We bumped into the owners of the retreat centre, Philip and January, standing outside their guest house. Philip, brown eyes twinkling beneath a mop of silvery hair escaping from under a woolly hat, warmly welcomed us, offering to make us a cuppa, much-welcome after our long ride (five hours from Bristol). We sat on the terrace, and let the waterfall work its magic. The constant sound began to smooth away the roar of the road – an incessant liquid lullaby. After we had finished our tea, I took the bike down to the field where we would be staying for the next three nights – in the picturesque Showman's Caravan. Our hosts showed us around; the beautifully-crafted wooden interior, decorated with painted details like a Romany barrel-top, had all we needed for our comfort: a cosy double-bed, a double-gas ring and coal-burner; a compost loo and shower wagon close by; plenty of space, peace and freedom – perfect. We felt like a lord and lady. I had heard of *glamping* – the latest buzz word for 'glamorous camping' (which has become increasingly popular with those who want to enjoy the great British outdoors without roughing it), but never thought I would succumb. Yet since this was our holiday, it felt nice to treat ourselves, and all the more important as it was our first time away together. We wanted to relax with each other, and to do so being comfortable would help. I went on the bike back to the nearest village – Llanrhaeadr – to buy our three days' worth of provisions, and then Jenni fixed a simple, but satisfying meal, which we ate outside on a picnic bench, surrounded by stunning mountains. We had arrived. We toasted our first night together and the week to come.

On the way up, we had stated our intentions – what we hoped to get out of the week – and this helped to make the whole experience more than just a holiday. It was a kind of rite-of-passage, a week-long ceremony exploring the mysterious, sublime and often hazardous landscape of love – that of our fledgling relationship. The wide spaces around us mirrored the wide spaces between us – we had much ground to cover. Fate, serendipity, chance, will – take your pick – had brought us together. But it was only through a conscious act of living, through conscious living, that we would choose to stay together. We had brought our bruised hearts to this natural crucible of elemental force, which would either unite or shatter them.

The Next Day
Making love breaks us open – makes us feel raw, vulnerable,

emotional and fully alive. After an intense day yesterday, where we experienced the 'full wave' (as Jenni called it, alluding to Gabrielle Roth's 5 Rhythms: flowing, staccato, chaos, lyrical and stillness), we had a subdued night's sleep, curled into ourselves. We both felt wiped out – earlier I had a kind of relapse, when I felt very weak, with a terrible headache. Jenni cradled my head in her lap and massaged my brow. It was wonderful to be held. It has been so nurturing. At first, we were overwhelmed with fatigue: from the long ride up; from the demands of life; from our vigorous lovemaking. We weren't keen to go far on our first full day, but we were both happy to sit and savour this astounding place we're in – to arrive and to allow our souls to catch up with our bodies. We've been gentle with ourselves – after all, we're still getting to know one another – but we've truly plunged in at the deep end! This is taking sacred time to a whole different level – every day, every hour, every minute, charged with awareness, with immanence. There is no division here between the secular and the sacred. Normally this would be challenging to sustain, but these are our holy days. We're in sacred time, because we've stepped outside our normal lives, picturesque, not following our normal routines of work, eating, sleeping, socialising. Everything here is conscious and highly selective. This is living for connoisseurs.

The clamour of the world is always there. Our commitments will be waiting for us when we return. But for a while we have stepped out of secular time. Pistyll Rhaeadr protects its pilgrims. Within its special zone (a SSSI among other things) time slows, senses sharpen, hearts and minds open.

Last night, we held a little ceremony on the evening of the new moon and the end of the recent Grand Cross – the end of an intense period. The ceremony consisted of two parts – Letting Go and Welcoming In. We decided to use a fire for this. We ordered a bag of logs from the owners, but they absent-mindedly forgot to put them out. I scavenged some but felt a bit weary and stressed (spending time in this place with my amazing companion was splitting me open). Despite my own lack of spark I somehow managed to get a fire going in the ashes of the TruthJuice festival central fire pit (who had used the field just before we arrived). I was feeling on a very low flame as I nursed the fire into life. Its few licks of flame seemed as tenuous as my own. It was soon dark – the way it is in the country – without light pollution, but even more so; it was the dark of the dark moon. Into this black bowl we cast what we wanted to let go of, using leaves tossed into the flames with our intentions. We took turns and watched the leaves sizzle and curl. I let go of pain, of the grief of love, of what could have been. I let go of any blockages preventing me from opening up. From any doubts. A new relationship can raise all kinds of anxieties but so far, it has felt good, so natural. It feels easy to open to Jenni, to trust. We are both in a place of truth, of authenticity, of wanting something real and sustainable. We talked of our dreams for community – for a place like Pistyll Rhaeadr where we could make a stand and put down roots, run workshops, hold retreats, and so on. In this place of spaciousness it felt like anything was possible. After we had Let Go, we raised the Awen, doing it a second time without words and with silent pauses (the Endless Syllable between the words), really feeling it flow through us – from our solar plexus, to our heart chakra, to our third eye: body, heart and mind connecting to spirit. Then I performed my praise poem, *Maid Flower Bride*, which felt especially apt, as I gazed across the fire to my beautiful woman, who seemed the very embodiment of the Woman of the Land. Then Jenni shared her story, *The Legless Fox*, in a lively, loose, natural way, using the space and her whole body well. And then I performed the Welsh Legend, *Lion of the Steady Hand*, which I associate with this time of year (its central protagonist, Llew Llaw Gyffes is a Welsh Lugh – the solar deity celebrated in the festival of Lughnasadh). Being a Leo, who feels a little sense of my own mortality as I approach my birthday this month, I have always related to the story, but this year it has gained extra resonance for me after a summer of heartbreak. I have really felt like Llew – 'assassinated' by an amoral fairy bride, who played me against an unwitting rival. Yet, I have done a lot of letting go already, and this sacred place, my companion's wise and beautiful presence, the fire, the stars, the endless song of the waterfall have helped to sing my soul back into my body, like Gwydion the magician does with his nephew, Llew – in the form of an emaciated eagle, shedding carrion from high up an oak tree. We gazed at the magnificent canopy of stars, which slowly revealed themselves, and beheld a shooting star each, the outriders of the Perseieds, due in a couple of days. We let the story settle as we held each other, wrapped in our blankets, gazing up into the infinitude. The last of the fire died away, embers glowing like jewels.

On the way back to the caravan I was blessed by another shooting star, over the waterfall, directly in line with Arthur's Wain, as though it pulled it (hitch your wagon to a shooting star...) – a magical end to an enchanting, cathartic night. Inevitably, after such a relatively intense sharing, we felt worn out and subdued. We were tired and went straight to bed. The dark moon often makes me feel 'flat' and it can raise all sorts of negativity, unless its ebb tide is worked with. We had gone with the flow. It felt good to mark this time with Jenni, to let go of what we needed to on the cusp of this new adventure together. The dark moon provides an effective 'ground zero'. From this place, this nadir, the solid foundation of truth, the only way *is* up.

The next day, we decided to go for a walk up to the top of the waterfall – to get some elevation. Having savoured being 'held' deep in the Druids' Bowl, as the valley below Pistyll Rhaeadr is called, we were ready to go higher. We prepared a packed lunch, put on suitable attire, and set off in the warm sunshine, full of high spirits – indeed high on the spirit of the place. We first went to the foot of the waterfall and hailed its mighty thundering spirit, then wended our way through the trees, and up the side of the mountain. We took our time, savouring the sunlight through the pines, the colours of the flowers, the suddenly revealed views. As we reached the top, we stopped at a stone by rowan trees and made an Awen as we gazed out along the valley.

I have noticed before (on my way to Llyn Geironydd, 'lake language', in Snowdonia) how the dramatic Welsh countryside, the deep valleys and brooding hills, seems to elicit sound from you – it feels like a natural response, to make sound in the landscape.

We continued on, hand in hand, descending into the groove of the river, a wooded fold. The waterfall did not reveal itself to us at first; we had to work our way towards it, slowly, in a serpentine manner. Jenni noted how this was like lovemaking – ontological foreplay, I called it. The landscape became eroticised – the rough feel of the bark beneath your fingers, the tickling of long feathery grasses against our legs, the squelch and suck of the peaty earth, the beads of dew on the blades, the silvery trickles catching the light. We sat higher up, at a smaller cascade, and ate some of our lunch, feeling caught in the spell of the place. The tiniest action seemed charged with significance and erotic power. We were lost in its dreaming, swept along by the fecund energies present – feeling as though we were expressing something of its ancient ageless magic, the miracle of Creation, unfolding in the eternal moment.

We walked to the brink, to where the waters suddenly plunged down the sheer cliff. I held Jenni's hand protectively, and we sat on a rock close to the edge, gazing out across the tree canopy below, seeing our recent home from a new perspective. We kissed on the precipice. Undertaking the journey of love is akin to the path of the Fool as depicted in the Tarot – stepping off the cliff edge, taking that leap of faith, hoping love (invisible, intangible) will sustain you. The dog of doubt, or of common sense, tries to pull you back, but the Fool steps out anyway, for that is his nature.

Lost in our love, we crossed the waterfall over slippery stepping stones and scrambled up into the woodland, amid the dripping ferns and moist mosses. I was hoping to find a path that would take us along the ridge to a smaller waterfall further on, which would afford us some privacy, for we both felt an urgent need to consummate what had been building in us all morning. I tried to bash my way through the slope of undergrowth, but gave up and headed back down – Jenni was waiting and took my hand. She told me to trust her and led me to a glade, guarded by two pine trees. Without saying a word, we lay down our coats, took off our clothes, and greeted each other, naked in the wild – like First Man and First Woman. My beautiful partner lay down and I adorned her with three ferns, like the rays of Awen. I had found a clump of soft white fleece, which I held to me – John Thomas and Lady Jane garlanded by nature – but our ritual attire was soon abandoned, as we were swept along by the waves of love. The sun broke through, bathing us in its warm benediction. Gentle rain fell upon my back, cooling, soothing. Our passion became more intense. We became like wild beasts. The undergrowth tore at our skin, yet still we continued. Feral cries echoed through the glade. We could hear visitors on the other side of the river, and we hoped the roar of the waterfall would disguise our ecstasy.

Time stopped. The world imploded with light.

We gazed at each other, the rhythm of our breathing, our beating hearts, slowing. Aftershocks tremored through our bodies. We quietly dressed and descended, wondering with surreptitious smiles whether people would know what we had done when they saw us. When we returned to the waterfall Jenni decided to go in. She stripped down to her undies and went in without hesitation – into a perfect little plunge pool into which streams of white water pounded. Seeing her there, gasping under the torrent, I couldn't resist her siren song for long and quickly joined her. It was shockingly cold, but exhilarating. As we emerged, laughing, our skin tingled and we felt wonderfully alive. A family arrived to behold us, standing there shivering and dripping. We felt like Adam and Eve in the Garden, but without sin or shame. We dried off as best we could, dressed quickly, and descended back down to our caravan, feeling deeply connected to each other after such a shared experience. Slipping under the duvet, we drank cocoa, ate buttered malt loaf, before nodding off in each other's arms – our ceremony completed with a siesta.

The next morning, after a peaceful night in our lovely caravan, we packed and prepared to leave. We had only been at Pistyll Rhaeadr for three nights, but it had rocked our world. We arrived as two people on their respective paths, and left as a couple on a shared journey, excited by what adventures awaited us, heartened by the solid foundation we had laid: complete openness, trust, gentleness, spontaneity, and respect. We had found we could make ceremony together in natural, spur-of-the-moment ways. We both venerated the Earth and felt compelled to express gratitude. We had been able to deeply savour the peace and sanctity of the place, feel fully connected to the land and each other, fully present in each immanent moment. We made love-making our prayer to the Earth. In the wild, it felt like we were making love with the spirit of the place also – blessing and being blessed by its genius loci. We had organically co-created what could be called *eco-tantra*.

Just before we left, after thanking our hosts – expressing how our stay at Pistyll Rhaeadr had so enriched us – Philip said that the place had also been enriched by our presences. I had been saying how much staying there had meant to us, how much we would take away – yet he suggested it was a two-way thing, that the site was similarly blessed by the pilgrims who come there with a good heart. It is a 'thin place', where the veil between worlds is porous. It opened up to us, and we had felt opened up by it. It felt like we had achieved a symbiosis with our surroundings, with the natural forces around us – making ceremony, making love, resting, eating, sharing, watching the stars, dreaming, being fully present, nakedly alive in the moment, living in sacred time – no separation, no demarcation between the mundane and the magical. All was numinous, all was significant – the slightest gesture or act, sign or sensation – yet none of it felt forced. It felt effortless, the natural flow of things. Perhaps we had achieved a consciousness akin the shamans or indigenous peoples, especially those who live in rainforests. We had been there for only a few days, but in a way it felt as though we had always been there. We had slowed time, perhaps even floated free of it entirely. In the numinous presence of Pistyll Rhaeadr, it all seemed possible.

And so we made our farewells and left physically, but it felt as though we took a little bit of the place with us – a waterfall in the soul. We wanted to preserve this amazing feeling we had, cherish it, savour it, hold it as long as possible – and so we headed deeper into North Wales, into Snowdonia, to take it to the mountains and other places of spirit. Using our improvised eco-tantric methods, the landscape presented itself in a completely different way. It felt like a deeper way of travelling – of arriving, and being. By constantly renewed acts of perception and devotion we return to the Garden.

St Melangell's Church, Pennant Valley

Leaving the deep peace and beauty of Pistyll Rhaeadr was difficult, but we didn't have to go far before our next soul spring. Taking a B road to Bala, we passed through a little village where there was a sign for St Melangell's church. On a whim, I turned off and decided to visit. My friend, storyteller and sculptor Peter

Please, had told me about it a few years ago and I'd been meaning to go for some time. We stopped off at the first church we came to, which turned out to be St Cynog's – still it was a pleasant church to visit. Jenni bought some cards (one bearing the message 'Death is the final healing') and we headed on. The lane wended its way deeper into the valley, and the further it went on, the more uncertain I became. Had we missed the turning? I wasn't expecting it to be so far down the lane, along an increasingly dramatic valley, steep sides flanked with woods. We passed a small convoy of cars and I suspected they had come from it; a popular pilgrimage site for centuries, it houses the oldest Romanesque shrine in Britain, dating from the twelfth century. Finally, we caught a glimpse of the distinctive square tower through the trees. Restored in the late nineteenth century (1876-78) and twentieth (1989), it looks surprisingly modern for such an ancient place of worship. Pulling into the simple car park, I killed the engine and let the silence settle. Leaving our helmets behind, we approached, heartened to see a fine hare carving on slate, one of many that adorn the site. This was no ordinary church. We entered through the stone lych-gate; two large stones incorporated into its walls might have been the remains of a Neolithic monument. A fragment of the original Melangell shrine is built into its arch. Stone seats line the interior. Local people recall the sexton standing here at funerals, holding out his spade on which people would place a fee – like the two coins given to Charon, but this figure an earth-bound ferryman of the dead. The other entrance, in the west, is known as Llwybr y Corph (the Corpse Path). We stepped through into the circular churchyard, another possible indicator of the site's age and sanctity – although this is apparently disputed. A surer sign are the mighty yew trees – five in total – four of which are up to two thousand years old. These are the original 'churches', predating the stone variety. Indeed, cathedrals emulate such groves with their branching vaults and tall trunk-like columns. As we approached the church, we could hear the rise and fall of singing – Anglican hymns – from a small congregation. We listened at the door and recognised *To Be a Pilgrim* – perfect for this important pilgrimage site. It had just gone noon and the parishioners were celebrating Eucharist. It was heartening to see such a remote church as this in use. And even more to see the many images of hares when we finally went inside (after the service was over) – beautifully-wrought hares on stone, on wood, on pew cushions and altar cloths: the pagan welcomed into the house of Christ, like the hare Melangell sheltered under her skirts, as recorded in the tantalising apocryphal tale of the saint. This is why I have a lot of time and respect for Celtic Christianity – the way the early Christians found common ground with the Druids and Heathens. They found a way to live – and worship – together.

We decided to have our lunch under the yew tree in one corner. Its dark canopy sheltered us like Melangell's skirts. The massive tree we sat under the west had a labia-like groove, into which it was tempting to slot, but first we shared our sandwiches and soaked up the thick sacred atmosphere of the place, feeling such joy at sharing the experience together. The whole journey has been like this – sacred time, sacred place. We once again made simple ceremony together – I stood in the tree and became 'Lord of the Yew'. In gentle role-playing spirit, Jenni supplicated herself before 'me' and invited me to share my yew-wisdom (put down roots – tap deep into the Earth's goodness – but reach up high; let in light, air, water; shelter all life; be strong and centred; bend, don't break; be at peace and endure). Then we swapped over, as she became 'Lady of the Yew', sharing her own wood-truth. We placed simple offerings in the alcove – a fallen bird's nest, some crumbs of bread and cheese – and left, feeling blessed. And then we went to explore the interior of the church, which was beautifully simple with a resonant sacred atmosphere that wasn't oppressive or stagnant, probably because it was charged by regular worship and acknowledged the divine in nature. The fifteenth century rood screen depicted the legend of St Melangell; the figure of the abbess is flanked by the noble huntsman and animals of the hunt weaving into the knotwork forest. This is her story:

Saint Melangell was an Irish princess, daughter of King Jowchel of Ireland, who, confronted with a forced marriage, left her native land with her chastity intact in 604 CE and came to Britain. Using what jewellery she had upon her, she purchased passage across the Irish Sea to Wales, fleeing the brutishness of men and her fate – or heading towards it. She journeyed through the mountainous fastness of Snowdonia, heading east as far as her legs would carry her until, in a steep sided valley, in a yew grove, she collapsed with exhaustion. When she recovered, she realised she was in a place already charged with sanctity. Here she decided to live her life in quiet prayer and devotion to God.

Soon after, Prince Brychwel Ysgithrog of Pengwern Powys, whilst hunting in a place called Pennant, started a hare and, with his hounds, gave chase. They came to a thicket of brambles and thorns wherein he found a beautiful maiden, given up to divine contemplation.

The prince's hounds snarled and growled about the young woman but she showed no fear.

The prince went to blow his horn and it stuck fast to his lips. The hounds backed away, whimpering, tails between their legs. It was as though Melangell, for it was she, was protected by a circle of light. A deep peace radiated from her. Spellbound, man and hounds watched on as the hare appeared boldly from under the hem of her garments. It gambolled around the clearing in a circle, returning to where it started, looked at them all with its unblinking eyes, twitched its nose, and slipped away into the undergrowth without harm.

The prince was astonished by this incredible woman. Moved by her piety and her serenity, the prince endowed Melangell with land and built for her a place of sanctuary for the service of God that it may be a 'perpetual asylum, refuge and defence', saying unto her: 'O worthy lady, for by your noble bearing it is clear you are one. I perceive that you are the handmaiden of the true God. You have given sanctuary, so let yourself find sanctuary here, and grant it to all who need it.'

Melangell passed the rest of her days in this lonely place, sleeping on bare rock. Many were the miracles which she wrought for those who sought refuge in her sanctuary with pure hearts. When she passed from this world, Melangell was reverently buried by her followers – for she had attracted many by her open arms and caring heart. A shrine was built and pilgrims came. All wounded hearts find healing there.

To this day, in honour of Saint Melangell, the hares are respected by the local hunters of Cwm Pennant and are never ever shot.

This tale seems more relevant today – in an age of ecological crisis – than ever. The feminine in the land, and in all human form, needs respecting. We were both to tell this tale over the next week, drawing much meaning from its symbolism and message. We reverently visited the actual grave (or site of the gravestone) in the circular Apse at the rear of the church, behind the shrine, where Melangell's relics are said to be (a skeleton of a female was found there relatively recently). The crude stone slab, adorned by a beautifully embroidered banner depicting the saint and a bulging-eyed hare, was so powerful in its simplicity. I lay my hand upon the slab and it tingled – with the temperature difference or its sacred charge, I could not say. Leaving and continuing our walk around the church we lit candles to loved ones – I to my mother, wishing her healing (she, in her own way had been a Melangell figure, in her love of animals, and her bringing up of three children and several grandchildren). We saw the carved stone tomb lid depicting Melangell, smoothed by time, but still clearly a spiritualised young woman. The two hares at her feet had been all but eroded by people sharpening knives, of all things – a telling sign that the conflict between man and nature has been 'won'. The struggle continues, and we will continue to harm ourselves until we learn to love our Mother.

Leaving, we felt uplifted and not a little 'spaced out', but the ride to Bala in the rain soon brought us down to Earth. We stopped at a popular bikers' cafe for a much-needed cuppa, before pushing on to Betws-y-Coed's overly dramatic terrain. Jenni grew chilled, so I lent her my padded waistcoat for the last leg of the trip – past Snowdon, over the spectacular Llanberis Pass, to Cae Mabon, Eric Maddern's inspiring eco-retreat centre overlooking the cool blue depths of Llyn Padarn. Here, like Melangell's fleeing hare, we hoped to find shelter, for the last section of our journey into the heart of the mountains/the mountains of the heart.

Cae Mabon
12-15th August
Hidden away on the side of a Welsh mountain, at the end of a long, narrow, winding lane that squeezes past looming buttresses of rock and plunges down improbably steep tracks – Sympleglades to deter the faint-hearted – Cae Mabon is an inspiring eco-retreat centre consisting of a dozen sustainably-built dwellings (hogan; straw-bale; green timber; round house; long house; cob; lodge and chalet) that blend into the hillside with their living roofs of turf and wildflowers, like a version of The Shire, 'but for real', as Eric (its founder, an Australian of Cornish heritage) likes to say. I have known about it for a number of years, but have only made it up within the last two, but since then have visited four times. This is the first time I brought somebody with me on the back of my bike. Balancing a

full-load and two passengers down the steep gradient and chancy surface of the dirt track took quite some skill and nerve, but we finally pulled up in the 'car park', the familiar features of 'Mabon' (which resemble Eric) beaming at us from the apex of the wooden archway entrance. We unloaded and lugged our kit down into the fairyland of Cae Mabon.

After the relative solitude of Pistyll Rhaeadr, where we self-catered and had a whole field to ourselves, our stay at Eric's place promised to be quite a contrast. It was one of the twice-yearly Open Weeks, when the programme is relaxed, and about twenty people were staying (a lovely collection of individuals, couples, families with gaggles of children). This temporary population shifted over the week, as people came and went at different stages. We had been half-expected – Jenni had contacted the host in advance, initially to make enquiries about availability. When it turned out we would have to share, we started to look at other options (and that's how we ended up in the Showman's Caravan at Pistyll Rhaeadr). Jenni's last email was to say that we were thinking of coming up on Thursday and would contact Eric then. This seemed to have slipped his mind (no doubt preoccupied with co-ordinating everything) because when I rang up from Bala, he sounded surprised to hear from me. He said one of the dwellings had become available – they were off to Dinas Emrys for the afternoon, but we were welcome to turn up. The weather was looking overcast, so the prospect of staying in a small tent with one sleeping bag between us (all we could fit on) wasn't appealing. Nevertheless, I purchased a sleeping mat in Betws-y-Coed just to keep our options open (we could always borrow some bedding if we did decide to camp). When we arrived, the hogan Eric said was available was clearly still occupied, as were the other dwellings and so I put up the tent in a little grove of trees (apple, birch, hazel, ash, oak). Despite such guardians, it wasn't the ideal pitch (flat ground was at a premium). The tent sagged sadly and Jenni laughed at my pitiful effort. I certainly had done better, but we were both feeling wiped out by the ride. If I had intended to make a sculpture of how I was feeling right then I couldn't have done better. We got a hot drink and attempted to arrive – slowing down and attuning to community life. We were to stay for two or three nights, and it would be a dramatic contrast to the sanctuary of Pistyll Rhaeadr, full of the vibrancy and challenges of community. In the early evening, folk started to arrive back from the numinous Merlin site of Dinas Emrys just in time for dinner, prepared for us by Eric's nephew, Sam and his girlfriend, Jaz. The fabulous food that appeared, filling the long table in the hall, was one distinct advantage to communal living – as were the lovely communal spaces. After dinner and doing the dishes, we heard the hot tub was ready and so we leapt at the chance of a good soak and were the first ones in the resurrected facility (having been recently repaired after a fire). The water was hot and we had to dip in the stream two or three times to compensate, but it was still bliss. Feeling a little restored, we joined folk as they gathered around the fire outside, to share stories, songs and poems and to perhaps spot some shooting stars – for tonight was the optimum time for seeing the Perseieds. When it finally came around to my turn, I managed to raise a few laughs with a lively version of *The Dragon of Llanrhaeadr*. We retired to our sagging tent and after a couple of minutes of trying to bear it, we caved into luxury – the lodge had become available and it seemed madness to rough it when we could sleep in style, and so we grabbed our bedding and scuttled across to the beautiful wooden structure. Constructed of thick interlocking trunks in a hexagonal shape, it felt like being held in the arms of the yew. We had found our 'Melangell' and slept soundly within its shelter.

The next day, we took it easy in the morning, enjoying the place, being still, being peaceful. I wrote and read some, which I always find soothing. After lunch, I took Jenni on a walk of the area – I intended a circuit of Padarn Country Park, which Eric's place abuts, but it turned out to be a little bit more dramatic than

I expected, as we ended up passing through the old slate quarry (once the largest in the world, employing 3000 men, which closed in August 1969 – a couple of days after I was born). We came upon a memorial to the men who had worked there for generations: its inscription read '*We won't see their like again, Quarrymen who did stamp this domain/God and labour here did reign, folk of genius did pertain*' (Norman Closs).

We carried on, coming upon the brutal but impressive post-industrial landscape of the quarry. Thousands of man-hours of labour had carved out the side of the mountain in steep grey terraces. It felt like an Arthurian wasteland, so it was interesting to hear that it had indeed been used as a location for a film about King Arthur in the nineties. By an enormous winch, at the head of a steep vermiculated rail-track, we had a break. Descending, we passed the National Slate Museum and Quarry Hospital. By the time we got back to Cae Mabon we were ready for a dip and so that's exactly what we did – stripping off to go in the cold waters of the lake. My partner was like a selkie returning to her natural element – swimming off towards the middle of the lake. Fortunately, she came back and we dried off.

We were glad to get back in time for the evening meal. That night, there was a puppet-show in the roundhouse, which we managed to miss, deep in conversation. Finally, we joined the circle but it was a bit subdued – the 'king' was in his chamber, and I felt too tired and not inclined to make a merry evening of it. We saved our energy for the next day, when we planned to climb Snowdon.

Climbing a mountain is more than just a physical act. Even a popular, accessible and relatively unchallenging mountain like Snowdon can still provide a powerful experience, a test of one's resolve, endurance, ability to work in a team and a metaphor for life's journey.

We set off at midday after making all the necessary preparations. We walked from Cae Mabon through Padarn Country Park to Llanberis, where we caught the Sherpa up to Pen-y-Pass. From here we took the Pyg Track ('rugged and very challenging'). Even with the head start, 1170 ft up, it is still a six hour walk. To make it more challenging, we decided to go across Crib Goch, the razor-sharp ridge, something I've been meaning to do for a while. It's good to test yourself. The weather wasn't great – it was misty on top and a little windy – but we took it easy and didn't lose our nerve. Jenni gamely gambolled on like some mountain goat. She has pluck, that gal! We attempted each obstacle as it arose and tried not to dwell upon what was behind or what was ahead. It was very similar to riding a powerful motorbike – you have to be fully present, and not lose your bottle! My Dad would've called it a 'bottle job', which he was fond of, having a predilection for jumping out of aeroplanes!

As we gained altitude, the visibility inevitably decreased, until we were stumbling along in the fog. But my trusty compass reassured us we were going in the right direction and sure enough, soon after, we intersected the Pyg Track, zig-zagging up the side of the mountain. We gratefully followed its stone steps up to the Finger Stone, and along to the summit. We were there just in time for a couple of snaps and a much-welcome tea from the visitors' centre. And then it was time to head back if we were to catch the last Sherpa bus back down from Pen-y-Pass. The summit was a predictable anti-climax. But it was, of course, the journey, not the destination. We had taken our time and savoured the walk up, stopping frequently to 'stand and stare'. And now we made our way down, with a little bit more alacrity.

As we descended, the sun broke through and we were treated to a glorious view of Llanberis Pass as it flooded the valley. Once more, the mountain looked benign and I envied a man walking back up it, laden with a rucksack, clearly intending to wildcamp. Still, a good meal, a fire, company, a hot tub, and a lovely soft bed awaited.

The session in the roundhouse was a packed one, with

another marathon set from our talented host, the shadow puppet show, singing, poetry and storytelling. I shared my poem written after climbing Snowdon last year then encouraged Jenni to share her version of the Legend of St Melangell. I followed this with a tale from my old home town of Northampton about saints and shrines, the Legend of St Ragener, inspired by our visit to the church in Pennant Valley. I said it was important to celebrate your own heritage, and the story clearly tells us that treasure can be found beneath your feet. It was empowering to tell a story from one's own past, even though it was late by the time my slot came up. Eric finished things off with the 'creation myth' of Cae Mabon, which was thrilling to hear. I had heard fragments before but not the whole story, and I was glad Jenni got to hear it, interested as she is in such ventures. Eric was Australian born, but moved to Britain aged ten, and went on to study at Sheffield University, before returning to Australia where he worked in Aboriginal communities. When he finally returned to Britain, he brought with him three principles, which provided the foundation for Cae Mabon: to provide Sacred Space; to offer rites of passage (especially for young people); and to explore the 'White Man's Dreaming' (that is, working with his own native tradition). Cae Mabon, the result of twenty-five years of hard work, embodies these principles, showing how one man with a vision, tenacity and skill can create something that serves a wider community, inspiring all who visit it.

Afterwards, we were more than ready for the hot tub, our weary bones in need of a soak. The skies had cleared, but the Perseids didn't show themselves. However, on the way back to the hogan I saw one and was content – a perfect end to a perfect week.

The next morning, we packed up, said our goodbyes and set off. The steep climb up to the car park made it a real effort to leave, as though the place didn't want to let you go. We loaded up the bike and headed along the track. In *The Hero's Journey*, as originally devised by Joseph Campbell, the final part, referred to as the 'Road Home', can be the most perilous part – in the same way descending a mountain can be. Tired and elated, that is when mistakes can happen – as the Babylonian king Gilgamesh bitterly discovered, returning from the Otherworld with the flower of life to resurrect his friend Enkidu. He fell asleep and the precious flower was eaten by a snake. We wanted to take what we had gleaned back into our daily lives, back into the 'real world', but first we had to get home! The bike's rear tyre was getting worryingly low on the way back, as a fellow biker pointed out. Although I had checked the pressure before leaving, I hadn't been able to inflate the tyre because the air pumps in petrol stations don't fit the valve (you need an adaptor, as I discovered). As a result, the rear tyre wore down rapidly – at the Oswestry Services, I noticed a worrying bald patch developing. At the Craven Arms it was twice as bad! Fortunately, the old-fashioned air pump fitted and I was able to inflate to the correct pressure (it was twenty when it should've been forty-two!). Praying I didn't have a blow-out or flat, we continued, hoping we would make Gloucester at least. The tyre held and in the golden evening light, we made it home. Exhausted, after seven hours of riding, I dropped Jenni off, in Bristol, and then got myself back to Bath. It had been a less than relaxing ride back for me, but what had been heartening was how we had coped as a couple, responding to the crisis with clarity and common sense. I think our climb up the mountain yesterday, negotiating perilous hazards, helped prepare us for 'the slings and arrows of outrageous fortune'. This week we had thrown ourselves in at the deep end and had not only survived, but thrived.

The critical part of experiencing sacred time is how we can incorporate what we have gleaned back into our 'normal lives'. The greatest challenge awaited us – the act of living consciously on a daily basis, making our sacred circle a movable feast. Within a week, our lives had completely turned upside down – I had gone on holiday with a relative stranger and had returned with the woman I love. We had turned the wheel, and now it was going to turn us, as we once more rejoined the circle of life.

Full Circle
18th August

As I reach the last day of my fortieth year, I feel it is an appropriate time to look back over the last twelve months and reflect upon what I have experienced, what I have learnt. This echoes what Philip Facey, owner of Tan-y-Pistyll said to me, soon after arrival at Pistyll Rhaeadr – to look back. He argues that we have spent too long looking forward, as the tellingly named human *race*, and it hasn't got us very far, going by the current state of the world – and it's time to look back. The answers are in the past, he says. We've raced ahead and left something of value behind. True wisdom doesn't come from being in a hurry. Nature takes it time. And maybe so should we. Everything these days is about speeding up, as though faster automatically equals better (once 'bigger' did, but that has dramatically shifted to 'smaller', 'sleeker'), but the growing popularity of the Slow Food Movement suggests otherwise. A dinner party with friends, lasting a whole evening, is infinitely better than 'Fast Food'. Value is returning to the homemade, the handmade, the well-made and enduring – as opposed to the mass-produced, the cheap and expendable. Built-in obsolescence is becoming, in itself, obsolescent. Everything contains its own quota of time – like the sands in an egg-timer – think of a tree with its rings. People do so as well, although fortunately we don't know our exact measure. Places sometimes do (or at least our time there, e.g. on holiday; as a pupil or student; as an employee, as a visitor). Experiences certainly have an expiry date. Their transience is part of their preciousness. Recently, on a trip to the Isle of Wight, I visited the area where John Keats wrote the famous line: 'A thing of beauty is a joy forever.' He wrote this on the Downs overlooking the magnificent Carisbrooke Castle, and I speculated that its ruins suggested to him that a manmade thing, however well-made, rarely lasts, whereas something as ephemeral as a 'thing of beauty' – a kiss, a smile, a sunset – is a joy forever, chiefly *because* of its transient nature. Pleasure that lingers indefinitely soon becomes unpleasant. Any bliss, if unending, would soon become unbearable. We have to learn to let go, especially of what we love the most. I certainly have a tendency to hoard, kidding myself that 'genius thrives on clutter'. But in the West, as a culture (in paradox with our throwaway habit) we have a tendency to cling onto some things longer than we should – our childhood; our adolescence; our youthful looks; our wealth; our destructive habits; past hurts and old scores. There is a distinct grace in letting go. As George Harrison told us 'All Things Must Pass'. That is not to cherish things in the present – to appreciate this world and all of its gifts. While we have bodies we should enjoy them, enjoy the realm of the senses. To do otherwise, to deny life, is an insult to creation. We should savour, then move on.

All of the experiences over the last year have been enriching and I'm glad I've had them, but part of their 'specialness' has been their transience.

Going to an unfamiliar location for an unusual experience is frequently equalled, often outdone, by the pleasure of returning home. This has been part of the pleasure of turning the wheel. Another is that I could let them all go.

Celebrating a year of sacred time has been immensely enriching; it's been a very conscious way to mark my fortieth year, but I don't feel compelled to repeat the experience every year. Some events I might do again, others, as yet unknown to me, I might enjoy, but I don't feel attached to any of them, including my birthday. On one level they are all artificial demarcations of time – lines in the egg-timer sands – things we impose upon the wheel of the year. Nothing should be set in stone. On another level, it could be argued that traditions seem to occur when people *stop* thinking, when they *stop* making choices, when, culturally, we fossilise. Every day, every waking moment should be a conscious act of awareness – not just something we do, because 'it's always been thus', because our forefathers did it and so must we.

Even if we're hard-wired to be like that.

Humans are pattern-making creatures; it's natural for us to see meaningful configurations in everything, from recognising our mother's face as a baby from the triangle of her features (eyes, nose, mouth); to seeing a man in the moon; cosmic codes in wheat fields; secrets in numerical sequences; zoomorphic shapes in stars; astrological significance to the happy accidents of birth, genes and relationships; simulacra in natural forms; to market trends in the stock exchange; and signs and wonders in every quirk of life. All fascinating in themselves, but patterns have a tendency of trapping us into certain ways of thinking, of behaving. And that includes odd customs and seasonal celebrations – however charmingly eccentric or reassuringly folksy they might be. The result: ossified modalities, a frozen way of living, or being, which is actually out of kilter with the organic way of things. If a seasonal celebration does not marry with what is actually happening in the natural world – for instance, a spring celebration when it's still plainly winter; a summer ceremony in the driving rain – then does it have any validity? We should always listen to nature, first and foremost, and respond accordingly, rather than impose our own narratives upon it, drowning it out. It should be a dialogue, not a monologue. To carry on regardless of the evidence of our senses is the height of folly. We need to listen to the Earth, and to our hearts – and then act with sensitivity to both.

I started this book by asking: why do we feel the need to celebrate? Over the course of a year I've looked at many different ways of making and marking sacred time – each with distinctive reasons, as quirky as the events themselves: to honour a place, a person, an anniversary; to celebrate the cultural heritage, diversity and creativity of the community; to break up mundane time and routines; to create holidays when revelry, rejoicing, and rest can occur; to step outside of our ordinary lives and feel part of something bigger, older, sublime or sillier; to synchronise with the natural cycles of the Earth, of the moon, of the sun and stars; to foster belonging; to connect to previous generations, to our ancestors; to create modern traditions that reflect the current cross-section of community and/or the zeitgeist; for fun – out of sheer folly, for its own sake, because its eccentric, absurd, obscure, wilfully non-corporate – socially permissive insanity that lets off steam, reinvigorates life with a sense of humour, and stops us taking things too seriously. And so on.

The reasons are as idiosyncratic and abundant as people.

Turning the wheel – with ceremony and celebration – is one of the peculiar things we do as humans that *make* us human. From marking the success of the hunt with a cave-painting to the latest state-of-the-art festival exhibition, we have created sacred space and time for as long as we've been on Earth and I can't see the tendency – what could be called social consciousness – to stop now.

***

There are inevitably many seasonal celebrations which practically I wasn't able to attend – weird and wonderful celebrations of local distinctiveness, such as the Marhamchurch Revels, Cornwall; the Old Green Championship to find the Knight-of-the-Green, Southampton; the Turning the Devil's Stone ceremony in Shebbear, near Holsworthy; the Abbots Bromley Horn Dance; the Bognor Birdman; Hoggin' the Bridge over the Severn; Coracle Races in Cilgerran, Pembrokeshire; the Puck Fair, Cillorglin, in the Republic of Ireland; the Burning of the

Clavie in the Outer Hebrides, and countless others – some recently started, others below the radar and open only to a small group of friends. New traditions are created or revived every year. They await another turning of the wheel, or other intrepid chrononauts and calendrophiles.

But for myself, I have to draw a line under my year-long journey around the seasonal wheel.

Closure is important. I like to finish things – to mark the end of a project. And so tonight I celebrate the last day of my fortieth year with a small group of friends, with a small gathering around the hearth, deciding to mark, for once, my birthday *eve* (I thought this was a satisfyingly quirky idea, until my German friend Ola commented that it was quite common in her homeland – not surprising in a nation that makes more of Christmas Eve than Christmas Day). At risk of reinventing the wheel, I went ahead anyway; for me, it was the start of a new personal tradition. At the stroke of midnight I can celebrate the start of my very own 'New Year' – and all that it will bring. Tomorrow is the beginning of a new phase of my life – in reality, a mere continuation of what has gone before, but hopefully a positive evolution. Each New Year we enter gives us the opportunity to 'start afresh' – to make a renewed commitment to our core values, our goals. This seems like a better time to make resolutions than in the hangover of Hogmanay. Maybe such intentions will fizzle quickly away like a firework, but it is good to make one's lifestyle choices conscious ones and not simply be swept along by the pre-existing pattern, which after all have been co-determined by us. Each day we have the choice to change the way we live. Are you alive, or merely in line? Strike out and forge your own path.

Step off the wheel.

13 Seasonal Poems

by Kevan Manwaring

January

Song of the North Wind

Wild north wind

frosty breath from the broken teeth of glaciers,
the breaching spume of sperm whales,
the endless stillness of the Targa,
the fey lightshow of the Borealis.

Wild north wind

unsentimental, austere,
you suffer no fools,
cut the wheat from the chaff,
stripping bare all illusions.

Wild north wind

your howling song sends men bosky,
makes seadogs batten down hatches,
become winter stay-at-homes, hearth-tenders, coal-biters,
lick wounds, recite sagas, nurse grudges.

Wild north wind

grey-cloaked raider, storm-herder,
all bow to your power,
mightiest of winds, bringer of the white death,
the cold kiss of eternal peace

Wild north wind

a grim giant striding the land,
heavy boots on rooftops, dislodging drift,
tile-clatterer, sky-strafer,
son of the midnight sun.

Wild north wind

when will you stop your restless search for vengeance?
when will your cease your blood-feud with summer?
when will your tundra heart thaw?

February

The Bride of Spring

In darkest hour of the year
she arises.
Casting off her shadowy gown
as she steps over the horizon –
by sun king kissed,
borne by his golden down.
A dress of frosted cobwebs
veils maiden skin.
Within a seasons turning
the crone has become virgin.
Snowdrops touch her and turn into flowers,
as the slumbering land stirs
in these formative hours.
The earth softens at her feet
where buds shake free their winter bed.
Newborn lambs begin to bleat –
insistent mouths by ewes' milk fed.
Rooster heralds her on the ground.
Above, the feathered chorus

make naked trees resound.
We awake to a changing world.
Her white magic revealed –
a petal uncurled.

Stone bound man
let your proud bells ring,
for we are welcomed into her garden
as she stand at the gates of spring.

The infant year she presents,
placing the future in our hands.
A gift of renewed innocence,
restoring the egg timer sands...

March

Blessed is the Mother

Blessed is the Mother –
honour Her on your day of birth.
Sacred is the Mother –
whose body is this precious Earth.
Find Her in the bend of a brook,
in the song of a secret spring.
Feel Her in a verdant vale,
in the joy of nature's flowering.

Follow Her contours
in the curved breast of a mound,
in the swollen belly of a hill.
Face Her in the fertile tomb of barrow womb,
in the dark and silence and still.
Mater Tierra, Prima Mater.

Earth Warriors, rise up!
Defend your Motherland.
The Dogs of Babylon
bite Her fair hand.
Mothers of the Future,
may your hearts be true –
tomorrow's generation
all depends on you.
Blessed is the Mother
of all Creation great and small –
Planet, animal, man and God:
the Mother Universal!
Mater Tierra, Prima Mater.
Mater Tierra, Prima Mater.

April

Pilgrim Song

Come wanderer and walk with me,
We have got so much to see...
Just listen to the forest for the song,
Stay on the path and you can't go wrong.
Ford the river, follow the stream –
Watch yourself flow by the banks of a dream.
Climb a mountain, ascend to the sun,
Go back to where we've all begun.
Offer your prayers to Grandmother Moon,
Look! The stars fall like a stellar monsoon.
Oh, we want to be where we want to be —
So far away, near infinity.
So far away, near infinity.

May

Heartwood

The arrow's loosed, the chase is done,
Dappled bushes, buds unfold –
The wand is split, the garland won,
Unlocking hoard of summer gold.

In the heartwood you wooed me,
The heart would, 'neath trysting tree.

Eglantine and apple blossom,
Meadowsweet and maytree white –
Spring is awakening in the wildwood,
Life returning after winter's night.

In the heartwood you wooed me,
The heart would, 'neath trysting tree.

With the dew the sap is rising,
Scented petals release their spell –
Robin's with Marian in his bower,
Honeysuckle and bluebell.

In the heartwood you wooed me,
The heart would, 'neath trysting tree.

The leaves are yearning for the sunshine,
The glade echoes with mating call –
For the rain the thirsty roots pine,
Love, the huntress, has us in her thrall.

In the heartwood you wooed me,

The heart would, 'neath trysting tree.

When we love the world it gladdens,
Leaf and fruit, milk and stream –
Faerie magic is all around us,
May we never awaken from this dream.

In the heartwood, Robin and Marian,
In the heartwood, we are one.

June

Solstice Sunrise

I awake
by a fire tended by a friend,
feeling the sudden quickening of dawn.
The misty air is alive with the white heat of bird song –
a thousand synapses firing,
the forest brain regaining consciousness.

Groggy, after a merry night
with flickering friends.
Entertaining the illusion
of the fullest moon, buttery and fat,
shining down upon us –
vast and silent – a full stop
at this still point of the year.

The world pauses for breath,
mops its brow
at the height of its labours,
girding its loins
to push the bronze cauldron of the sun

back down the hill
from its northern arc to its nadir.

After a breakfast of black coffee and treacle tart
we circumnavigate the hill fort,
greeting nonchalant cows.

With clothes of woodsmoke
and feet of dew
we wend our way down to earth,
to a dreaming city
slowly rising.

July

Culbone

Sitting on the Lovelace Seat,
on a summer's evening –
the last rays of sun gilding the coombe
with honey. The dusk chorus sings
the Last Post of the day. A wood pigeons
coos its melancholy Morse code
across the shadowed grove.
A river of sky above –
clouds mottled, distant, slowly
drifting. The stream's constant
whisper the sole dialogue.
and yet not alone, in this solitude's bliss.
Numberless ghosts crowd
this humble parcel of land,
angels of place dancing
in the palm of Culbone's hand.
The smallest church, a grey fist –

open it up to find the people. Thirty, a modest flock.
Each feature, a century.
A steeple like an inverted ice-cream cone.
Its thin iron cross, God's punctuation.
Gravestones, wafers of lichened rock.
Geological records of lives –
generations of Reds: Ambrose, Ethel – were they ready?
A Welsh Guardsman taken too soon.
Joan Cooper, guardian of vision,
speaking stone tongue:
'Let not your heart be troubled'.
The slow silent explosion of a yew tree
millennia long,
limbs amputated by a tree surgeon,
bows unstrung.
Yet peace comes in thick waves,
undisturbed by the ramblers,
preying mantis poled,
who clatter through the gate, stay for a snap,
a plastic cup of tea from a flask,
talk as if to drown out the sacred silence
they have come to seek – afraid
what it might say to them. Perhaps.
Gone in an automated flash,
the moment digitised,
leaving the vale inviolated, eternal,
itself.

Mantled in the jealous wings of its mystery.

August

Last Rites for John Barleycorn

Twilighters,
Roam with me...

Through the Gates of Herne
To find a kernel of truth,
Confront the stag of the seventh tine,
Decode the marks of his horned hoof.

Down the familiar paths we trod,
Frequenting our earlier selves;
Sharing our picnic of the past –
Feasting with Pooka and his Elves.

Then over the bloodstream
And through the iron turnstiles,
Two into one –
Led by the Maiden of the Corn
To the barrow to be reborn.

Along a tunnel to the light –
Spurred on sperm, a wheaten worm,
Wisely upstream wriggling;
To germinate where we are but a gleam –
Prodigal suns returning.
Walking between the worlds,
Through fields of alien wheat,

To the place of all hallowed dreams,
Whence all our tomorrows meet.

Rising to that yawning cleft –
Between that baked earth, right,
And bearded barley, ripe –
Beyond all that is left.

Demeter mourns for her lost youth,
Russet cloak unleavening
The burgeoning Lammas-scape
In her widowed wake.

Yet, if she lifted up her downcast eyes
They would glimpse a gladdening light
That could de-mistify those
Night-stung tears of dew.

Rekindle a faltering love
Which was once so bright;
Tinderbox heart sparked ablaze
By this Promethean view.

Look! His dazzling smile already melts
Her frosty gaze –
The heartening land smiles welcome

As the colour returns to her cheeks.

With a God's eye view
We discerned the canvas
Upon which he painted –
Pigments selected from a divine palette,
Sable-soaked, laden with morning hue –
As elegantly across the vast vista
he swept it.

Drowsy textures arose –
Dormant tints, awoken by his touch.
As our orbs imperceptibly peeled
An earthairfirewater colour
Was unveiled.

Rich vermillions, sombre umbers,
Occult ochres, verdant viridians,
Were presented by this prismatic parade
As if such a spectrum had never before
Dared to emerge from the shade.

Blinded by an unearthly faith,
We now rubbed our eyes
At this dawning creation
With a renewed belief.

Breath taken, we breathed it back:
Pulling the sky towards us
In lungfuls of light – then exhaling,
The clouds dispelled like dandelions.

An impromptu pantheon,
Recreating the world
In our image –
Raise an eyebrow to influence the air,
Lift a finger and the crops would soar,
Invert a thumb and harvests fail…

But who are we to judge
When from afar, we appear mere
Dot-to-dots,
Yearning for a common thread?

Yet the lionheart's golden mane
Is not ours to wantonly flay;
Braided bails of spiralling corn
The only evidence
Of a God that passed this way.

Now hush – for fields have ears
And silence is as golden as the sun.

From the dancing trees
Our forest kith could be heard;
Amongst the bustling stalks
The flower kin spread the word.

It was a choral dawn like no other –
The morning eavesdropped upon by Adam
when first he emerged from the
All-Mother.

A myriad of voices chattered away,
But in the same tongue spoken.
Revealed! The lost language of the fey
our ears had awoken!

The gloaming star winked green:
It knew a secret – we did not.
The champion waited for
Was finally seen, borne in his sacred cot.

Lugh! He soars by bronzed chariot.
Lugh! He strums with a solar lyre.
Lugh! He sings with honey lyric.
Lugh! He sees through eyes of fire.

We toasted the rising king
With wide eyes and barley wine,
Our joy expressed in sundancing –
Jumping alive with acid mime.

Lost in the landscape of Lughnasadh,
The moment telescoping,
Outside time.

It was ourselves looking at our elves,
which the Outsiders insighted –
a frame within a frame.
The burning gallery ignited.

Rocketed by déjà vu (again)
A product of eternal combustion,
This glimpse of infinity's spark?

For the answer to that endless question
We had to go where none return:
Down amongst the dead men,
Hoping in the dark.

Skull walls leered in silent mockery,
A sarcophagus whistled
A deadly tune;
Lulled, rolling into the barrow,
Returning to the tomb...

Way, way down there:
A rag, a bone, a hank of hair –
Would that be all that is left
To resurrect us?

O Lazarus, O Lazarus.

Ashes to – what then – Ashes?

Dust to – nothing more than – Dust?

As cold clay kissed awake,
Mannequins of the Fire Drake.

Charged in this earthen kiln,
Ossified, lacquered and brittle,
Until dropped, and shattered
At the marriage of the Quick and the Dead.
Each shard indicative
Of the punishment or pleasure
Stretching ahead..?

No,
Not whilst friends remain
To keep one's memory alive –
Though tempests torment us,
Storms in our cracked cup.
Join hands

and we shall endure.

The dead talked
Amongst themselves;
Thick as thieves –
They kept their secrets,

We kept our lives.

For now we had descended

To the summit's peak,
Casting our reflections
Upon the waters of the deep.

It was time to go,
To leave a votive offering behind.
Confronted,
The past's shadow was exchanged
For something of worth to find.

The sacred place resanctified,
By rites of passage outworn,

We emerged remembered,
Reconciled, reborn.

Crawling into the cotton-budded world,
We learnt to see again, through fields of vision.

Back down to earth
The cloudwalkers gently floated.
The grease of our harvest supper
Still upon empty mouths –
Terra firmly devoted.

The Bacchanalia was over –
Boozy God of derangement
Rent asunder: his goodness shared,
Blood into wine, flesh into bread.

John Barleycorn is dead!
John Barleycorn is dead!

The parched soil drank him dry:

The Goddess takes back what once was hers.

The power returns to the Mother,
The power returns to the Mother,

As we turn to the crimson-smeared day,
Imbibing the drunken sun,
Whetstone-slicked sickle in hand,

Ready to make hay.

September

Summer's Wake

The Earth is ablaze with flaming tears –
Shedded in grief as Her sun disappears.

For this is the time of the annual sunset,
When man must savour lest he forget.

A cauldron that tips its molten load –
As it touches the land, Midas glowed.

Reforging the world in a different vein,
Making us appreciate whatever will wane.

Leaves become gold to impress their presence –
Precious to us in their newfound transience.

Their weight, like their value, seems to have altered –
Heavy now they fall, as if indeed moulted.

Gravity and time take their toll,

Casting off weight in this seasonal cull.

The reaper scythes with relief –
Cutting the chaff from the wheatsheaf.

We reward our labours with indulgence,
Seducing our senses with Nature's opulence.

Her dark bounty tempts us to dine,
Enticed to sin on the fruits of the vine.

Its bouquet we judge as connoisseur –
Our tastes informing us of a good year.

The party is over, the revellers scattered,
The place where it was, in legacy, littered.

A lonely breeze comes to sweep it away –
The rest is absorbed in silent decay.

The garden is a film set deserted,
Yet still it is haunted by those departed.

Phantoms flicker of a glory past –
Images in sepia fading fast.

We thumb through the album but must let go –
Forgetting yesterday, remembering tomorrow.

As the evening arrives, our nostrils flare –
A season has passed, scenting night air.

The vessels absence still ripples make,
As we stand gently rocking in summer's wake.

The dying king sails to the Isle in rest
where he shall remain the Goddess' guest.

The holly resumes his thorny crown,
At his queen's side of blacker gown.

Briefly, the balance is maintained,
As we must gauged what has been gained.

Until the scales begin to sway,
And night takes over what once was day.

So rejoice! The year has come of age.
Our shadows stretching – like ink down the page.

October

The Wild Hunt

When mad mushrooms bloom
And dream mists still linger
Then restless souls will hear a horn
The call of Herne the Hunter.

He waits at forest threshold
Astride snorting stallion –
Garbed in skins,
Bow on back,
Bright-ringed horn in hand,
A crown of antlers upon his head –
King of the Wood, Herne.

His bestial huntsman gather
With their phantom pack.

The only sound a ragged chorus of crows
Scattered by a second blast.

The Wild Hunt Rides!
Hoof beats shake dew from cobwebs,
Leave a whorl of bloody leaves.
They harrow the hollow lanes,
The old straight tracks,
Over hedge, through field,
Knowing no boundary –
Heeding not the law of the land-grabber.

Steed steaming,
Breath ragged,
You reach the edge of the grove
Where the quarry is cornered.
Dismounting,
Spear poised,
You close in for the kill.

Herne waits,
Arrow ready,
Aiming at you.
He shoots –
Then all around the baying of the
Gabriel Hounds
As they tear your soul to tatters.

First,
Wormfodder,
Earth turning,
Earth turning...
Then, reborn –
Robin in the berry bush,

Otter in the weir,
Owl scrying from her bowl,
Mouse hushed on wheat ear,
Fox skulking at red dusk,
Bristled boar with deadly tusk.
Rutting stag of the royal tines,
Rex Nemorensis,
Herne –

The Hunter
Became the hunted.
Animals are we all –
So bless your beast
In time for the feast
And desecrators of the sacred wood
Beware!
When winter's tang
Sharpens our appetite
And the wild hunt rides!

November

Fireworks over Bath

Stars, upward shooting,
busy sperms
struggling to inseminate the night.

Vying for the egg of the moon.

Qabala
tree of life
suspended
in plain sight.

Sephiroth of light,
the way illuminated by
a criss-cross of paths.
Star-fruit,
hanging in the dark vineyard
almost within reach.
Faces upturned
softly lit by the glow,
eyes shine with distant fires.
Crowds excited
spilling onto the road,
normal rules suspended.
Gaggle of teenagers
guzzling booze.
Cozened toddlers,
watch their first fireworks
with awe, as proud parents watch them.
Grandparents and grandchildren,
all generations.
Friends, tourists.
A city watching the sky.
A hearth in the air,
in the absence of a bonfire.
People wrapped up against the
November chill.
Mufflers and 3-D glasses – take my photo –
a kooky kind of ritual garb.
Everyone filming it on their phones,
or taking endless digital snaps.

Deletable memories.

What meaning for people,
the candyfloss pyrotechnics,

except the wide-screen spectacle,
the ultimate IMAX?

Celebrating a terrorist?
The execution of a Catholic martyr?
Freedom fighter or freedom's frightener?
The Fall Guy,
Society's bogeyman.
Over Parade Gardens,
disturbed from their topsy-turvy sleep,
bats flit in terror,
their echo-location shattered
unable to find home,
A pigeon flaps about in panic.
Countless small animals petrified,
hear the palpitations of tiny hearts.
Whoosh! Boom! Crack! Fizzle!
A Ragnarok for pets.
In a thousand flats, old dears fretting over
their budgies and lapdogs,
Compose letters of objection to the local rag.

Yet it is still beautiful,
every explosion of fizzing colour,
eliciting sounds of satisfaction and wonder
from the Twenty First Century audience,
wearied by the world,
sporting their cynicism on their shoulders,
sarcasm the safest option. The coward's way.

Yet
fireworks make children of us all.

Briefly we are taken back

to the place of innocence
when the world was full
of magic and miracles.

December

All Heal

Between the earth and the stars
it hangs – like a threat
of love,
a promise of bliss.
White bubbles that could
burst on your lips like a kiss.

This is old druid magic – ancient fertility
rite in your living room,
live in front of plasma screen.
Raise a glass to the golden bough,
to Baldur's bane,
Aeneas' passport to Hades and back.
On oak and lime and apple
how the mistletoe glows
like a swarm of green bees,
berries of awen waiting
for the glint of sickle
in the virgin midwinter sun.

Follow the Sun Road Home

Awakening to a dreaming world –
The road winding,
The mist rising,
Shadows in the valleys,

Ancient shapes in the land.

Crossing the faerie bridge with a kiss,
The brook running deep and clear –
Climbing through fields wet with tears,
To the slumbering barrow on the hill,
The door to the Otherworld is there still.

Follow the sun road home
Called by the song of the Sidhe.
Follow the sun road home,
Over the westering sea –
Beyond this world of bones
To the place where the spirit is free.

Within the chambered tomb
We wait for the crack of dawn.
Within the dripping darkness
We wait to be reborn.

In the stillness and the silence
We listen to our forefathers.
Before the horn of solstice blows
We heed the heartbeat of the mother.

Then we feel the thrill of Earth's quickening.
The gathered hold their breath,
Gaze through the grey –
Wordlessly praying for
A Grail for the sickening.

Follow the sun road home
Called by the song of the Sidhe.
Follow the sun road home,

Over the westering sea –
Beyond this world of bones
To the place where the spirit is free.

A swift kestrel takes wing
The new sun has risen.
Friends depart and wheels turn –
May we meet over the
horizon.

Follow the sun road home,
Follow the sun road home.
Down the hollow lanes,
And shining leys,
Following the sun road home.

About the Author

Kevan Manwaring is an author of over a dozen books, including poetry, fiction and non-fiction. He teaches creative writing for the Open University and Skyros Writers' Lab. As a professional storyteller he has performed in many venues across Britain and abroad, including USA, Italy and Malta – appearing on BBC TV. In 2010 he was Writer-in-Residence in El Gouna, Egypt. He lives in Stroud, Gloucestershire.

His website is: www.kevanmanwaring.co.uk

Selected Works

The Way of Awen: Journey of a Bard, O-Books, 2010

The Immanent Moment: poems for now, Awen, 2010

The Book of the Bardic Chair, RJ Stewart Books, 2008

Lost Islands, Heart of Albion Press, 2008

The Bardic Handbook: The Complete Manual for the 21st Century Bard, Gothic Image, 2006

The Long Woman, Awen, 2004